MEANING
AND
CONTEXT

An Introduction
to the
Psychology of Language

COGNITION AND LANGUAGE
A Series in Psycholinguistics
Series Editor: R. W. RIEBER

Recent Volumes in this Series:

COGNITIVE DEVELOPMENT AMONG SIOUX CHILDREN
Gilbert Voyat

CRAZY TALK: A Study of the Discourse of Schizophrenic Speakers
Sherry Rochester and J. R. Martin

DEVELOPMENTAL PSYCHOLINGUISTICS
Three Ways of Looking at a Child's Narrative
Carole Peterson and Allyssa McCabe

DIALOGUES ON THE PSYCHOLOGY OF LANGUAGE AND THOUGHT
Edited by Robert W. Rieber

LANGUAGE AND COGNITION: Essays in Honor of Arthur J. Bronstein
Edited by Lawrence J. Raphael, Carolyn B. Raphael, and
Miriam B. Valdovinos

MEANING AND CONTEXT: An Introduction to the Psychology of Language
Hans Hörmann
Edited and with an Introduction by Robert E. Innis

PSYCHOLOGY OF LANGUAGE AND LEARNING
O. Hobart Mowrer

THE USE OF WORDS IN CONTEXT: The Vocabulary of College Students
John W. Black, Cleavonne S. Stratton, Alan C. Nichols, and
Marian Ausherman Chavez

A Continuation Order Plan is available for this series. A continuation order will bring delivery
of each new volume immediately upon publication. Volumes are billed only upon actual ship-
ment. For further information please contact the publisher.

MEANING AND CONTEXT

An Introduction to the Psychology of Language

Hans Hörmann

Late of Ruhr University
Bochum, Federal Republic of Germany

Edited and with an Introduction by

Robert E. Innis

University of Lowell
Lowell, Massachusetts

PLENUM PRESS • NEW YORK AND LONDON

13395342

2-89

Library of Congress Cataloging in Publication Data

Hörmann, Hans, 1924–1983.
    Meaning and context.

    (Cognition and language)
    Rev. translation of: Einführung in die Psycholinguistik.
    Bibliography: p.
    Includes indexes.
    1. Psycholinguistics. I. Innis, Robert E. II. Title. III. Series.
    BF455.H62813 1986   401′.9   86-8126
    ISBN 0-306-42197-6
    ISBN 0-306-42296-4 (pbk.)

© 1986 Plenum Press
A Division of Plenum Publishing Corporation
233 Spring Street, New York, N.Y. 10013

Original edition © 1981 Wissenschaftliche Buchgesellschaft
Darmstadt, Federal Republic of Germany

Printed in the United States of America

Hans Hörmann
1924–1983

Preface

At the time of his death Hans Hörmann, then Professor of Psychology at the Ruhr University, Bochum, West Germany, was preparing an English language version of his *Einführung in die Psycholinguistik*. The goal of this book, in both the German and English editions, was to present in compact and readily accessible form the essentials of his approach to the psychology of language. Basing his work upon the materials treated at length and in depth in two previous comprehensive and more technical works, *Psycholinguistics: An Introduction to Research and Theory* and *To Mean—To Understand*, Hörmann had made a selection of themes and problems suitable for beginners and for those who wanted a convenient introduction to the specific framework within which Hörmann thought psycholinguistics was to be pursued.

The result is a remarkably clear, succinct, and provocative account of central issues and options of the psychology of language, that broad and not strictly delimited part of psychology that takes as its domain the multiform conditions, processes, and structures involved in the acquisition, development, production, and grasp of linguistic meaning. Hörmann's approach is admittedly contentious and goes directly against a great deal of Anglo-American psycholinguistics. In particular, it radically devalues the relevance of certain types of theoretical linguistics, principally, though not exclusively, Chomskyan, for the psychology of

vii

language. Its principal fault, Hörmann claims, is its overconcentration on syntax and its logicism, its presupposition that language is ultimately structured like a formal calculus or as a system of idealized competencies which linguistic performances merely inadequately realize. Hörmann also saw the philosophical presuppositions and implications of research in psycholinguistics, for by focusing on the overall primacy of meaning and understanding at every stage of language use and development as central, he makes the points of intersection between philosophy and psychology abundantly clear. Hence, linguistic, psychological, and philosophical considerations distinctively interact and mutually enrich one another in Hörmann's approach and bear witness to the centrality and scope of the problems treated in this book.

My task as editor of the book has been threefold.

First, I have smoothed out the language and rid it of a number of Germanisms that echoed too closely the German original upon which the book is based. The manuscript of the present book was not strictly speaking a translation. Although it followed closely, sometimes exactly, the German version, often the order of discussion had been modified, new materials added, some materials deleted. I have tried to turn the text into idiomatic, clear, if not elegant, English.

Second, I have inserted section divisions into the chapters. These correspond, with a couple of exceptions, to Hörmann's "running heads" as they appeared in the German edition. I have also inserted relevant supporting and illustrative materials into the text, mostly in the form of block quotations that encapsulate or express in particularly striking fashion positions parallel to or identical with the main thrusts of Hörmann's argument. Because of their often ringing aphoristic character they will be able to function as nodal points for discussion and reflection. Many of them, but by no means all, were cited by Hörmann in his two more technical books. They give the present book slightly more density and body without changing the introductory character that Hörmann sought and attained.

Third, I have added an introduction that tries in synthetic, compendious fashion to highlight the main lines of Hörmann's approach and to pinpoint in particular the relations between psychology, linguistics, and philosophy that Hörmann thinks must be adverted to if we are to get a proper bead on language as it is actually learned and used by living human beings.

I want to thank my wife Marianne and my friend Elaine Ober for their helpful suggestions concerning the editorial interventions and Kelly Lambert, of the University of Lowell libraries, for digging out references. I am greatly indebted to Eliot Werner and Harvey Graveline of Plenum Press for the detailed and thoughtful editorial attention they have given to the physical realization of this project. R. W. Rieber proposed a felicitous modification in the title. Finally, Mrs. Hans Hörmann generously supplied us with a photograph of Professor Hörmann.

ROBERT E. INNIS

LOWELL, MASSACHUSETTS

Contents

Introduction

ROBERT E. INNIS

The *intentional act* by which the self-conscious mind
establishes a relationship with the world around it is . . . a
principle beyond which there is no sensible inquiry.

Hans Hörmann

Sense-Giving and the Critique of Objectivism

The chief presupposition and organizing principle of this book, which is devoted to studying the real psychological processes involved in the human use of language, is encapsulated in I. M. Schlesinger's striking phrase: "Human nature abhors a semantic vacuum." At every point and at every level in human intercourse with language we find operating a drive toward sense and meaning, a "pull of meaningfulness," which is not restricted to language and articulation as such but is also delineated in perception and action as well. One of Hörmann's main theses is that just as a size constancy, a color constancy, a brightness constancy, and other constancies account for the presence of an organized and coherent world within which the human organism operates, so there exists in the human intentional system a factor of "sense constancy," an ultimate semantic function, an overarching interpretative and constructive mechanism, which permeates all attempts to render linguistic utterances intelligible. It underlies all comprehending dealing with language, supporting our ability to apply language to novel situations, to make semantic anomalies perspicuous, and to grasp the point in a metaphor, whether creative, when discourse makes itself visible, or in the normal

3

processes of concept formation which are themselves permeated by metaphorical factors.

Hence, language for Hörmann is subsumed into the general semiotic matrix of "sense-giving" as such. It effects, to be sure, a revolution in the human apprehension of the world, but it in no way abrogates the overarching orientation toward meaning and expression that marks the human animal as such. This giving of sense through a system of linguistic signs oscillates between two poles and hence has a double orientation: toward one's communicative partner, whose behavior or consciousness one is trying to influence, and toward oneself as a being gearing into the world through perception and action, whose perception can be channeled and whose action can be steered and facilitated by the construction of a linguistic device (see Wegener: 1885/1971 and Gardiner: 1932/1951). This device is thematized by Hörmann, with reliance on Karl Bühler's *Sprachtheorie* (see also Innis: 1982), as a tool or organon which is shared by the social group and appropriated by each individual. The "work" done by this tool is hence not just communication and the effecting of a participation in a pool of preexisting meanings, but the mastery of the world of objects, the conscious control of the behavior of others, and the consolidation of one's own consciousness or *interiority*, which takes on human form by being assimilated to the semantic powers of language systems. Hörmann's picture of language then is, in the broadest sense, praxeological, rooted in the totality of concrete interactions between the human organism and the world. With this slant, Hörmann breaks with the epistemologically freighted notion that language's innermost trajectory is toward a cognitive or contemplative "mirroring" of a preexisting world, fundamentally for the satisfaction of the individual consciousness. As Hörmann constantly insists, language is first of all the continuation of action by other means, and this action takes place within a social field, a point made with great force and strength by V. N. Vološinov in his *Marxism and the Philosophy of Language* (1929).

Perhaps the chief opponent of the arguments and selections of data that Hörmann adduces in this book is the rationalistic, monadological orientation that ascribes primary importance to the admittedly massive cognitional achievement of language and contends that, ultimately, not only does language as an independent system of signifiers exist independently of the language user but also the study of its formal structure in itself supplies us with the guiding principles, chief questions, and heuristic clues for a specifically psychological study of language. It is precisely this thesis that Hörmann claims has stifled and misled research in psycholinguistics since the great attack by Noam Chomsky on Skinner's behaviorist language theory.

The irony of the historical aftermath of the ascendancy of Chomsky's model is that in place of an objectivistic behavioristic model of the language animal, which was the object of Chomsky's critique, there was put, in effect, another objectivistic model, oriented now toward formal logic. Chomsky shared with the structuralist tradition, attaining self-definition in Saussure's thematization of language as an autonomous system of differentially related signifiers, the assumption that to explain the functioning of language one had to have recourse exclusively to language-immanent factors and elements. Although Saussure took as his theme the existence of the language system as a social institution, a position he derived from the American linguist Whitney and the French sociologist Durkheim, Chomsky was impressed by language's putative correspondence to logical structures, being in fact an instantiation of a formal system and explicable on the model of a logical theory. It is this logistical orientation that led to the primacy, not to say overweening predominance, of syntactic problems in Chomskyan linguistic theory and in the psychological investigations flowing from it. Echoing the work of Karl Bühler, whom he considers to be the greatest psycholinguistic scholar of the century, Hörmann resolutely rejects the guidance of formal logic. Bühler's ringing slogan pithily summarizes the thrust of Hörmann's whole approach: *lingua docet logicam* [language teaches logic].

Hörmann's book is one long argument against linguistic objectivism in the psychology of language. This critique of objectivism appears first of all in Hörmann's rejection of the competence–performance distinction which underlies the whole intellectual trajectory of the Chomsky school. One of Chomsky's key theses was that the main task of linguistic theory was to formulate the system of rules that constitute the linguistic "knowledge" of the language user and that enable him or her to produce or recognize grammatically correct or well-formed utterances. This system of rules did not have to be consciously available to the linguistic subject. The rules remained for the most part "tacit" and had only to be operative. The peculiarity of Chomsky's position was that syntax, the formal structures that govern the assembling of linguistic strings, was considered to be the core of language and that there was an innate core of syntactical constraints underlying the empirical constraints resident in concrete individual languages and which had to be learned through a process of hypothetical reasoning on the basis of fragmentary evidence and instances. This process Chomsky reckoned cognate to C. S. Peirce's "abduction," one of the three main forms of inference. This system of syntactical rules makes up the idealized speaker and his competence but is not meant to describe the performance of any individual speaker who is subject to the thousand natural shocks that flesh is heir to.

Hörmann strives to show that the fatal weakness of the whole Chomskyan approach is the subordination of semantics to syntax. The relation, in his opinion, is to be reversed. It is rather the drive toward sense, the semantic dimension, that governs the acquisition of and evolution of syntax. Syntax itself must not labor under the domination of formal logic nor, as a matter of fact, must semantics do so. Hörmann accordingly also takes direct aim at the notion of an ideal lexicon as the locus where the semantic and circumstantial markers that constitute the meaning of a word are to be found. It is not at all clear whether such a lexicon has any psychological reality and is not instead a construct due to the philosophical commitments of the researcher. The chief defect of the lexicon is that it does not appear to be accessed in the postulated way in the normal, pragmatic use of language. Such a use is not dependent on a rigid, structured world of semantic features. Rather, it displays the most remarkable selectivity, fragmentariness, shiftings and turnings, depending on the situation in which the language user finds himself. Hörmann draws attention in many places to numerous experiments that call the role of such a lexicon into doubt and reveal it as the correlate of the attempt to found a pure, idealized theory of syntax independent of semantic factors, no matter how nuanced the various approaches to this problem within the Chomsky-inspired school have been. Word meanings are not structured in the consciousness of the language user as tree diagrams which are accessed according to logically formalizable routes of derivation or paths of superordination and subordination.

Linguistic objectivism is also manifested by a school of thought with which Hörmann does indeed have a real affinity, perhaps even more than he would have been willing to admit. I am referring to all those positions which have been lumped together under the rubric of the "linguistic relativity thesis," represented most notably in the English language scholarly world as the so-called Sapir–Whorf hypothesis. In the German world out of which Hörmann worked the equivalents were already present in the writings of Herder in the late eighteenth century and of von Humboldt in the early nineteenth century. In its most radical form, this thesis asserts the identity of thought and language, with the consequence that not only does thought master the world through language, a world that would be inaccessible without it, but that ultimately language masters thought, in such a fashion that thought forms are strictly speaking functions of language forms. As Humboldt put it in his *Academy Treatise on Comparative Philology*: "The mutual interdependence of thought and word makes it evident that languages are not really means of representing already known truth; they are means of discovering hitherto unknown truth" (cited by Hörmann 1979: 272). Indeed, as Humboldt puts it later:

> Intellect and language permit and develop only forms which are mutually compatible. Language can be said to be the outward manifestation of the mind of nations. Their language is their mind, and their mind their language. One must imagine them as completely identical.
> (Cited in Hörmann 1979: 272)

Although Hörmann agreed with Humboldt that "language is the thought-forming instrument" (cited in Hörmann 1979: 156)—which is completely in accord with his organon or tool model of language—his mentalism in psychology as such and in

the psychology of language did not extend to a complete identification of the two. He allowed room for many perceptual factors
which are not formally and explicitly mapped into the linguistic
system, although many obviously are, as for instance in the system of color terms that have so occupied the linguistic relativity
theorists. Language for Hörmann is in its sense-constituting
character both productive, that is, "going beyond the information
given," as Bruner put it, and reproductive, that is, oriented toward a world of pregiven and preinterpreted objects and meanings. It is the subtle relationship between these two dimensions
of language and their realization by the various systems wherein
human beings apprehend and create meaning that Hörmann
calls attention to throughout his book. Although, to be sure, the
book focuses primarily upon language, the perceptual system as
well as other prelinguistic, translinguistic, and extralinguistic
cognitive and action systems also play varying roles. As Hörmann's analysis, which parallels that of G. H. Mead, will show,
"the nucleus of the knowledge from which language emerges is
contained in *the perception- and action-based act*" (1981: 211).

Perceptual Presuppositions

In fact, there underlies Hörmann's whole approach a certain set of
perceptual postulates which are not made completely clear in this
book but which he has presented quite extensively elsewhere.
They impact directly on his image of the language animal. Hörmann's main point is the active, constructive character of perception. Perception is, as von Allesch put it, a comprehending and
complementing of perceptual data, that is, of percepts, "in terms
of available knowledge. The complementing seems to proceed step
by step, and we are guided closely by the subjective need to round
off our perception" (von Allesch 1909: 498, cited in Hörmann
1981: 4). Here we have the perceptual roots of sense-constancy,
which plays a critical role in Hörmann's work. In support of von
Allesch, Hörmann cites (1981: 48) a passage from Rudolf
Arnheim (1947: 69), which also intersects with a position es-
poused by Manfred Bierwisch:

> Perhaps perception consists in the application, to the stimulus mate-
> rial, of 'perceptual categories,' such as roundness, redness, small-
> ness, symmetry, verticality, etc., which are evoked by the structure of
> the given configuration. . . . There is a fitting of perceptual charac-
> teristics to the structure suggested by the stimulus material rather
> than a reception of this material itself.

"These categories," Arnheim claims "are the indispensable prerequisites which permit us to understand perceptually." They
are, in fact, on the order of "anthropological constants" which
are the foundation of all language acquisition and use.

It is these categories, and our powers of bringing them to
bear on the sensory array, that make perception an interpretative, creative process that is potentiated by the achievements of language. Hörmann cites in his *To Mean—To Understand* (48) another long passage from Arnheim (1947: 70) which
must be kept constantly in mind as one reads the following introductory book:

> Our assumption is that the individual stimulus configuration [in
> analogy: the word as received by the ear—H. H.] enters the perceptual
> process only in that it evokes a specific pattern of general sensory
> categories, which *stands* for the stimulus [as the cluster of the re-
> spective semantic markers stands for the meaning of the word—H.
> H.] in a similar way in which in a scientific description a network of
> general concepts is offered as the equivalent of a phenomenon of
> reality. . . . If this theory be acceptable, the elementary processes of
> perception, far from being mere passive registration, would be cre-
> ative acts of grasping structure. . . . Perceiving would represent indi-
> vidual cases through configurations of general categories.

This process—described here by a Gestalt theorist in semiotic
terms—is hence far from being automatic or arbitrary. Perception strives to find "the relevant joints" (in Plato's sense) in experience, and for this to occur the perceiving agent must let itself be
led by the natural cues and clues which are found in the perceptual field. But the field is not self-assembling as such; there is
always, as Polanyi put it, a logical gap between the sensory particulars and the focal unity upon which they bear.

It is the interpretative achievement of the perceptual subject
to cross this gap and to wring from the flow of sensory contents
the significant units that occupy the center of attention and that

make up the realm of physiognostic meanings upon which the teleognostically contrived linguistic signs as vehicles or carriers of articulate content bear (see the essay "Sense-Giving and Sense-Reading" in Polanyi 1969). Hörmann's deepest commitments with respect to perception are to the findings of Gestalt theory and, as it will become very clear in the book, to the universal relevance of the figure–ground structure. Linguistic utterances themselves not only have a figure–ground structure but are really themselves, in their complex reality, figures over against a ground made up of contexts, fields, shared situations, and so forth, which make up the great background of presuppositions over against which the linguistic form effects its predicational novelty.

Another aspect of the perceptual roots of linguistic meaning is found in the work of Manfred Bierwisch, whom Hörmann cites frequently in *To Mean–To Understand*. These roots function both as conditions of the possibility of linguistic meaning and as a set of antecedent constraints upon the range and variability of the meanings articulated in linguistic forms themselves. They are anthropological constants which ground the semantic markers that make up, though not in the way conceived by proponents of the semantic feature approach, the zones or spheres of linguistic meaning. They constitute a kind of biological-perceptual *a priori*. In Bierwisch's (1967: 3) words:

> Semantic markers in an adequate description of natural language do not represent properties of the surrounding world in the broadest sense, but rather certain deep-seated, innate properties of the human organism and the perceptual apparatus, properties which determine the way in which the universe is conceived, adapted, and worked on. (In Hörmann 1981: 47)

There is a qualification, however, which Bierwisch (1967: 4) makes in order to avoid what both he and Hörmann would consider the trap of the radical linguistic relativity thesis:

> The idea of innate basic elements of the semantic structure does not entail a biological determination of concepts or meanings in a given language, but only of their ultimate components. These components can be combined rather freely and differently in different languages.

This whole problem of semantic or linguistic universals lies outside the strict problem space of the present book, but it constitutes the indispensable background to the full investigation of linguistic meanings which Hörmann's approach would entail.

Fields

Hörmann shows clearly that linguistic actions are stratified events that are embedded in contexts or fields. These contexts or fields make up another aspect of the conditions of sense. They constitute the ultimate socially shared, public frames within which the acts of linguistic communication and use take place. All contribute, in varying ways and to varying degrees, to determining the meaning of a linguistic action.

The perceptual field is the genetically first determinant, for the original linguistic actions refer to components within this field within which the infant is acting and striving to satisfy its desires and needs. It is because the speaker and hearer dwell in a common world of objects (I am using *object* in a non-philosophical, everyday way) that are in important ways preunderstood that the infant is able both to generate and to understand linguistic utterances. Hörmann has many interesting things to say on this process, both in its developmental aspects and in the role of perceptual fields in determining the meaning of linguistic utterances in adult use of language. This topic has not only psychological but also social-psychological importance and is in addition one of the places where Hörmann's approach intersects with the philosophy of language in particular and with the general theory of signs or semiotics in general (see Innis 1985b). The perceptual conditions of sense can never ultimately be avoided, although, as he himself points out, it would be a gross mistake to claim that language always refers to perceptual units as such.

This perceptual field is itself embedded in an action field, a pragmatic field of material gearings into the world and of goal-directed activities. It is a world of mutual adjustments and coordinations that is potentiated through the use of linguistic signs. In this sense language is a significant gesture which inheres in a larger social act as one of its phases. This is another place where

Hörmann's theory comes close to the positions elaborated by the great American symbolic behaviorist, George Herbert Mead. As Mead writes, "language as such is simply a process by means of which the individual who is engaged in co-operative activity can get the attitude of others involved in the same activity" (1934: 335). Karl Bühler placed the point of origin of signs in social life precisely here: in the social space occupied by participants in a common undertaking (see Innis 1982). Language arises as a di-acriticon which effects a shift either in action or in perception, and it does so over against a field which is shared by the partici-pants. The steering function of language, which plays a predomi-nant role in Hörmann's whole approach, is particularly evident here, as it was in Philipp Wegener's *Investigations into the Fun-damental Problems of the Life of Speech* (1885/1971), cited by Hörmann in his more technical books, but not in the present work (see Innis 1985a). Looked at this way, language does not merely transfer information through a channel structured by a code, but is rather a participation in and constitution of a com-mon "world."

Besides the extralinguistic fields of perception and action we have properly linguistic fields: syntactical fields and semantic fields. Syntactical fields are composed of those intralinguistic or-dering devices that relate the various word classes to one another and differentiate the formal aspects in which the world is ap-prehended. Linguistic strings are generated according to rules which control the combination of signifying units. One of the great debates in modern linguistic and psychological theory con-cerns the psychological status of our knowledge of these syntac-tical and grammatical rules and their function in the acquisition of linguistic "competence." The Chomsky school, which func-tions as a kind of permanent interlocutor for Hörmann through-out his book, has always insisted on the special place of syntax in linguistic analysis and on the specificity of the type of knowledge involved in the language user's command of syntactic rules. Chomsky claimed that the language user had a fundamentally "tacit" knowledge of these rules which it was the job of the lin-guist to thematize by a process of rational reconstruction. The empirical rules of grammar which govern the well-formedness of any concrete linguistic string must, however, correspond to the conditions of a universal grammatical competence, which is distinctively human.

Syntactical rules make up a system of constraints which the language users have to share in order to communicate successfully and which putatively make it possible, for example, to know, independently of meaning, that the famous sentence "Colorless green ideas sleep furiously" is an acceptable utterance from the point of view of syntax. Hörmann tries to elucidate the processes by which syntactical knowledge arises by rejecting out of hand the main Chomskyan assumptions: idealized linguistic competence thematized fundamentally as belonging to the domain of syntax, the secondary role of meaning in the generation of a linguistic string, and the logicism of an approach which isolates language from the great matrices of action and social life out of which it grows and within which it always functions. The arguments against all of these assumptions makes up a continuing and central part of the book and of Hörmann's whole psycholinguistic project. As he put it in his *To Mean—To Understand*:

> To proceed with proper linguistic analysis, the language user must first make certain decisions concerning the linguistic aspects of the utterances on supralinguistic grounds. Stretching the point a little, we might say that we can understand language only when we understand more than language. (123)

The focal point, however, of Hörmann's whole procedure is semantic. The category of 'meaning' or 'sense' is placed at the very center of all his analyses. It is by no means an exclusively linguistic concept but extends, as Merleau-Ponty (1945/1962) demonstrated, all the way from the primary achievements of motility to the highest reaches of articulate abstractions (see Cassirer 1929/1953). Hörmann points out in an important footnote (Chapter 5, note 2) the variability of the concept of meaning, for it is possible to speak of the meaning of a gesture, of an action, of a word, a sentence, a text, and so on. All of these domains are subject to different formal and material constraints and have different expressive powers, which would be thematized and systematized in a full-fledged, comprehensive model of language and of semiosis (see Innis 1985b). The furnishing of such a model is no job of an introductory text on the psychology of language. Language exists for the sake of meaning, which is a more comprehensive category than language. Moreover, linguistic meaning is in no way to be modelled after the types of domains and ideal entities which are investigated by a logistically oriented philosophical semantics which is obsessed by a particular conception of how the representational function of language operates. These domains exist, to be sure, but they are a derivate from a more encompassing matrix of sense and relevance within which the intentional engagements of the human being for the most part take place.

Hence, 'meanings' are just as much instruments employed by the linguistic subject in coming to master the world and to influence it as something to be grasped as the term of an interpretative act. Hörmann's resolutely mental and social approach to meaning is epitomized in his relentless critique, here as well as in his other writings, of the notion of a completely structured lexicon which makes up the actual field of meanings used by the linguistic subject. As Hörmann put it in his *Psycholinguistics: An Introduction to Research and Theory*:

> We have to abandon the view that semantic categories are simply compartments into which everything, characterized in terms of the features, fits equally well. It is more likely that semantic features form a focal center with a slowly blurring surround. The definition of a crime in the vocabulary of the layman is not characterized by a listing of common features shared by *all* crimes, but is instead centered around a definite configuration, 'murder.' (228)

The same point was developed by Vygotsky in his essay "Thought and Word" in his classic *Thought and Language*, where the semantic peculiarities of inner speech are easily transferable to normal functioning speech in everyday linguistic intercourse. The basic peculiarity, which he himself derived from Paulhan, is "the preponderance of the *sense* of a word over its *meaning*." For Paulhan, as well as for Vygotsky:

> The sense of a word . . . is the sum of all the psychological events aroused in our consciousness by the word. It is a dynamic, fluid, complex whole, which has several zones of unequal stability. Meaning is only one of the zones of sense, the most stable and precise zone. A word acquires its sense from the context in which it appears; in different contexts, it changes its sense. Meaning remains stable

> throughout the changes of sense. The dictionary meaning of a word
> [that is, the codified, structured account of its meaning—REI] is no
> more than a stone in the edifice of sense, no more than a potentiality
> that finds diversified realization in speech. (146)

Indeed, as Vygotsky paraphrases Paulhan once again, "the sense of a word . . . is a complex, mobile, protean phenomenon; it changes in different minds and situations and is almost unlimited" (146). It is precisely the dialectic between sense and meaning, as here understood, that makes up the living semantic reality of language for Hörmann. His is a sophisticated voice from psychology warning us of the dangers of imposing antecedent restrictions upon the types of actual semantic structures that one ought to look for or that one could possibly find. These dangers have their source in letting the psychology of language be guided too rigidly by linguistics in general and by linguistic models in particular that rely upon the notion that language is fundamentally a concretization of an essentially abstract calculus.

Supporting Linguistic Theories

There are, however, other language theories that are not antithetical to Hörmann's approach, and he himself notes in particular the work of Chafe and Fillmore, both of whom offer more grounds of support for the psychologist of language than either the now discarded behaviorist model or all those models that rely on formalization techniques. Still, the greatest source of inspiration for Hörmann is undoubtedly Karl Bühler, whose great untranslated masterpiece *Sprachtheorie* is an incomparable synthesis of linguistic, semiotic, psychological, and philosophical materials and insights.

Many of Bühler's main points are constantly mirrored in Hörmann's analyses and most have already been alluded to: the so-called organon model of language and the multiplicity of language functions inherent in or able to be read out of a language event, with the representational function being only one of them, the necessity of a mental "set" and processes of abstraction in the constitution of the linguistic sign, the role of fields and surrounding contexts as semantic determinants, the primacy of the social matrix in the origin of semantics, the mutual conditioning of subjective and objective factors in the genesis of linguistic meaning, the primacy of the thing-meant over the mediating and essentially instrumental word-meanings, the necessity of application, of determining the "fit" between an expression and the experiences upon which it putatively bears (see Innis 1982, 1984b, 1986). All of these themes receive a clear, if not complete, discussion in Hörmann's book. Hörmann explicitly situates his own work within the Bühlerian framework, of which it is both a continuation and an application, as well as, in places, a criticism, the details and validity of which, however, have no place in an introduction to an introductory text.

In addition, in his two more technical books Hörmann refers, as I already mentioned, to the work of Wegener. It is easy to see the presence of Wegener's pivotal themes in the present book, too: the necessity of shared situations (called by Wegener the situations of perception, of remembrance, of consciousness, and a cultural situation, all of which play a large role in Hörmann's project) wherein the essentially diacritical act of speech occurs, the multiple lines of orientation—whether "altruistic" or "egoistic"—of an utterance toward the speaker and the hearer and its effects either upon behavior or upon the contents of consciousness of the participants in the linguistic exchange, the goal of language use as the effecting of mutual understanding or the realization of common ends rather than an essentially monadological "mirroring" of the world "in" consciousness (the world is, in one sense, mirrored or at least mapped in consciousness, but the process is really social in essence, for the linguistic tool which makes it possible is social through and through), the essentially predicative nature of utterances, that is, their foregrounding as figures the semantic novelty in the situation, which functions as a ground, and the emergence of grammatical structures through a process of emendation, through the attempt to eliminate ambiguities, to correct misunderstandings, and to supplement through properly linguistic means the inadequacy of a prior articulation, showing forth in this way the primacy of use and intention over form (cf. Innis 1985a).

Not mentioned, however, in Hörmann but eminently relevant to and supportive of his whole argument is a continuation of Wegener's work by the British language theorist and Egyptologist, Sir Alan Gardiner. His *A Theory of Speech and Language* presents in lucid and systematic form, with historical sophistication and theoretical acuity, a strong case for mentalism in language theory and a nuanced account of the situation-dependent aspects of speech (see also Innis 1984a). Although Gardiner was not concerned with psycholinguistics, which as such did not exist when his book was first published, the rootedness of his work in the actual facts of language and its avoidance of a logistical and monadological approach give it extraordinary pertinence to and heuristic fertility for the psychology of language. From a specifically linguistic and not at all genetic or developmental point of view, we find a thorough examination of fields, of the nature of word meanings and sentence meanings, of the nature of predication as the essential act of speech (a position which intersects with Fillmore's case grammar), of the primacy of function over form, that is, of meaning over syntax, and a continual awareness of the *steering* function of language, with both the speaker's and the hearer's consciousness being steered by the linguistic tools.

The relatively nonformal semantic approaches of Bühler and Gardiner especially give strong support to many of Hörmann's main themes. Nowhere is this more clear than in the thesis that words are bearers of *meaning-areas* rather than of strictly defined ideas of a quasi-Platonic sort. As Gardiner (1932: 36) put it: "We can perhaps best picture to ourselves the meaning of a word such as *horse* by considering it as a territory or area over which the various possibilities of correct application are mapped out" (36). Although *horse* excludes *cow* as "off the map," since they have no overlapping areas in common, "within the legitimate range of the word-meaning *horse* the various things meant will be differently grouped, some rather near the borderline, and others distinctly central" (37). Prancing steeds, towel-horses, gymnasium horses all fall within the domain of application but not all certainly lie close to the center of the semantic space. As we move from toy horses through gymnasium horses to towel horses there is an increased feeling of strain—a distinctive reference to subjectivity—since "in terms of our map, these applications grow increasingly peripheral" (37). Hence, "the meaning of a word is not identical with an 'idea' in the Platonic sense" (44). "Word-meanings possess nothing of that self-consistency and homogeneity which are characteristic of 'ideas'. Ideas, if attainable at all, are the result of long and toilsome search on the part of philosophers" (44). This is certainly not the case with everyday use of language.

Bühler makes the same points, relying on both the analysis of mature language and of materials from the psychology of language itself. Exemplary are his notions of a "meaning-sphere" and of a "synchytic" concept. As Bühler (1934: 22) put it:

> The appearing of an ordering sphere in our knowing points universally to the fact that in many cases of the actual use of a word it is enough if, instead of the content, the scope of a concept, that is, the domain of application of the ordering sign, be in some way marked out.

The way in which this is so depends on the interest structures of the language user's consciousness as well as on the objective contexts, linguistic or otherwise, in which the language sign is located. Most nonscientific concepts, as borne by words, have in fact no sharp boundaries. They are made up of a bundle of different semantic features which are related to one another by family resemblances. Bühler calls such a concept a *synchytic* concept, a notion that bears a remarkable similarity to the ideas developed by Wittgenstein, whose thought was deeply influenced by the idea that word meanings coalesce around prototypes, models, paradigmatic examples, typical instances, which intersect with one another in sets of features the way family members share features which clearly join them together but which still let each member be identified for itself (see Eschbach 1984).

Philosophical Background

This is indeed one of Hörmann's main philosophical semantic presuppositions, and he is indebted to two concepts that Wittgenstein (1958) developed most fully in his *Philosophical Investigations*: that of family resemblances and that of language being embedded in "forms of life" wherein various "language games" are played. Wittgenstein's most famous, though certainly not only, example to illustrate family resemblances is that of the criteria for classifying something as a game: board-game, card-game, ball-game, Olympic games, and so on. Looking for, rather than postulating, common features leads one to the conclusion, so argues Wittgenstein, that what we find are similarities, correspondences, and relationships, but no isomorphically possessed set of common features. "We see a complicated network of similarities overlapping and criss-crossing" (§ 66). It is impossible to find a boundary determining with logical strictness the inside and the outside of the game concept. We can stipulate one or draw one, but it is not found in the nature of the concept itself which would have a putatively stable place in a rigid, dictionary-like lexicon. To determine the range of application of the word *game* or to explain to someone what the word means, it is necessary to give examples in such a way that the other will get the point, not through seeing what all these examples putatively have in common but in his now being able to employ these examples in a particular way. Hörmann's whole approach to describing how the language user really "possesses" meaning runs substantially parallel to Wittgenstein's position and shows an important point of intersection between psycholinguistic investigations and the philosophy of language.

The notion of a language game also intersects with Hörmann's chief contention that language is a continuation of action with other means and also that, within limits, it *is* possible to see language as a set of rule-governed processes, although we must resist the temptation, as Wittgenstein puts it, "to think that if anyone utters a sentence and *means* or *understands* it he is operating a calculus according to definite rules" (§ 81). The role of rules is extremely flexible and depends on the type of language game one is playing. We are entangled in our own rules, but they are not rigid. They are context-dependent and emerge from the need of the language subject for some regularity. Now, as Wittgenstein says with regard to philosophy but with equal relevance to the project of the psychology of language, "This entanglement in our rules is what we want to understand (i.e., get a clear view of). It throws light on our concept of *meaning* something" (§ 125).

To mean something, as well as to understand something, is to make a move in a game, precisely the game of meaning and understanding. Such a notion is fundamentally functionalist. As Hörmann put it in *To Mean—To Understand*:

> In line with our functionalist approach to language, we cannot fail to notice the frequent overdetermination of what is the goal of language use. Instead of treating speaking as representation of knowledge in action, we prefer to see it as an intricate complex of interrelated means of action that are used in highly variable ways for purposes of conveying and grasping meaning. (239)

Here we have an echo of Wittgenstein's oft cited remarks that "the word 'language-game' is supposed to emphasize here that the speaking of a language is part of an activity, or of a form of life" (§ 23) and that "I will also call the whole—consisting of language and the activities with which it is interwoven—the 'language-game'" (§ 7). Hence, there is an intimate connection between meaning and use, a point important not just in philosophical semantics but also in the psychological treatment of semantic problems. A long and technical treatment, which should be turned to after this book has been digested, will be found in Hörmann's *To Mean—To Understand*.

Besides these obvious and fruitful points of intersection between Hörmann and Wittgenstein, at which I have only hinted here, there are further parallels in the philosophical literature to many of Hörmann's chief themes and also other philosophical supports to his procedures and substantive conclusions. The two most important, which are not emphasized in the present book but which play a more critical role in his other treatises are K. Adjukiewicz and M. Polanyi. Adjukiewicz's work on mutual understanding of sentences "surpasses Wittgenstein's in precision," according to Hörmann (1981: 153) and is "of paramount importance for the psychologist of language because it brings us close to the process of understanding" (153).

For Adjukiewicz (1934: 106) "the sense carried by the expressions of a language determines in some way the rules of their uses" (cited by Hörmann 1981: 153). But how can we determine that the sense is the same for the partners in the language game?

> We try to find for this sentence a particularly salient type of experiences, a type in whose nature it is that experiences of this type warrant a determined acknowledgment of the sentence. If we then find the person to reject the sentence in spite of becoming aware of an experience of this type, we conclude that the sentence has been associated with a different sense than in our case. (Adjukiewicz 1934: 10, as cited by Hörmann 1981: 154)

This position results in emphasizing what Hörmann calls "an eminently psychological aspect" which is rooted in agreement in forms of life and not merely in opinion. In Adjukiewicz's words (1934: 110) once again: "The connection between, e.g., the sentence 'It hurts' and the sense attributed to it in the particular language can be established only by someone who, becoming aware of the experience of pain, is ready to acknowledge the sentence" (cited in Hörmann 1981: 154). This corresponds, as Hörmann points out, to Deese's interpretation of understanding as "the inward sign of the potential for reacting appropriately to what we see or hear" (1969: 516).

It is only, Hörmann claims, the problematic character of the very notion of *sense* as used in connection with the issue of the rules of language use that makes him hesitate to employ Adjukiewicz's conception more explicitly. Adjukiewicz writes (1935: 166):

> As to the question whether one should say that sense is determined by the rules of language or rather that the rules are determined by sense, I observe that there is mutual determination. That is to say: if the sense of an utterance is such and such, then such and such rules apply to the utterance, but also conversely, if such and such rules apply to the utterance, then its sense is such and such. (Cited in Hörmann 1981: 154)

It is true that *sense*, like *meaning*, is a plurivalent and rather slippery concept. But in line with Hörmann's attempt to show that language is only one component in a large and highly differentiated matrix of sense giving and sense reading, his hesitation only points out the need to engage in a large-scale philosophical and semiotic investigation into the modes of signifying in every domain of human life, from perception through action to the highest reaches of artificial sign production. The synthetic nature of Hörmann's approach already indicates how, in the specifically psycholinguistic research area, this would be done.

Polanyi's influence on and importance for Hörmann's approach are perhaps even more marked than Adjukiewicz's. The main points taken over by Hörmann from Polanyi's extensive and comprehensive theory of "tacit knowing" are the following: the universal from–to structure of consciousness exemplified in skills and thematized through the distinction between focal and subsidiary awareness, the concomitant generalized notion of meaning, as identical with wholes of all sorts, rooted in Polanyi's exploitation of Gestalt theory for his own use in constructing a cognitional theory, and a model of emergence, of higher levels and boundary conditions, which Polanyi developed for purposes of a philosophical ontology but which Hörmann took over to illustrate the relations between the various levels in language.

As to the first, Polanyi (1962: 601) writes:

> We perform a skill by relying on the coordination of elementary muscular acts, and we are aware of having got these right by accomplishing our skillful performance. We are aware of them *in terms of this performance* and *not* (or very incompletely) aware of them *in themselves*. . . . There are vast domains of knowledge . . . that exemplify . . . that we are generally unable to tell what particulars we are aware of when attending to a coherent entity which they constitute. Thus, there are two kinds of knowing which invariably enter jointly into any act of knowing a comprehensive entity. There is (1) knowing a thing *by attending to it*, in the way we attend to an entity as a whole and (2) knowing a thing *by relying on our awareness of it for the purpose of attending to an entity to which it contributes.* (Cited in Hörmann 1981: 15–16)

In accordance with the general conclusions of Gestalt theory, which Polanyi was concerned to expand into a model of knowing as such, we attend to focal wholes, figures, forms, coherences in the experiential flow. They lie at the focus of attention and, in Polanyi's terminology, are the intended terms of "focal awareness." The "parts," "elements," and "particulars" which go to make up these comprehensive wholes are vectors which carry the sense-oriented consciousness toward completion. They are not attended to in themselves but are dwelt in and fused or integrated into a unity by the synthetic power of consciousness, the great "tacit" power that Polanyi put at the base of all dealing with the world, both practical and cognitional, the rigid distinction between which it was one of his aims to abolish. They are "subsidiary" to the whole upon which they bear (for a discussion of Polanyi's model as a whole see Innis 1973, 1974, 1977).

Knowing quite generally, then, in Polanyi's conception, is "an action which requires skill" (1958: vii).

> Skilful knowing and doing is performed by subordinating a set of particulars, as clues or tools, to the shaping of a skilful achievement, whether practical or theoretical. We may then be said to become 'subsidiarily aware' of these particulars within our 'focal awareness' of the comprehensive entity that we achieve. Clues and tools are things used as such and not observed in themselves. They are made to function as extensions of our bodily equipment and this involves a certain change in our own being. Acts of comprehension are to this extent irreversible, and also non-critical. For we cannot possess any fixed framework within which the reshaping of our hitherto fixed framework could be critically tested. (vii)

The implications for Hörmann's language theory of the ideas encapsulated in these texts are manifold. The distinction between focal and subsidiary awareness—its from—to structure—accounts for the so-called transparency of language signs which is manifested in the phenomenal irrelevance of the material carrier of meaning. It disappears from the center of consciousness and is replaced by a thematic consciousness of meaning. It is also illustrated in our ability to master and utilize at the same time a large set of subsidiary rule systems—phonetic, phonological, syntactic, semantic, stylistic, pragmatic—in the construction and interpretation of a sense-filled expression, of no matter what degree of complexity. Each one of these rule systems leaves open a set of boundary conditions which are employed on the next higher level, which, although dependent for its emergence on the lower level, still operates according to laws of its own and in fact constitutes the meaning of the lower level. And "as we ascend a hierarchy of boundaries, we reach to even higher levels of meaning" (Polanyi 1968: 1311, cited in Hörmann 1981: 168) for meaning is the "bearing which a particular has on the comprehensive entity to which it contributes" (Polanyi 1962: 601, cited in Hörmann 1981: 15–16).

Thus, we are presented with a model for understanding the essentially hierarchic structure of language. Hörmann's account of the various levels within which the speech act, as the fundamental unit of analysis, operates and is constituted must be seen within this comprehensive schema of Polanyi's. Each level allows its own investigation, but the lower levels exist for the sake of the higher and are subject to different degrees of formalization.

The whole process is under the control of semantic factors. In his essay "Sense-Giving and Sense-Reading," found in *Knowing and Being,* and in his monumental chapter "Articulation," in *Personal Knowledge,* Polanyi attempted to delineate the essential contours of the ultimately nonformal conditions surrounding the genesis of meaning in general and the apprehension of language in particular. Moreover, by identifying meaning with any comprehensive entity or whole—through a generalization of the figure–ground distincton in Gestalt theory—he managed to offer a philosophical framework which not only contributes to clarifying the problems of psycholinguistics but also sheds some light on the philosophical implications of its findings.

It is ultimately, however, the vectorial nature of understanding and of the linguistic instruments that promote and effect this understanding that Hörmann wants to highlight. The linguistic subject exists in a directed field of semantic forces and is carried along by them. On the one hand, he receives these linguistic instruments from without—they are something social, objective, and handed down. On the other hand, they must constantly be endowed with new meaning by the speaker and the contexts in which the speech event takes place. As Bühler (1934: 68–69) put it:

> To employ linguistic structures in intersubjective communication . . . to employ them as all other members of the speech community do, is one thing; another is to give them the precise meaning prescribed by language structure from case to case, and, moreover, to endow them with a uniquely modified meaning here and there. (Cited in Hörmann 1981: 169)

This position is echoed in a pregnant passage from Polanyi (1958: 81):

> To classify things in terms of features for which we have names, as we do in talking about things, requires the same kind of connoisseurship as the naturalist must have for identifying specimens of plants or animals. Thus the art of speaking precisely, by applying a rich vocabulary exactly, resembles the delicate discrimination practised by the expert taxonomist.

This subtle oscillation and dialectic penetrates every speech act and also bears directly upon the whole issue of the creation and comprehension of metaphors.

Metaphor as a paradigm of linguistic meaning, which has been discussed in an enormous literature, plays little role in this introductory book, for a number of reasons; but the principles for dealing with it, from the point of view of psycholinguistics, are laid down in Hörmann's account of sense-constancy: the effort at sense giving and sense reading is under an unrestricted demand for intelligibility. An act of understanding experience will employ every available means to bring it under an intelligible unity and the gaps in the already existing semantic space will be filled with new combinations and fusions when we *have* to construe it linguistically. Karl Bühler spoke of a drive toward drastic characterization (*Ausdrucksdrastik*) when the semantic system needs to be rearranged or wrenched out of its normal patterning in order to handle novel experiences (*Ausdrucksnot*) which have no equivalent in the existing system. From the point of view of the addressee of a metaphorical utterance the "interpretative center" which makes up the "mechanism" of the cognitive subject is able to find the necessary means to render it comprehensible. Although Hörmann does not explore the problem of metaphor in any great detail in this book, it seems to me that a fusion of his notion of sense constancy with an approach that relies on the parallels between perception and linguistic apprehension, such as, for example, Karl Bühler has done with his binocular model of overlapping filters or matrices or in the Polanyi text cited above, can take us a long way in clarifying both the special place of metaphor in language and its universality. For, as Quintilian rightly noted, *paene omne dictum metaphora est.*

Conclusion

Quoting Uhlenbeck (n.d.: 107) to the effect that "the trouble with language is that it is such a complicated, many-sided phenomenon," Hörmann (1981: 16n) rejects the notion that there is some unified model that can handle all the phenomena, structures, systems that make up language as such. The implication of this is that language is not itself something unified, but rather the result of a vast array and combination of biological, social, historical, and psychological preconditions. As, for example, Bühler and Toulmin (1971) have pointed out, it employs and arises on the base of a humanly specific constellation of different types of functions and abilities, of which tool use is also an essential component.

Bühler wrote in 1928 (48):

> It used to be said that speech was the beginning of hominization [*Menschwerden*]; maybe so, but before speech there is the thinking involved in the use of tools, i.e., comprehension of mechanical connections, and devising of mechanical means to mechanical ends, or, to put it more briefly still, before speech appears, action becomes subjectively meaningful—in other words, consciously purposeful. (In Hörmann 1981: 174)

This position is echoed in Mead's contention (1934: 237) that the hand which isolates physical things is as essential as speech for the development of the human animal and helps constitute the social human being as such. Tools and speech as exosomatic organs make up the two great systems of media within which human society develops. They potentiate as well as arise from the natural human capacities with which human beings are endowed at birth.

But it is not the dialectic between these two systems that is central in the present book, but rather the dialectic between *to mean* and *to understand*. Everything in this book is dedicated to illuminating their manifold relations, conditions, ranges, and implications. Its main point is expressed in the following text (Hörmann 1981: 257):

> From our psychological analysis of presupposition it follows that understanding can be conceived as a motion originating in a definite

cognitive state. The speaker who means something may be said to implant certain magnetic points in the hearer's presupposed cognitive field in an effort to modify it in the desired manner.

Hörmann's book contains a theoretically efficacious set of such magnetic points. By its candid discussion and questioning of positions it is an ideal introduction to the core issues in the psychology of language and lays the foundation for a detailed and more advanced study, to which it inevitably leads.[1]

References

Adjukiewicz, L. "Sprache und Sinn." *Erkenntnis* 4 (1934): 100–138.

———. "Die wissenschaftliche Weltperspektive." *Erkenntnis* 5 (1935): 22–30, 165–168.

Allesch, G. J. von. "Über das Verhältnis der Ästhetik zur Psychologie." *Zeitschrift für Psychologie* 54 (1909): 401–536.

Arnheim, R. "Perceptual Abstraction and Art." *Psychological Review* 54 (1947): 66–82. [Reprinted in his *Toward a Psychology of Art*. Berkeley: University of California Press, 1966.]

Bierwisch, M. "Some Semantic Universals of German Adjectivals." *Found Lang* 3 (1967): 1–36.

Bühler, K. *Abriss der geistigen Entwicklung des Kindes*. Leipzig: Quelle und Meyer, 1928.

———. *Sprachtheorie*. Jena: Fischer, 1934. [Reprinted with an introduction by Friedrich Kainz. Stuttgart: Fischer, 1965.]

Cassirer, E. *Philosophy of Symbolic Forms*, 3 vols, translated by Karl Manheim. New Haven: Yale University Press, 1953–1957. [Originally published 1923–1929.]

---

[1]A handy place to begin is with *Dialogues on the Psychology of Language and Thought*, edited by R. W. Rieber in collaboration with Gilbert Voyat (New York: Plenum Press, 1983). This volume, which could be used as a companion text to Hörmann's fine synthesis, contains clear and incisive discussions with Noam Chomsky, Charles Osgood, Jean Piaget, Ulric Neisser, and Marcel Kinsbourne about pratically all the topics and themes broached in Hörmann's book. It gives a focused presentation of the interlocutors' specific positions, and Rieber's and Voyat's general introduction gives a solid and accessible overview of the controversial issues in the psychology of language and thought.

Eschbach, A. "Verstehen und Interpretation. Karl Bühlers synchytische Begriffe und Ludwig Wittgensteins Familienähnlichkeiten." In *Bühler-Studien*, vol. 2, edited by Achim Eschbach. Frankfurt: Suhrkamp, 1984.

Gardiner, A. *The Theory of Speech and Language*. London: Oxford University Press, 1932; 2nd edition 1951. [Reprinted by Greenwood Press.]

Hörmann, H. *Psycholinguistics*. 2nd edition, revised. Translated by H. H. Stern and Peter Leppmann. New York: Springer, 1979. [First edition, 1971.]

_____.*To Mean–To Understand*. Translated from the German by Bogusław A. Jankowski. New York: Springer, 1981. [Originally published by Suhrkamp, 1976.]

Innis, R. "Polanyi's Model of Mental Acts." *The New Scholasticism* 47, 1 (1973): 147–178.

_____. "Meaning, Thought and Language in Polanyi's Epistemology." *Philosophy Today* 18, 1 (1974): 47–67.

_____. "In Memoriam Michael Polanyi." *Zeitschrift für allgemeine Wissenschaftstheorie* 8/1 (1977): 22–29.

_____. *Karl Bühler: Semiotic Foundations of Language Theory*. New York: Plenum Press, 1982.

_____. "Bühler und Gardiner: Von der Indikation zur Prädikation." In *Bühler-Studien*, vol. 2, edited by Achim Eschbach. Frankfurt: Suhrkamp, 1984a: 116–155.

_____. "Perception, Abstraction, and Subjectivity in Bühler's Language Theory." In *Rassegna italiana di linguistica applicata* 16, 1 (1984b): 2–23.

_____. "Articulation as Emendation: Philipp Wegener's Anti-formalist Theory of Language." In *Semiotics 1984*, edited by John Deely and Margot D. Lenhart. Washington, D.C.: University Press of America, 1985a.

_____. *Semiotics. An Introductory Anthology*. Bloomington: Indiana University Press, 1985b.

_____. "The Thread of Subjectivity: Philosophical Remarks on Bühler's Language Theory." To appear in *Karl Bühler's Theory of Language*, edited by Achim Eschbach. Amsterdam: John Benjamins, 1986.

Mead, G. H. *Mind, Self, and Society*. Edited and with an introduction by Charles W. Morris. Chicago: University of Chicago Press, 1934. [Reprinted as Phoenix paperback, 1962.]

Merleau-Ponty, M. *The Phenomenology of Perception*. Translated by Colin Smith. New York: Humanities Press, 1962. [Originally published, 1945.]

Polanyi, M. *Personal Knowledge*. London: Routledge and Kegan Paul, 1958. [Reprinted by University of Chicago Press.]

_____. "Tacit Knowing: Its Bearing on Some Problems of Philosophy." *Rev Mod Phys* 34 (1962): 601–616. [Reprinted in M. Polanyi, *Knowing and Being*.]

_____. "Life's Irreducible Structure." *Science* 160 (1968): 1308–1312.

_____. *Knowing and Being*. Edited by Marjorie Grene. Chicago: University of Chicago Press, 1969.

Toulmin, S. "Brain and Language." *Synthèse* 22 (1971): 369–395.

Uhlenbeck, E. M. *Critical Comments on Transformational Generative Grammar 1962–1972*. The Hague: Smits, n.d.

Vološinov, V. N. *Marxism and the Philosophy of Language*, translated by Ladislav Matejka and I. R. Titunik. New York: Seminar Press, 1973. [Originally published 1929.]

Vygotsky, L. *Thought and Language*. Translated by Gertrud Vakar and Eugenia Hanfmann. Cambridge, Mass.: MIT Press, 1962. [Original Russian edition, 1934.]

Wegener, P. *Untersuchungen über die Grundfragen des Sprachlebens*. Halle: Max Niemeyer, 1885. [English translation in D. Wilfred Abse, *Speech and Reason*. Charlottesville: University Press of Virginia, 1971.]

Wittgenstein, L. *Philosophical Investigations*. Translated by Elisabeth Anscombe. Oxford: Basil Blackwell, 1958. [American edition, New York: Macmillan.]

Perspectives on Language

An Introduction

HANS HÖRMANN

Well, but surely . . . you do not suppose that you can learn, nor I explain, any subject of importance all in a moment; at any rate, not such a subject as language, which is, perhaps, the very greatest of all.

Plato

. . . this alloy of speech and action.

L. Vygotsky

The trouble with language is that it is such a complicated, many-sided phenomenon.

E. M. Uhlenbeck

Everybody knows, of course, what language is, what speaking is, what understanding speech is. We know that grammar tells us to talk "correctly." But—*how* does language work? How do we operate to get a listener to know what we want him to know? How does language function?

This is an introductory text book. Its first aim is to make you see problems, to make you ask questions. Only a few questions will be answered—and these only very tentatively. What you should acquire by reading this book is a cognitive map of the psychological problems pervading man's use of language. The problems become abundantly visible as soon as explanation begins to go beyond the most superficial layer of verbal communication. Speech being the most human of all human faculties, there are many questions to be asked.

Cynthia and Billy T. are twins; a few days ago they celebrated their third birthday. When I visited the T.'s on that day, Cynthia opened the door with, "Hi, uncle, you bring us something?" and she did most of the talking for the next half hour. Billy was always a step behind her, silent, his eyes on his sister, only once or twice muttering some incomprehensible sounds. "It's always like this", their mother complained, "Cynthia is quite advanced in speaking, but Billy says nothing, or I don't understand what he says. But I think he understands us adults quite well. And of course he understands Cynthia perfectly. And she understands him and often tells me what he means. What am I to do? He is not dumb. Why can't he learn to talk like other children do?"

Can he really not learn to talk? Does he lack some of the prerequisites for this venture? If so, what, and why? Or was it, until now, just not necessary for him to learn to talk, because his sister understands him and acts as a kind of interpreter? What does he comprehend of the verbal utterances addressed by an adult to the twins? He shapes his behavior to that of his sister—is this proof of comprehension? *What* actually is proof of comprehension? Are there *degrees* of comprehension?

Here is a first block of questions addressed to the psychologist of language.

Teacher (old Mr. M.) enters the classroom. There is the usual noise and he shouts, "How often did I tell you: when I come in by the window, you are to close the doors"—a slip of the tongue. He confused *window* with *door*. Why and how did he do this? Can he not distinguish between a door and a window? Of course he can. Are the words we know stored in our brain as in a vast array of pigeonholes, and did Mr. M. catch hold of *window* and *door* in the wrong order? But planning an utterance and executing this plan cannot be a simple left-to-right ordering of words, because in Mr. M's utterance the mixed-up words are not immediate neighbors. Is the selection of nouns planned in one stage, and the integration of these nouns with the predicate in another? Are there different (and nonsimultaneous) stages of producing an utterance?

Here we encounter more questions for the psychologist of language.

John is a high school student. In history class today, Sean gave a talk on Europe in the Middle Ages. Afterward the students were told to write a one-page summary of the talk for class for the following week. And now Johnny is groaning that he cannot remember that awful talk, and that Sean's talks are always a chaos in which nobody can find a connecting thread.

What do we mean by saying there is no thread in a text? Do texts have an internal structure, which is neglected or violated by people like Sean? And is the existence or nonexistence of this internal structure responsible for our remembering—or not remembering—that text? Are there different structures in a history paper, a fairy tale, a recipe, a report of a baseball game? Can we learn more about these structures in order to write, for example, better textbooks?

Here are more questions for the psychologist of language.

Dotty has witnessed a rather bad traffic accident at an intersection. In court she is questioned by the prosecution. "In your opinion, how fast were the cars going when they crashed?" Counsel for the defense gets up and objects to the use of the word *crashed*, because this word implies a higher velocity than, for instance, the words *collided* or *bumped*.

What does a word mean? How is the meaning of a word to be described in a way which allows one to assess, for instance, the similarity of words? Obviously, there is often more to the meaning of a word than is noted in the dictionary. How are we to find out what a speaker using this word means? How rigid and unchangeable is the meaning of a word? In the utterance "a few paperclips" *a few* means more than in the utterance "a few elephants"—the meaning of the whole utterance is not pieced together from the meanings of the individual words in this sentence. What *is* a sentence, anyhow? Is it a complex structure of slots into which we insert words referring to who did what to whom in what circumstances? Is this structure perhaps the primary unit of communication—so that the individual words have to play different roles assigned to them by this encompassing structure?

These are further questions for the psychologist of language: questions we have to consider when we reflect on what goes on in an utterance and in the speaker and the listener connected by that utterance. While she was doing a crossword puzzle a few days ago, my wife asked me, "What's the word for a Chinese type of ship, used on rivers and estuaries, flat-bottomed?" I knew immediately that I *did* know the word, that it was on the tip of my tongue, but I could not name it. How are we to conceptualize this peculiar state of mind? This state of knowing and yet not knowing? I knew that *junk* was wrong, that it had to have two syllables, that the same vowel appeared in both syllables. What can we learn from this phenomenon (R. W. Brown [1973] calls it the tip-of-the-tongue phenomenon) about what goes on in our heads when we listen to a speaker? Are there different levels to traverse in the course of going from the sound in the ears to what the speaker means? If so, levels of what? And what is it, in the tip-of-the-tongue phenomenon, that obstructs the smooth progression from one level to the next?

On the TV news, the verbal utterances of the speaker about the latest *coup* in a Central American state are accompanied by some still pictures. How is the visual information of these pictures "connected" to the verbally conveyed information—and to my store of knowledge about this country and about *coups d'état* in general? Is this general knowledge about a revolutionary event a kind of schema which controls *what* I take up from TV and *how* I use it in constructing what I now actually know (and believe) about this particular event? Is this act of construction involved in what is called *understanding*?

And if this is so, what factors are important for facilitating this constructive understanding?

Laila is the ten-year-old daughter of a Turkish foreign laborer in Germany. She came to that country with her family two years ago and had to learn German as fast as possible to be able to attend school. Is there one "best method" for learning a foreign language? Or are different methods best suited to different cases: the very young child learning two languages at the same time (Laila's sister Fatima, then two and one-half years old), the scientist interested in acquiring a *reading* knowledge only of the foreign language? What is the difference between acquisition of one's native language when one is a child and acquisition of a second or foreign language in later life? Probably the young child is learning not only what his native language is like but to a large extent also what the world he lives in is like. And the adult foreign language learner already has this knowledge of the world, so he has only to acquire a second set of labels for the items in his store. Is this correct? Or do different languages (such very different languages as Turkish and German) "cut up" the world into non-congruent items and connect these different items according not only to different but also to sometimes incomparable rules of syntax, and so on? And if so, again, what are the differences between first- and second-language learning?

My cousin has suffered a stroke which destroyed some parts of his brain. Speaking is severely impaired. When the doctor showed him a pencil, he could not name it but said, after some hesitation, "for writing." Why? Is there a mental representation of some action "beneath" the mental representation of the object? And if so, should this theoretical conception tell us also something about how language is structured in the healthy speaker/listener? And about how this structure is formed in the course of language acquisition by the young child? Can we make use of this theoretical conception when we try to retrain the stroke victim?

These too, are questions for the psychologist of language. There are, of course, many more questions to be gathered from our experience and from a superficial analysis of this experience. In this book only a very few of these questions will be touched upon directly, because this book is not on what might be called "applied psychology of language." It is a textbook introducing you to the basic psychology of language. Because we are not satisfied with the perfunctory statement that everybody knows what language is, we should have a closer look into the processes going on in the speaker and in the listener while they use language. Learning more about the prerequisites and the conditions of these processes should—later on—help us also in thinking up tentative answers for the more "practical" questions. Above all, however, it should help us in discovering the problems which are still hidden in those very ordinary and apparently banal activities of speaking and of listening.

CHAPTER 1

Psychology and Linguistics

I am not yet so lost in lexicography, as to forget that words are the daughters of earth, and that things are the sons of heaven.

Samuel Johnson

Language acquires life and historically evolves here, in concrete verbal communication, and not in the abstract linguistic system of language forms, nor in the individual psyche of speakers.

V. N. Vološinov

Verbal thought is not an innate, natural form of behavior but is determined by an historical-cultural process and has specific properties and laws that cannot be found in the natural forms of thought and speech.

L. Vygotsky

Beginnings of Psycholinguistics

In almost every science there are branches or subdisciplines which are revived, so to speak, after having been considered extinct or just dormant for decades. Within psychology this is hardly anywhere as clear as in psycholinguistics or the "psychology of language" (we shall use these two terms, at least for the time being, as synonyms). Psycholinguistics was born, ostensibly from nothing, in the beginning of the 1950s in a series of symposia in the United States and developed at a rapid rate in the Anglo-American language communities, but psycholinguists discovered only after twenty years of this development that there had already been some "psychologies of language" in Europe, in Germany, for instance, notably in the last third of the nineteenth and the beginning of the twentieth centuries. They discovered at about the same time that there was and still is a rapidly developing psychology of language in Russia.

This nonexistence of what might have been a fruitful tradition can be easily explained: the emigration of many scientists from Germany and Austria during the Nazi regime and the Second World War destroyed a number of promising beginnings. Karl Bühler,[1] who is in my opinion the greatest psycholinguist of this

---

[1]Bühler's major work, *Sprachtheorie* (*Language Theory*), originally published in 1934, has not yet been translated into English. Such a translation would have

41

century, was deprived of his scientific influence by the political events of 1938 in Vienna. And because of the lack of knowledge of foreign languages on the part of many American scholars, a compartmentalization or isolation of what was to be American psychology developed.

In addition to the factors which result from general history, there are also those which result from the history of psychology proper: the triumph of behaviorism, which had advanced through Anglo-American psychology since 1920, was not advantageous to the scientific study of the phenomena and processes of language, for these cannot be reduced to a stimulus–response formula, and this formula was the basic model according to which behaviorism worked. It was only after this orthodox behavioristic approach had advanced to what is now called neo–behaviorism (Osgood) that major contributions to psycholinguistics became possible.

On the other hand, behaviorism's rival school of psychology, Gestalt psychology, was rather uninterested in language. Thus, since the beginning of what was to be modern psycholinguistics in the 1950s was rather poignantly new, the developing field of study showed a great number of the characteristics prevalent at this time in linguistics on the one hand and in psychology on the other. Awareness of these characteristics should facilitate our understanding of what psycholinguistics is today and of what it can (and cannot) do. We shall start with an evaluation of the psychology of that time.

In the 1950s psychology was thoroughly established as an empirical science and had just reached the end of its behavioristic period. This means that only those results were considered as scientifically meaningful and valid which were collected in a ver-

---

saved the developing field of psycholinguistics from many unnecessary detours. [An account of Bühler's language theory may be found in Robert E. Innis, *Karl Bühler: Semiotic Foundations of Language Theory* (New York: Plenum Press, 1982), which also contains a translation of Bühler's seminal essay, "The Axiomatization of the Language Sciences," a revised version of which became part one of *Sprachtheorie*. A translation of *Sprachtheorie* is in preparation, to be edited and introduced by Achim Eschbach and Robert E. Innis (Amsterdam and Philadelphia: John Benjamins).—Ed.]

ifiable and repeatable manner, but that the field of things thus found was no longer restricted to outwardly recognizable stimulus–response data but could also include experiences, desires, and consciousness as far as these can be empirically assessed. During the behaviorist era, psychology had been little concerned with language; now the fact that language serves as a tool in the field that encompasses man and the world was beginning to come back into focus: a tool (it was already called an *organon* in classical antiquity) which is employed in the field of force between the ego and the world to master the tasks which existence sets before man. Language can fulfill this task because it is a system of signs.

Semiotic Aspects

In the use of language it must also be considered that words are signs for things, and that we need signs not only to convey our thoughts to others, but also to help us to think. For just as in large centers of trade, in games, and so on, one does not always pay with money, but instead makes use of slips of paper or tokens, in the same way the mind uses representations of things. . . . The mind is content to put the word in place of the thing. . . . And just as a master of arithmetic who refuses to write a number which he could not carry in his mind would never complete his calculation, in the same way we would have to speak very slowly or remain silent, if in speech or even in thought we attempted to use a word without forming a clear picture of its meaning. . . . That is why words are often used as cyphers or counters in the place of images of things, until step by step the sum total has been attained and thus only at the logical conclusion the thing itself is reached.

G. Leibniz

The sign which stands for something else is the vehicle of the phylogenetic progress which culminates in the spiritual nature of man. We find many cases of signs even in prelanguage areas—wherever there is goal-oriented behavior. Signs are possible and are used "before" human language. A bird alerts his young to the approaching cat with his cries. A Pavlovian dog, conditioned to the sound of a bell, takes this sound as a sign that food is being delivered, and he reacts to this sign. The rat in a maze learns to expect signs and to be guided by signs. The sign points to something which is not the sign itself. This animal capacity to react in the same way to a sign as to the biological agent which the sign stands for was called the *first signal system* by Pavlov. The full potential of the sign, its anthropological efficiency, however, is first manifested in human language, because only here does it become a systematically available sign. It is then possible to formulate generalities and thus to create an order which extends beyond the individual concrete event. Thus knowledge can be gathered in a representative medium, and finally culture can be created. Human discretion and human reason are based on the ability to operate with signs, with representations, and so to plan action, to consider acts.

This is achieved by what Pavlov called the *second signal system,* a system freely available to humans to a much higher degree than the first system is to animals.

Signs occur wherever there is goal-directed behavior. The act of substitution of the sign for something else is distinct from direct action. It originates at a prelinguistic level, but the sign comes truly into its own only in human language—here it can be used at will to make the not-here and the not-now available. With the signs of language we may make generalizations which transcend the actual events. We may give the single event its place in a hierarchy and treat it as "a case of this" or "an instance of that"—a case of bread or an instance of kindness or of schizophrenia, and so forth. These higher–order entities—kindness, schizophrenia and the like—are first of all facts of language. We create those facts or we can take possession of them because language with its signs is available to us.

But now back to our sketch of the psychology of the 1950s: at this time, psychology was again beginning to recognize more clearly than before that man's use of language belongs to its field of study. It was turning itself toward this task on a methodological level, which in the meantime had become extraordinarily high: the theoretical bases were being discussed, the statistical, descriptive, and testing procedures were being developed further than in many other empirical sciences.

Chomsky's Revolution and Its Limitations

> . . . it turns out that 'knowledge' does not imply action or
> behavior of any sort; neither the ability to act on the knowl-
> edge, since the actual use of language is in the domain of
> performance; nor the awareness of ability to formulate the
> grammatical rules. The knowledge is 'tacit' or 'implicit'; in
> fact, it must be understood as knowledge in an epis-
> temological rather than in any psychological sense.
>
> E. Ingram

If one wants to describe the situation in which linguistics found itself at the end of the 1950s, one comes upon the middle of a scientific revolution. The conquerer who was to emerge from this revolution, Noam Chomsky, seemed so congenial to the psychologists of that time that they developed the discipline which first bore and earned the name of *psycholinguistics* as a bridge to him.

Before this revolution the study of linguistics had generally been divided into three parts: philology (the study of literature), the investigation of the history of the language (diachrony), and the structural description of language. The revolution began in this last area.

Structural linguistics, which generally gained dominance around 1955, sees language as a closed system: individual phenomena and processes may not be isolated, but must be seen within their context.[2] The systematic structure of language is described by means of a presentation of, for example, the constituents of the sentence, which will be discussed in Chapter 2. The function of language (as a tool) does not play any role here.

The revolution in structural linguistics begins because a new essential question is asked: Chomsky (1957, 1965) no longer inquires directly about the structure of sentences, but rather about what knowledge allows the speaker of a language to differentiate between grammatically correct (well-formed) and grammatically

---

[2]This mainly goes back to the Swiss linguist F. de Saussure (1916/1959), who sees language as a system of signs, each of which is defined by means of what differentiates it from other signs, and to the so-called Prague school of N. Trubetzskoy and Roman Jakobson at the end of the 1920s.

incorrect (not well-formed) sentences, even when he has never before heard the particular sentence.

This knowledge can certainly not be understood as a catalogue of all grammatically correct utterances which are possible in the particular language, because something can always be said (and understood) which has never been said before. This knowledge can thus only be a system of rules according to which grammatically correct sentences—and only such sentences!—are constructed, are *generated*. The goal of linguistics is accordingly reformulated by Chomsky: a generative grammar as a theory of language must present the intuitive knowledge of the speaker of this language as a system of rules which functions completely without intuition and only according to the laws of logic or mathematics.

The theoretical basis upon which the linguist designs his grammar also changes with this. If until now it was practical knowledge, which was never further questioned, that moved the linguist to attribute a certain structure to sentences, now the writing of a grammar becomes a rational construction of theory. This follows the model of Descartes: the mysterious intuitive knowledge of the living speaker should be reproduced as the theory of an automaton and thereby made understandable.

Three points were decisive for the fascination which this rationalistic, constructive tendency of generative linguistics held for psychology at that time:

- It is emphasized that grammar is the rational formulation of the knowledge of rules which the speaker/listener of a language has—even though in an unconscious way. Such knowledge, however, also undoubtedly belongs to psychology's field of research, as soon as it does not limit itself, behavioristically, to mere behavior but rather also takes interest in cognitive facts.
- The basic characteristics of this knowledge of rules must, according to Chomsky, be innate, because the small child already needs it to *learn* the individual language in the environment in which he grows up. These basic characteristics thus belong to the biological, or better, an-

thropological, "basic equipment" of man, and it is the task of psychology to clarify and describe this equipment.

- If the grammar of a language is a system of rules which allows one to produce and understand (correct) sentences, then it becomes the goal of psychology to make the function of this system of rules recognizable in man's use of language.

Therefore, generative linguistics, which originated at the beginning of the 1960s, seemed at that time well-suited to provide psychology with those linguistic units and constructs that psycholinguistics must be aware of if it is to clarify the act of language use. A division of labor seemed to present itself: linguistics furnishes the *description* of language; psycholinguistics employs the terms and theoretical approaches of this description in order to examine the *use* of language.

Today, more than twenty years later, this view proves to have been a mistake. Linguistics, and with it generative linguistics, was exclusively interested in language-in-and-of-itself; it conceived of language as a closed system of signs. The combination of signs, that is, syntax, is the focal point of linguistic endeavour. It is only in recent years that a scientific description of language *usage* (pragmatics) has been added to that of the self-contained system-as-such.

For the psychologist, however, the sign must always be an applied sign, a sign-in-use. If the basic anthropological characteristic of language is its character as a tool, then this function of language must also be the basis and focal point of the psychology of language. Looking back over the first twenty years of modern psycholinguistics, we see that the only theory of language which could arise from the linguistic approach (language-as-system) is one which has not been optimal for the psychological approach (language as a functioning tool). (See also, e.g., Kintsch 1980; Hörmann 1976, 1981.)

Psychology of language has today only managed a part of what is becoming a necessary emancipation from linguistics. What psycholinguistics is today, what its interests are, and what understanding it has thus far achieved only become completely comprehensible when one sees the psycholinguistic questions of the last two decades against the background of the history of the science which has been sketched here. In the following chapter we will work out what portions of structural and generative linguistics have been important and will continue to be important for psychology of language.

CHAPTER **2**

Language-as-Such

Or, What the Psychologist of Language Should Know about Linguistics

There is nothing isolated in language. Since structure is the essence of language, each individual item results from structuring; it is determined in its nature and function by its position in the whole of language.

J. Trier

The task of grammar as one of the most ancient studies of humanity borders almost on the impossible: it attempts to create an awareness of a mental condition of human existence. Not only is the range of this condition beyond our grasp but its inner workings are also impenetrable.

L. Weisgerber

Language is . . . mental organization within a community. It is based on the fact that mental concepts and attitudes to experience are defined by being linked with characteristic sound patterns. But this mental organization, however pervasive its effect, is in general not consciously experienced by the language user. Grammar, since its beginnings in ancient Greek times, sets itself a threefold task. It makes the user conscious of this common mental organization; it elaborates its structural laws and fundamental units, and it elucidates its overall organization down to the *minutiae* of each determining quantum, if one may use this analogy from physics.

H. Glinz

In the first chapter we sketched the rise of modern psycho-linguistics out of the historical constellation of postbehaviorist psychology and generative linguistics. We contrasted the working tendencies in linguistics with those in psychology by means of two key phrases: on the one hand, language as a self-contained closed system, on the other, language as a tool used by man. In the past, psycholinguistics worked mainly with concepts that come from this system-oriented linguistics and tried to use these concepts in the psychological explanation of the phenomena of language use as well. Psycholinguistics has tried to establish what was called the "psychological reality" of linguistic concepts and linguistic theoretical assumptions. In this chapter we will present such concepts and theoretical assumptions, as far as they are necessary for our purposes, without further maintaining the division between structural and, in the narrow sense, generative linguistics.

The Phoneme

What is language-as-such like? A first answer to this question could be: certain sounds appear in a certain order. A description of language should thus begin with a description of the speech *sounds*.

51

If one wants to describe speech sounds, one must first establish what *one* sound is: in the continuous flow of language, where does *one* sound begin, and where does this sound end? One must also establish which criterion to use in order to decide that "these two sounds are identical, these two are different." One faces the question of what should be taken as a *unit of sound.*

To answer this question, we have to decide on what level our description should operate. Theories in this area have at least two levels of representation: a level on which the sounds are described in as detailed and as concrete a fashion as possible (called phonetics), and a more abstract level where the variance encountered on this first level is reduced to "what actually counts" (called phonology).

The necessity for having several levels of sound description becomes easily evident. If we ask a series of people to say a particular word, for example "car," into a microphone, then analyze the acoustic event with respect to the physical dimensions of intensity, frequency, and time and make this analysis visible by means of an oscillograph, we notice that these records of the different speakers (all of whom pronounce the same word, "car") look quite different. This exact acoustical or phonetic analysis is thus apparently not suitable for clearly showing us the sound units which come together to form the flow of language and which we now want to describe. The different speakers have said the *same* thing; therefore, our analysis must be adjusted to determine "the same thing" in different speakers. It follows that we must *categorize,* that is, we must compile physically different events in such a way that their unity—since indeed all represent the word "car"—will become clear. We must go from the phonetic to the phonological description; we must identify the—at first sight unobservable—sound units (see Diver 1979).

This problem of identifying invisible units appears, by the way, at several points in linguistics: what is *one* sound, *one* meaning, *one* word, *one* sign? The Swiss linguist F. de Saussure (1916/1959) has suggested a solution to this problem which has become very influential: he defined a sign as that which differentiates itself from other signs. A sign is an independent unit if it signals something different from all other signs. (This consideration is a basic component of both so-called structural linguistics and of information theory.)

A process of categorization is, of course, not only necessary for the scientific *description* of language sounds; something similar must also occur in human *perception*. Otherwise, we could not perceive that the different speakers (male, female, southern, a child, one with a cold) all said "car." For example, we must categorically group the different realizations of *a* in "car" (the male, the female, etc.) together in such a way that they are differentiated from the sound in "care" that is in this position and from the sound in "core" that is also in the same position, although the words are different.

This means that we must categorize according to those aspects of the sound which make a difference for the code. We define the unit *phoneme* in that sense as a unified category of sound: phonemes are those smallest units of sound which are responsible for the significant differences between different utterances in a language. In every language there is a limited number of phonemes. Within each phoneme there are other acoustic differences (so-called *allophones*) which do not, however, cause a difference in understanding. For example: whether or not a *t* in English is pronounced with aspiration does not play an important role, the word "stop" is not different from the word "top" because of the kind of *t* used, even though the acoustic characteristics of the two *t*'s are completely different (by saying the *t* in *top* we can blow out a match, by saying the *t* in *stop* we can not).

When one looks at both *t*'s on an oscillograph, one would hardly think that it is really the same phoneme in English. In Chinese and in some other languages, on the other hand, aspirated *t* and unaspirated *t* are two different phonemes. In English, the two *t*'s are allophones belonging to one phoneme. Language operates with sound categories in which certain acoustic details play no important role. Phonemes are, on the phonetic level, not directly observable. Their existence—and their boundaries—are brought to light by observing on the phonological level a human speaker/listener using his language. Inspection of the spectrographic data makes it clear that there is no simple one-to-one relation between the physical description of what is actually uttered by the speaker and the discrete phonemes that are the building blocks of communication.

This fact is, as we will see in Chapter 8, a major problem for all theories of speech perception or comprehension: how is the listener, who receives at best the physical stimuli produced by the speaker, to go from these phonetic data to the units on the phonological level, that is, the phonemes?

At this point one could ask whether it is possible to analyze a phoneme into still smaller "elements" which could be used for systematically describing what distinguishes between two different phonemes. The answer to this question are the so-called *distinctive features*, phonetic properties which are claimed by most theories to be binary: a phoneme is either +voiced or −voiced, either +nasal or −nasal, and so on. And it is further claimed that these distinctive features are universal, that is, they may be used for describing the sounds of any language (see Schane 1979).

The fact that a phoneme can be seen as a class or category of allophones involves two interesting ideas. The production and perception of language apparently must occur through a system of classification, a system which ignores irrelevant nuances and which sorts out sounds according to those aspects which are important in this language. When we say "in *this* language," it means that we are dealing with learned aspects; a baby growing up in China will learn different phonemes (with different divisions between phonemes) than one growing up in England.

The second idea which suggests itself here brings this classification into the context of the phenomena of sensory or perceptual constancy, which are familiar from general psychology. The constancy of shape of a table, which appears square to us, even though it is reflected in a distorted way on the retina, is analogous to phoneme perception: the *t* in English may sound like anything—as long as it is clearly different from, say, *p* or *d*, we will ignore distortions and differences. Although we earlier described language as a series of sounds, we can now see that this is only correct if we define a series of sounds as a series of phonemes. It is not linguistically relevant what the sounds are physically, but rather the way they are classified by speaker and listener. The physical characteristics of a phoneme are, however, rather important for the ease of learning and producing this phoneme. Articulations which are easy to learn to control will be preferred over articulations that are more difficult to learn to control, and more difficult articulations will be used where high distinctness is essential, for example, at the beginning of words (see Diver 1979).

Phonology sets the limits for how a speaker is permitted to articulate what he has to say and the limits on the sound variations a listener can expect to hear in comprehensible speech.

Phonemes signal differences in meaning. They themselves, however, have as yet no meaning.

Morpheme, Syllable, Word

The difference in meaning is found chiefly at the next highest level. In order to be an appropriate medium for the transfer of information, language must present a finite number of distinguishable, mutually exclusive sound utterances, that is, language must be describable in linguistic units, which have the property that they change the meaning when one unit is replaced by another. In order to find such units of meaning, we need to analyze the decision-making processes that occur in the speech events. The speaker must, in the process of speaking (and the listener in the process of listening), decide over and over again what he is saying (what he is hearing).

We may now define as follows: *one* decision must be made for every unit, and the converse: that which is chosen by *one* selection process is a unit. Let us take as an example the sentence "The beer is good." There was a selection necessary, for example, before "good." At the time of speaking one could have decided on "bitter" or "bad" or "yellow." Another choice had to be made before "is." The speaker could have said "tastes" good or "was" good; instead of "beer" the choice could have been "house" or "child." The units which are delineated in this manner are called *morphemes*.

Morphemes are not identical with words. The sentence "He looked at the flashlight" is made up of 7 morphemes: he / look / ed / at / the / flash / light, where -*ed* means past tense. If we break up a morpheme further, then according to our definition it must lose its meaning. The meaning of "look" is not a composite of the "meaning" of the phonemes /l/, /u/, and /k/. We can only break up the form of the sound of the morpheme, namely, into the phonemes. The morpheme is, therefore, the smallest unit that *carries* meaning or *has* meaning. (Remember: the phoneme is the smallest unit which *signals* [differences of] meaning.)

Thus we have in linguistics several levels to describe language. The phonetic level is concerned with an exhaustive description of the actually produced speech sounds—this description may be undertaken in terms of acoustic or of articulatory features. This level is, as it were, the surface of the spoken utterance. Below this surface level we have two levels where the material or data of the higher level are categorized to form units: the phoneme and the morpheme. The same principle is valid for both these levels: a selection must be made for each unit. What is chosen by *one* selective decision is *one* unit. From a small number of units, which are themselves not signs, namely, phonemes, we can build signs, namely, the morphemes, and we can say everything that was ever said or will be said with a few thousand morphemes. This double articulation is the essence of human language.

From the morphemes, we can now look in the other direction, that is, toward larger units. This is the syllable, which holds a very specific position in respect to the morpheme. Both syllables and morphemes are usually made up of several phonemes, but a specific meaning is not definitely assigned to a certain syllable. The word "marbles" in the sentence "He's lost his marbles" consists of two syllables: *mar-bles*, neither of which are units which carry meaning alone, in this case. The same word, however, is made up of two morphemes, namely, the morpheme *marble* and the plural morpheme *s*, which by definition both carry meaning (*s* means plural). Linguistically, the division into morphemes is certainly more important than that into syllables. Whether this is also true for the actual speaker and listener is, of course, doubtful, since the syllable plays a major role in breath-regulated pro-nunciation and probably also in the perception of language.

Communication surely does not consist of an unordered pile of morphemes. The next object for the linguist's inspection must therefore be those structures which govern the occurrence of morphemes. How can morphemes be combined into sensible ut-terances in a certain language? Supplying the answer to this question is the work of *grammar*, that is, the description of or the theory of the admissible combinations in a language. Within the topic of grammar we usually differentiate between morphology and syntax. *Morphology* is concerned with the combinations within words (their internal structure), *syntax* with the combina-tions of the words themselves.

With that we have arrived at the role that the unit *word* plays in linguistics. The nonlinguist obviously considers the word to be the best delineated unit because he can see such a clear separa-tion in the printed text—whereas for all linguistic and psycho-linguistic research, spoken language and written language are two separate matters which are not always closely connected with each other; of primary interest is, of course, the spoken language. The linguist who works, for example, with syllabic script, or with languages written in hieroglyphics, would certainly have diffi-culty in finding an operational definition of "word" adequate for all languages. The best approach for the linguistic lay person is to look for a semantic definition in which to identify the word as that which indicates a separate, unified object or concept. This leads us rather quickly into difficulties. In English we have the word *justice*—is justice a unified concept?

When it becomes difficult to define words by their content, then we must rely on a formal definition. Bloomfield's (1933) defi-nition is widespread: a word is a minimal free form (here a free form is that which can stand alone). "Child" is according to this a free form. What about "childish"? The syllable *ish* is indeed a morpheme, because it expresses the meaning of, among other things, "having the qualities of . . . ," but it cannot be used inde-pendently; it represents a "bound form." According to the above, "childish" is *one* word because it cannot be broken up into any more parts which are *all* both meaningful and independent.

The Structure of the Sentence

The largest linguistic unit is the sentence. The organizational rules of a language have their main effect within the sentence. The selection of sentence components influences the construction of the best sentence only indirectly. Bloomfield, one of the leaders of structural linguistics, called the sentence a construction which is not a dependent part of a more inclusive construction.

This statement has to be qualified in the light of modern developments in linguistics: a sentence is often—according to some theories, always—a dependent part of the text in which it is included. However, the rules that have power within one sentence (mainly the syntactic rules) are qualitatively of a different kind from those rules that constitute a text: the one who does not follow the rules of syntax makes a grammatical mistake according to a binary standard (right/wrong). Texts are not right or wrong, but rather more or less acceptable. (See de Beaugrande, 1980.) The sentence is, so to speak, the playing field of grammar.

When we try to grasp the structure of a sentence we start by analyzing the morphemes of the sentence into form classes on the basis of how they "behave" in combinations with other morphemes. Thus we find what we call nouns, adjectives, verbs, and so forth. We will illustrate this *immediate constituent analysis* with the sentence

(2.1) The woman killed the dog.

When we look at this sentence, we can intuitively realize that certain words (or better: certain morphemes) belong more closely together than others: "The" and "woman" belong closer together

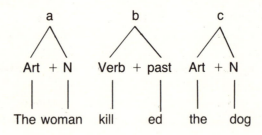

than "woman" and "kill"; "the woman"—or the unit which we call (a)—could be replaced by *one* word ("she") without changing the structure of the whole sentence. Also, "the dog" could be more easily replaced by one word ("it") than, for example, "killed the."

We see that the higher-order unit which we called (a) is of the same kind as the unit we call (c). Both have the ability to function in many similar environments:

$$\left\{ \begin{array}{l} \text{The woman} \\ \text{The dog} \end{array} \right\} \text{found a slice of bread}$$

$$\text{He heard} \quad \left\{ \begin{array}{l} \text{the woman} \\ \text{the dog} \end{array} \right\} \qquad \text{(etc.)}$$

What we have called (a) and (c) are units of the same type because they have the same combinatorial properties. This type of unit is called a *noun phrase* (NP). "Killed," on the other hand—the unit we have called (b)—has quite different combinatorial properties; we cannot say

killed found a slice of bread.

The unit (b) is a verb. Our linguistic intuition tells us, however, that on a different level (b) and (c) form a unit, too: "killed the dog." This unit is called a *verb phrase* (VP).

The second NP of our sentence ("the dog") is, as we see, a dependent part of the VP, whereas the first NP ("the woman") is not. The first NP and the VP form together the highest grammatical unit, the sentence. The internal structure of this sentence may, therefore, be presented by this *tree diagram*:

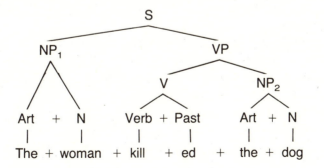

In this immediate componential analysis of the structure of the sentence, we proceed, so to speak, from the bottom to the top, from the words to the phrases (the woman, the dog, killed the dog) and finally to the sentence. It can be shown fairly easily that such a procedure can become quite arbitrary, arbitrary, that is, with respect to what is considered as belonging together and combined in that way. Consider the sentence

(2.2) He killed the man with the club.

Does "with the club" belong to "man" or to "killed"?

Generative Grammar

In order to be able to identify properly the constituents of this sentence, one should really already know the principles which were used to construct, or, as we say, to generate, this sentence. Whoever hears the sentence, "He killed the man with the club," knows that in the depth, so to speak, two different structures are to be found in it. He cannot, however, differentiate between these two structures if he starts with the surface of the sentence, that is, from the words that are uttered one after the other, as the primary data. He knows, though, about this double structure because he has a command of the English language. He must put this knowledge into action so that he can understand the sentence correctly—understanding all of the words of the sentence is not enough. Even if the listener knows what the phrase "with the club" means literally, he can only understand what the speaker means by it if he assigns the sentence *one* specific structure.

But it is apparently not possible to assign this whole sentence *one* specific structure, if we analyze from below, from the phonemes and the morphemes and words, that is, if we first describe the smallest and then the larger units of the sentence. The analytical description of the sentence must begin at the top.

At this point, seen under the aspect of the history of science, begins that revolutionary change in linguistics which we mentioned in the first chapter when we discussed the relationship between linguistics and psychology. According to Chomsky (1957, 1965), the description of the structure of a sentence should not begin with the smallest elements, but rather with the sentence as a whole.

In addition, the old key question of structural linguistics— how can the sound units in a sentence and their structure be described?—is superseded by a new and rather revolutionary question: what does the adult speaker know about his native language that enables him to differentiate between grammatical sentences and ungrammatical strings of words? He knows intuitively that

(2.3) Colorless green ideas sleep furiously

is a sentence, whereas a similarly nonsensical string of words

(2.4) Ideas furiously green sleep colorless

is *not* a (well-formed) sentence.

This contrast has strongly influenced the development of modern linguistics. With it Chomsky wants to show that the meaning of an utterance does not play any role for the *grammaticality* of that utterance. Accordingly, generative grammar strives toward the construction of a purely syntactic theory of language, without recourse to meaning. (In this abstention lies *one* of the reasons why the psychology of language cannot afford to follow this line of linguistics indefinitely.)

When Chomsky asks what the speaker/listener "knows" about his language in this manner, we must immediately define what is to be understood by the word "know": it does not need to be any kind of formulated knowledge; what we call "tacit knowledge" is enough (see Polanyi 1966). On the basis of this knowledge, the speaker/listener of the English language can determine that the two sentences

(2.5) The president determines political guidelines

and

(2.6) Political guidelines are determined by the president

express generally the same idea, whereas this is not the case for the following two sentences:

(2.7) The president determines political guidelines.
(2.8) The president is determined by political guidelines.

Thus it is this kind of intuitive knowledge which that person "has" who is in command of a language. With the help of this knowledge he can form sentences and understand those which he has never heard before. This knowledge allows him to differentiate between grammatical and ungrammatical sentences.

If it were possible to formulate this intuitive knowledge in a strictly logical system of rules, this would be the grammar of the particular language. For Chomsky, then, grammar is a theory of the ability which makes it possible for a native speaker[1] to form all the grammatical sentences possible in his language and no ungrammatical one. (It should at least be noted in parentheses that this goal is unbelievably narrow: we are not dealing here with a theory about the way language is used and understood, but rather with one which merely investigates how grammatical sentences can be differentiated from ungrammatical sentences.) On the basis of this concept, Chomsky (1957, 1965, and later) builds up an impressive structure, *generative grammar,* also called *transformational-generative grammar* (TGG—we will explain both terms directly), the fundamental characteristics of which we will outline now.

Chomsky calls his grammar "generative" because it is supposed to be a theory of the logical development of grammatical sentences. It must be generative, that is, it must consist of rules and not of a complete list of all grammatical sentences, because language is creative; that is, new sentences which have never before existed but are nevertheless grammatical can be continually generated. It is generative (and this must be especially emphasized) logically, not psychologically, speaking, that is, in the sense that the formula $2x + 2$ generates the series 2,4,6,8, 10 . . . . . when x is an integer.

In generative grammar several distinctions and postulates play an important role which have also been used in psycholinguistics and must therefore be briefly presented here.

First there is the pair of terms *competence/performance.*

---

[1] A native speaker of a language is a speaker/listener who has that particular language as his mother tongue.

Chomsky is interested, as is every linguist, in language as a system, not language as a tool. That is, he wants to describe this system before it is used for any (e.g., communicative) purposes. He wants to describe it without dealing with the fact that the speaking person perhaps does not always use this system correctly. This agrees with his basic theoretical approach, as already mentioned: he does not proceed empirically, but in terms of a rational reconstruction. He does not describe what he actually discovers, but rather he constructs a theory.

> Linguistic theory is concerned primarily with an ideal speaker/listener, in a completely homogeneous speech community, who knows his language perfectly and is unaffected by such grammatically irrelevant conditions as memory limitations, distractions, shifts of attention and interest, and errors (random or characteristic) in applying his knowledge of the language in actual performance. (Chomsky 1965:3)

Chomsky calls the linguistic knowledge that is the basis for the accomplishments of the errorless ideal speaker/listener *competence.*

This is contrasted to *performance,* namely, what an actual speaker/listener, one influenced by all sorts of physical and psychological factors, reveals in the use of his language.

The relationship of these two concepts to each other has proved to be the source of far-reaching theoretical difficulties and conflicts, which will not be further discussed here.[2] Let us only mention that during a certain period of its development psycholinguistics considered it to be its task to prove, by means of research into performance (only this can be examined by empirical research), the "psychological reality" of processes and concepts which had been postulated by linguistic competence theory.

Surface Structure and Deep Structure

The second pair of concepts which we need for the understanding of TGG is the difference between *surface structure* and *deep structure.* The two sentences

[2]An extensive discussion may be found in Hörmann (1976/1981); a shorter one is presented by Langendoen (1979).

(2.9) John is easy to please

(2.10) John is eager to please

have at first glance very similar structures. When we look more closely, however, we see that John is the active subject in the second sentence, whereas in the first sentence he represents the passive object of the action. The deep structures of the sentences are thus different.

With this distinction between surface structure (SS) and deep structure (DS) generative grammar takes into account the fact that linguistic utterances are structured on different levels.

The description of these structures is developed or generated from the beginning symbol S (sentence)—we stated above that the structure of a sentence must be generated from the complete sentence, not from the elements in ascending order. We will now do this for the sentence

(2.1) The woman killed the dog.

The structure of this sentence is unfolded by using what is called the *rewrite rules* of generative grammar:

1. S → NP + VP
2. NP → Art + N
3. VP → V + NP
4. Art → (the, a . . .)
5. N → (woman, dog, boy, fallacy . . .)
6. V → (kill, like, feed . . .)

With these six rules we can generate the grammatical structure of sentence (2.1), or, as we might say, the use of these rewrite rules allows the phrase structure of the sentence to become apparent. There are, of course, more than six such rewrite rules; for more complicated sentences we need more rules. We have also ignored the fact that our sentence describes action in the past, which is not actually included in the rules we used.

If we look at these six rules more closely, we can divide them into two different kinds: rules 1–3 end in elements that must be further rewritten, whereas rules 4–6 lead to the words that are actually spoken. The latter are called *terminal,* the former *nonterminal rules.* This division corresponds to an idea that is widespread in linguistics, namely, that the linguistic competence of a person is divided into two departments, so to speak: the rule system of *syntax* and a storehouse in which words (or morphemes) of a language are stored according to their meaning. This storehouse is usually called the *lexicon* (rules 4–6 thus concern themselves with the use of the lexicon). Although the rule *NP → Art + N* requires and thus determines that a noun must appear at this point in the structure, it is only in a later step (namely, *N → [woman, dog, boy, fallacy . . .]*) that it is determined what these *N* are. Also, it is not determined with this rule *which N* should be chosen. Application of rule 5 might also lead to the sentences

(2.11) The fallacy killed the dog

or

(2.12) The dog killed the fallacy

or

(2.13) The woman killed the fallacy, etc.

Application of rules 4 to 6 might also produce

(2.14) The idea hurt the fallacy

or *any* sentence at all with the structure

$$Art + N + V + \text{past tense} + Art + N$$

With this we have the greatest achievement and at the same time the decisive weakness of Chomsky's generative grammar: it is interested (almost) entirely in syntax, that is, in the systematic combination of linguistic signs, without taking meaning into account, the content of these signs. The structure that we find for

(2.15) The boy kicked the ball

also characterizes the sentences

(2.16) The ball kicked the boy

and

(2.17) The girl found the cowslip.

Chomsky himself sees this limitation of the goal of his theory of grammar. He accepts it because he believes that only in this way can he accomplish what he wants to: to construct a system of rules that functions *without* intuition, which can generate all grammatical (and no ungrammatical) sentences of a language. Thus it is also understandable why the sample sentence "Colorless green ideas sleep furiously" (2.3) plays such a key role for Chomsky: its purpose is to show that the grammaticality of a sentence is not dependent on our understanding the meaning. If the sequence of the words is changed, the grammaticality is destroyed.

Up until now we have discussed the way that the sentence S is structured in individual phrases. Such a *phrase structure grammar* has a weakness that bothers Chomsky. The native speaker of the English language intuitively says that the sentence:

(2.5) The president determines political questions

is more or less the same as the sentence

(2.6) Political questions are determined by the president.

He would say that both sentences mean the same. This equivalence is not expressed in a pure phrase structure grammar. According to it, the two sentences would be structurally quite different. How can we do justice to their similarity; how can we form a grammar that expresses this intuitively perceived similarity?

Transformational Generative Grammar

Chomsky does this by adding a transformation section to his phrase structure grammar, one which intervenes between deep and surface structure. A transformational grammar would generally say here: the two sentences just mentioned have the same deep structure but different surface structures. More specifically: one and the same deep structure is *transformed* once into an active sentence, once into a passive sentence. The differentiation which a transformational generative grammar (TGG) presents in comparison to a mere PSG (phrase structure grammar) can be explained as follows: the phrase structure rules generate the deep structure. The transformational rules change the deep structure into the surface structure. Transformational rules can also be presented as rewrite rules, but to the left of the arrow there appears not *one* element, as in the formation rules of the phrase structure grammar, but rather a *chain* of elements. Also, the operation which is put into effect by the transformational rules is relatively complicated. For passivization, for example, it includes the interchange of the two nominal phrases, and so on. There are different kinds of transformations. In Chomsky's original essay, the change to question form (Did the boy kick the ball?), negation (The boy did not kick the ball), and so on are also viewed as transformations. Thus all of the following sentences are derived from one and the same deep structure by means of different transformations:

- The man opened the door.
- The man did not open the door.
- Did the man open the door?
- Didn't the man open the door?
- The door was opened by the man.
- The door was not opened by the man. (passivization plus negation)
- Was the door opened by the man?
- Wasn't the door opened by the man? (passivization plus negation plus question form)

With the help of a transformational grammar, the inner structural relationship can be shown between sentences which have different surface structures but an identical deep structure. With the help of a transformational grammar, however, it can also be shown that sentences like

(2.2) He killed the man with the club

are structurally ambiguous, because here the transformations of two *different* deep structures lead to the *same* (and therefore ambiguous) surface structure.

Let us summarize what we have said so far about Chomsky's transformational grammar in a flow chart (Figure 1) which shows the generation of a grammatically correct sentence.

The generating of a sentence begins with a syntactic component which is made up of two subcomponents, namely, the phrase structure component and the transformational component. The output of the phrase structure components (the DS) is taken as input for the transformational component; the transformational component then processes the SS to the *phonological component* of the sentence. This determines which sounds are spoken in succession. The output of the phrase structure component, namely, the deep structure, is also used for a second purpose: it is *interpreted semantically*. Here, at this vague point which Chomsky has not worked out with the same meticu-

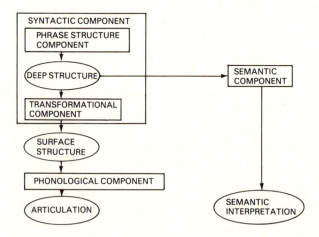

Figure 1

lousness as he has his other ideas, meaning comes into play, meaning now seen as a connection between a sign and what it points to. The deep structure is interpreted by the so-called semantic component. In this way the sentence obtains its meaning. What kind of a process this semantic interpretation is remains unclear.

In psycholinguistics, later also in linguistics itself, this syntax-centeredness of Chomsky's model has proved to be its major difficulty and weakness. Meaning cannot be something that is secondarily tacked on to an utterance which is already completely structured.

Chomsky could, of course, refute this obvious objection by saying that his concept of generating was not meant psychologically; he does not maintain that his model describes the temporal relationships of the conception or the understanding of a sentence. The clearer this becomes for the psychologists, the more the importance of Chomsky's model for psycholinguistics is weakened—a process which has of course taken years.

We started on our tour through grammar because of the question, What does an adult native speaker/listener know about his language? Chomsky's answer was: he knows the rules which make it possible for him to generate all the grammatically (and that means here: syntactically) correct sentences of this language.

But he evidently also knows completely different rules, for example, rules which, when used, prevent the creation of an otherwise (syntactically/grammatically) correct sentence like:

(2.3) Colorless green ideas sleep furiously.

The research program of linguistics must thus be expanded. It is not enough to formulate rules for the systematic combination of linguistic signs, but the rules according to which the *meaning* of the units (words, morphemes) and of the complete sentence is constituted must also be formulated.

Analysis of Meaning

Linguistics, in its prominent schools, has hesitated for a long time in beginning this task. The "content side" of language is much more difficult to express in laws or rules than the formal side, that is, the order of the appearance of signs.

The difficulties that linguistics is having with incorporating meaning become clear from the fact that Fillmore could still write in 1976 that grammar consists of those parts of linguistic knowledge which can be formulated as rules; the parts which cannot be described in this way, which are item-by-item knowledge, are called the *lexicon*. Is meaning really not amenable to rules? Or are there rules to be discovered in the organization of the lexicon?

If we look for a starting point for the inclusion of the content side in a particular system of rules, we should remember that the constituent analysis began with the question, What belongs together? Let us take this question with us for the clarification of the structure of the lexicon (which involves the vocabulary of our speaker/listener). How is it organized? What belongs together for what reason? Are there thematic complexes (intelligent, bright, wise, clever . . .) or rather hierarchies of categories, from "animal" to "mammal" and all the way to the individual species of "dogs" and to my neighbor's Rover? Are there similarities in the historical development, similarities in the possibilities for usage, similarities in their effect on the listener? In the following we will show several such approaches in brief, none of which achieves the level of precision or are as well thought out as TGG but which are interesting for the psychologist of language, for whom the contents of what is said and what is meant are naturally at least as important. The concepts which are handled here in their linguistic aspects will be taken up again in their psychological aspects in Chapter 5.

Let us reformulate the main question in our search as follows: how is the lexicon, which the speaker/listener of a language "has," ordered? What structures pervade it? (It is probably not in alphabetical order.)

A first approach, so-called componential analysis, arranges words in the following way:

man	woman	child
bull	cow	calf
stallion	mare	foal

In this method of grouping certain similarities become apparent; we could call them dimensions of our lexicon. Horizontally, they are "human," "cattle," "horse"; vertically, they are "male," "female," and "offspring."

What is expressed in this approach? A grouping or order is pointed out in the lexicon in which we view the words as combinations or points of intersection of individual, elementary dimensions of meaning. Such dimensions thus present features which are each attributed to several words. The feature "male" does not only appear in "man," "bull," and "stallion," but also in "boar," and also in "knight," "grandfather," and so on.

Such an analysis of the meaning of a word into meaning elements or *features* leads us very soon to the problem of what we "can do with" this kind of feature. The linguist now asks, Can we conceptualize the semantic features so that we can explain the ability or skill of the speaker/listener to form "normal" sentences with them?

Semantic Anomaly, Metaphor

If we follow this thought further, we again approach generative grammar and its encompassing goal of describing the intuitive linguistic knowledge of the speaker/listener in a scientifically precise way. Again we come to Chomsky's famous example:

(2.3) Colorless green ideas sleep furiously.

Chomsky said that this sentence is grammatically correct—where grammar and syntax are seen as synonymous. However, many people who hear this sentence perceive it as being abnormal, as a *semantic anomaly.* Ideas can be neither colorless nor green, they cannot sleep, and one cannot sleep furiously. That is, the features of the words combined in this sentence are incompatible.

Can one propose a theory in which some kind of precautionary device can prevent words with semantic features that are incompatible from being united in one sentence? Can we take theoretical precautions against the appearance of a semantic anomaly?

The semantic theory of Katz and Fodor (1963) begins at this point. The authors want to construct an addition to Chomsky's TGG of such a kind that semantic anomalies like "colorless green ideas" are avoided in the same way that an ungrammatical sentence is avoided by (the use of) TGG. They suggest a differentiation of the lexical entries which characterize the words and which direct the "access" of the terminal rules. In Chomsky's grammar, the word *man* is represented by the symbol N (= noun) alone; for Katz and Fodor it is represented by a series of syntactic *and* semantic features:

> man: N
>   physical object
>   living
>   animate
>   human
>   adult
>   male

To these features are added several "selection restrictions"; that is, specific combinations are forbidden in order to assure that only those words are combined with each other in a certain syntactic manner that are compatible according to meaning. Thus the word "green" will have "color" among its semantic features, and "color" will have the selection restriction that it "may only be said about physical objects." Since "idea" does not have the feature "physical object," "idea" cannot be combined with "green" to form "green ideas."

At first this seems to be an elegant solution to a problem that had not been handled satisfactorily (namely, not at all) by Chomsky! It also faces difficulties, though, when, for instance, such selection criteria are nullified without hesitation for metaphors or idioms ("The sun smiles down . . ." or "Fritz bit the dust"), and must be nullified for proper understanding.

Naturally we should not ignore the fact that the avoidance of semantic anomalies—and the difficulties with metaphors and idioms that are connected to it—themselves becomes a problem in linguistics only when dealing with language-as-such. As Schank and Wilks (1974) have said, a speaker will generate a semantically deviant sentence only if he wants to make an utterly sensible statement in an unusual form.[3]

For Katz and Fodor, semantic features play a clearly secondary role in a primarily syntax-centered model. The structure of a sentence is determined here, too, by purely syntactic rules; the semantic features with their selection restrictions become effective only when the lexicon is accessed by the terminal rules, for example, $N \rightarrow ball, boy, woman. \ldots$

Thus the assumed division between the (syntactic) system of rules and the lexicon is not lifted here. This dichotomy is less acute in the third approach we will look at in order to grasp the problem of meaning from the linguistic side, so-called generative semantics. Here the description of deep structure is undertaken in a manner which stands, as it were, *before* the conceptual division of syntax and semantics.

The sentence

(2.13) The man cuts the bread with the knife

can be described, as Fillmore (1968) argues, in a more appropriate and more meaningful way than by the orthodox analysis of $S \rightarrow NP + VP$, etc., in that one begins with the description of the structure of the sentence with the *predication* anchored in the verb ("to cut"). To the verb are tied one or several noun phrases, each of which has a specified *case* relation to the verb. For "to cut" we expect an *agent* who cuts, perhaps an object or a patient, perhaps an instrument. Depending on which cases in a sentence are realized, they take different positions in the surface structure. In our sample sentence, if the agent role is not filled, the instrument in nominative can appear as the subject of the sentence: "The knife cuts." If the agent is realized, however, then the instrument must be introduced with the preposition "with":

(2.14) The man cuts with the knife.

Generative semantics is, as will become clear in Chapter 5, much closer to psychology than the syntax-centered model of orthodox TGG, because the basic relations therein (agent of an action, ob-

---

[3]See also Hörmann (1973 and 1976/1981).

ject of an action), which are here defined linguistically, are very similar to the relations in which a growing child's relationship to the world probably organizes itself.

Proposition and Speech Act

Very similar and hardly further from psychology is a widespread approach which organizes deep structures into *propositions*. If we compare the sentences

(2.15) The poor man fears the hunter's large dog

and

(2.16) The poor man fears the large dog that belongs to the hunter

we notice a large "inner similarity," even though the ownership of the dog is expressed differently in the surface structures. Both sentences have, as we say, the same propositional content. A proposition is a *declarative unit* which combines a verb with one or more nominal components. In the two sentences mentioned we find the propositions

> The man is poor.
> The dog belongs to the hunter.
> The dog is large.
> The man fears the dog.

Paraphrases can thus be made by means of different combinations of the propositions.

Case grammar and the propositional approach (and this may not be overlooked) no longer fit naturally into the linguistic pattern with which we began: that the speaker/listener knows the (syntactic) system of rules and possesses a lexicon which gives him the component parts which are to be set into the syntactic structure. Case grammar and the propositional approach place part of the structuring forces of the linguistic event in semantics, that is, in the study of meaning. The dividing line between syntax and lexicon appears in a different place than it does in the

Chomsky—Katz—Fodor approach; indeed, we can no longer actually talk about a dividing line of this kind.

In this chapter we have adopted the basic question of TGG: what does the speaker/listener know about (the rules of) his language? Our answer has already gone beyond that of TGG; he knows more than just the system of rules which determines the syntactically correct order of linguistic signs in the sentence. He also knows something about the relationships of the meaning of the words of his language.

The speaker/listener of a language "knows" still more. Let us clarify this with an example from Fillmore (1976b). The speaker who says "Good morning, sir" to a listener knows not only how he must pronounce the words. He also knows that he accomplishes an act of greeting with them. Here the language philosophy of Austin and Searle proposes the *theory of the speech act*—that this statement is appropriate only during a certain part of the day, that the person spoken to must be a male adult, that the speaker wants to express a certain amount of respect, and that such a greeting may be given only one time per day per person spoken to.

The theory of the speech act just mentioned is, strictly speaking, not a linguistic theory; it is not concerned with language-as-such, but rather with the connection between the structure of a sentence and the fact that this sentence is spoken.

Speech acts are the basic and smallest units of communication, not of language.

What constitutes a speech act? This can best be shown by an example: when someone says

(2.17) It's raining outside

(a) a sentence is uttered, (b) perhaps a warning is given to the listener who wants to go out (it can also be a joyful statement that it is finally raining after a long dry spell!), (c) it perhaps has the effect that the listener takes an umbrella with him. These are three aspects which are realized in and through an utterance. (In the philosophy of language they are called *locution*, *illocution*, and *perlocution*). All these aspects are taken into account by a speaker when he makes a statement in this way.

The integration of these aspects in one speech act is the clearest when so-called performative verbs are used, verbs which accomplish a specific act when they are uttered. The act of baptism is accomplished by uttering the words, "I baptize you." The act of promising is accomplished by the statement, "I promise you that. . . ." The speech act of promising is constituted or executed not only by the utterance of a certain series of words; a series of nonlinguistic requirements must be fulfilled, too, as an example will reveal. When the speaker S says to the listener L, "I promise to pay you $5.00 tomorrow," he has accomplished the speech act of promising only when the following requirements are also fulfilled:

- The speaker S must himself believe that he can pay the $5.00 tomorrow.
- He must assume that the listener L would rather see this promise kept than not kept (otherwise we are talking about a threat!).
- It cannot be self-evident to the speaker or the listener that S will give L the $5.00 tomorrow no matter what.

If these requirements surrounding the utterance are not fulfilled, the utterance "I promise you . . ." does not accomplish the speech act of promising, but rather a deceit or an error has perhaps occurred. The speaker and the listener must thus have knowledge of a certain schema in order to make and understand a promise.

A speech act is a kind of schema. Schemata or "frames" are available for the language user to help him to understand his environment. There is, for example, an "economic" frame, to which "buy" and "sell," "money," "pay," "cost," "bill," "loan," "allowance," and much more belong (see Fillmore 1976a,b). The meaning of these words becomes clear to the language user when he relates them to their frame, and by this relation the listener of an utterance learns a great deal which is not verbalized in this utterance itself. It may be debatable whether and to what extent such knowledge is *linguistic* knowledge, but we cannot naturally argue that such pragmatic requirements are any less important for the success of an utterance in language than the requirements which syntax, and in a narrower sense semantics, would like to see fulfilled.

Accordingly, in recent times linguistics has added to phonology, syntax, and semantics, a separate study of usage, *pragmatics*. It seems to me, however, that the reason why the step from linguistics to the psychology of language is such a difficult and large one lies in the character of this (additive) assistance: can we really divide the scientific description of a system used for a specific purpose into the description of the system and the description of its use? Can we divide up the impression that a painting makes on us for description's sake into the impression that the colors make and the impression that the figures make? We can without a doubt. But what have we actually described?

The *psychology* of language must definitely, if it wants to do justice to its task (namely, to describe those psychological processes which occur in the speaker and in the listener during the use of language), not only consider linguistic information in the narrow sense but also nonlinguistic factors which are important for the success of the communicative event. The influential psycholinguist G. A. Miller said in 1965, in complete agreement with the leading opinion of the times, that one must differentiate between a description of language and a description of the language user. He left the description of language to the linguist, whereas the description of the language user was limited to the psychological presentation of a person who "realizes" those linguistic concepts which the linguist has created to characterize language. Today the psychology of language has almost completely dissociated itself from the dichotomy between the description of language and that of the language user. Now the speaker/listener in the act of using language is the point of interest most linguistic considerations have only a value as a stimulus for genuinely psychological approaches. As a recent statement says: "Language is not learned in isolation and it is not used in isolation—why should it be described in isolation?" (Derwing and Baker 1978: 206.)

Text as Unit

Even in linguistics itself several approaches have recently been published which no longer intend to describe language "as such" (this requires an additional study of usage) but which rather define the object of description as an *actualized* system. These approaches appear partially under the heading "text linguistics"; a particularly consistent one is suggested by de Beaugrande (1980). For them text is a "many-leveled unit" of language which consists of fragments which can have the character of a sentence but need not necessarily have it. A text must be relevant to a situation in which a constellation of strategies, expectations, and knowledge is active. A text is a manifestation of a human action; this action is directed by the intention to instruct someone (Schmidt 1973) or to change the consciousness of a listener (Hörmann 1976/1981).

With this, the borderline between linguistics and the psychology of language, which was so reassuringly clear (and so detrimental for research and theory development), is abolished. Linguists must become accustomed to thinking psychologically. Psychologists of language must break the habit of allowing "pure" (i.e., nonpsychological) linguistics to give them their concepts, constructs, and theories.

CHAPTER 3

Language as a Tool

The Basis of Language Acquisition

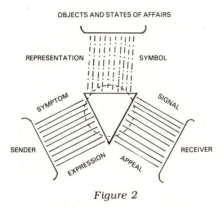

Figure 2

The circle in the middle symbolizes the concrete sound phenomenon. Three variable moments on it are capable of raising this phenomenon in three different ways to the rank of a sign. The sides of the drawn-in triangle symbolize these three moments. The triangle encompasses, in one respect, less than the circle (the principle of abstractive relevance). In another direction, however, it surpasses the circle, in order to indicate that the sensibly given constantly experiences an apperceptive enlargement. The multitude of lines symbolizes the defined semantic relations of the language sign. It is a *symbol* by reason of its being coordinated to objects and states of affairs; an *index* (*indicium*) by reason of its dependence on the sender, whose interiority it expresses; and a *signal* by reason of its appeal to the hearer, whose outer and inner behavior it directs just as other communication signs do.

K. Bühler

Bühler's Organon Theory

Until now we have viewed the sign as something that represents something else. The relationship between the sign and what it stands for must now be made more specific. First we will follow Karl Bühler, who proposed in 1934 in his epoch-making book *Language Theory* an *organon model* of language or, more specifically, of the sign. It is called an *organon* according to the Platonic principle: language is a tool, an instrumental auxiliary, by means of which one person can communicate something about something to someone.

One—to the other—about things: these are three points among which this model establishes relationships. Bühler's example: one person hears a pattering sound outside and says to another, "It's raining." The latter hears the words and looks out of the window.

That which is uttered here in speech has different relationships:

- to the one who says it
- to the one who hears it
- to what is being spoken about.

In order to make this clear, Bühler uses a stronger amplification, so to speak, which allows him to recognize the differences of these three relationships. In the center is the concrete linguistic event, the phenomenon. Three different aspects are called up from this phenomenon to make it a sign in different ways: the phenomenon is a *symbol* in its relationship to objects and events which it represents; it is a *symptom* in its dependence on the sender, whose inner situation it expresses; it is a *signal* by power of its appeal to the receiver, whose behavior it directs.

Representation, expression, and appeal are, according to Bühler, the three characteristic accomplishments of language— today we would say, somewhat more carefully, the three characteristic functions of the sign. If we want to understand the conversation of two people in a foreign language, the analysis can follow three "lines of sight": we can place the linguistic patterns in relation to what is happening in the environment (whenever it rains, he produces these sounds); we can place them in relation to the speaker (whenever he is afraid, he produces these sounds); or we can place them in relation to the way the listener reacts (whenever he hears these sounds, he comes over here). In the first case, the pattern of sounds is seen in its representational function, that is, as symbol; in the second case it is taken as an expression or symptom, and in the third case as a signal which makes an appeal to the receiver.

The relation between the sign and that for which it stands can also be seen in another aspect which has interested man since antiquity: is the connection between the sign and what it stands for a natural necessity? Or is it learned—and learned differently in every cultural and linguistic environment? In Plato's view, the connection between the linguistic phenomenon and that for which this linguistic phenomenon is a sign contains a moment of natural necessity, and therefore there is truth or correctness in this connection: words are names which conform to the things. Offshoots of these kinds of considerations can still be found in today's psychology of language and in ethnopsychology under the headings of sound symbolism and word magic.

The view that words are naturally and by necessity related to

some specific thing outside of language is replaced by the Aristotelian approach: the connection between language and things
outside of language does not consist of a substantial necessity but
rather is arbitrarily set by man. For Plato, the claim to truth for
language was guaranteed by the natural appropriateness of the
sound form. For Aristotle this claim to truth becomes a problem.
Since man takes part in the consummation of the relation between the sign and what is represented, and because this relation
(called meaning) is thus arbitrary, there remains here a moment
of insecurity.

To return to Bühler: a weakness in his model, which grew out
of the philosophical situation of his time, is that the world of
objects and events is viewed as completely independent of language. The Aristotelian idea that language represents the world is
contained in the above. What they fail to take into consideration
is that many things in our world are actually first *made* with and
through language and therefore that the view of a true representation, in language, of a (language-independent) reality is questionable. Here a new function of language is touched on: that of
constituting objects. It was emphasized by Humboldt (1963) (and
after him by many others): "Language is the producing organ of
thought," not the *reproducing*.

Also neglected in Bühler's organon theory is the question
whether the sign has of itself a specific function (or many), or
whether a specific intention of the user of the sign actually *makes*
the language phenomenon *into* a sign, points it in a specific direction. Thus we must now ask, In which way does a sign "have"
"its" meaning? Is the word *table* a name tag, so to speak, which
the object *table* always wears around its neck, and by saying it we
can call it up, call it into consciousness? Definitely not, because
we can, according to the situation, also call it a "low thing" or "the
ugly thing" or the "wooden thing" or only "that thing"—how
many meanings does the object wear around its neck like a
name?

Also, what is the case with a sign for something that is not an
object in the physical sense? What is the relationship between the
word *love* and that for which it stands?

In the attempt to answer questions of this nature, we would enter difficult philosophical and psychological terrain. We should not do this here, except to say very generally of the last example: the word love means something because the speaker means something by it. It develops its function or action as a sign only at the time of its use by the speaker. We cannot separate *sign* from its use. An utterance is only a sign if and as long as it is intended by the speaker in a certain way. The intention of the speaker, his intentions with respect to the listener,[1] makes the sign a sign. The listener *understands* what the speaker *means* if he is successful in realizing that a warning is intended with the spoken words, "Careful, the dog bites." Understanding assumes that we realize that a sound or a combination of sounds is meant, is *intended* as a sign. The understanding of an utterance in language already assumes a certain preunderstanding—one that is still uncertain, undecided, only a frame, which is not yet completely determined—which is then differentiated and made precise by the meanings of the words actually used, by the structure of the message, and by many other things.

Linguistic communication assumes that the receiver understands the utterance of the speaker as an intended act and allows himself to be seized by the force,[2] so to speak, which carries through the mere utterance and beyond it to the place where the speaker wants the consciousness of the listener to be.

This recognition of the intention of the speaker also presents the basis for the acquisition of language by the small child.

In the following sections we will show how, in the "business of learning to talk," many problems arise which are also, apart from the aspect of language acquisition, pervasive problems for any psychology of language. We shall see that this "business of learning to talk" becomes understandable when we view it as happening between two people who live and function with one another.

[1]This includes the case in which the speaker is talking to himself, e.g., verbalized thinking.

[2]In the philosophy of speech acts this force is called illocutionary force.

Predialogical Activity

> Gestures, if carried back to the matrix from which they
> spring, are always found to inhere in or involve a larger
> social act of which they are phases. In dealing with commu-
> nication we have first to recognize its earliest origins in the
> unconscious conversation of gestures. Conscious commu-
> nication—conscious conversation of gestures—arises when
> gestures become signs, that is, when they come to carry for
> the individuals making them and the individuals responding
> to them, definite meanings or significations in terms of the
> subsequent behavior of the individuals making them; so that
> by serving as prior indications, to the individuals responding
> to them, of the subsequent behavior of the individuals mak-
> ing them, they make possible the mutual adjustment of the
> various individual components of the social act to one an-
> other, and also, by calling forth in the individuals making
> them the same response implicitly that they call forth ex-
> plicitly in the individuals to whom they are made, they
> render possible the rise of self-consciousness in connection
> with this mutual adjustment.
>
> G. H. Mead

Let us begin with a report of the German child psychologist Meumann, whose small son had learned to reply to the question, "Where is the window?" (in German: "Wo ist das Fenster?") by pointing to the window. Had this little boy really already learned the meaning of the words "Where," "window," and so on? Had he learned the syntactic form of the question? Meumann comes closer to the solution to this problem by asking the child, who had never heard a word of English, "Where is the window?" Again the child pointed to the window, and he asked, "Où est la fenêtre?" and the child pointed to the window. Finally Meumann asked, "Wo ist die Tür?" (Where is the door?) and the child pointed again to the window.

What can be concluded from this report? In the first round it was shown that the child "understands" what the speaker "means." The speaker wants to turn the attention, the con-sciousness, of the child to the window. He does this by turning

himself with the child toward the window, carries out a specific
pattern of behavior with the child, and he accompanies this event
at a specific moment in time with a specific utterance.

This situation of attending to something together (Bruner,
1978, calls it "joint attend") is one of the basic situations in
which and from which language develops. The precursor of
speech events proper is, as we see, a kind of predialogic activity
involving adult and child—the child who is guided and the adult
who, in his turn, fits into the unitary sequence of events comprising that group of two.

A very early manifestation of such predialogic activity is reported by Kaye (1977): in the first month of life bursts of infant
sucking alternate with bursts of mother's jiggling the bottle to
stimulate the infant further to suck. Infant sucking—pause—
mother jiggling bottle—pause—infant sucking . . . is the sequence which is established in this predialogue. The pauses are
necessary parts of it, because they stress the systematic nature of
the pattern.

At the age of three or four months a gazing interaction between mother and child develops, which need not be a single
alternating system. It is (Jaffe *et al.*, 1973) rule–governed to the
extent that what happens next is a function of the state currently
prevailing in the group.

Later on, the joint attending or predialogic activities include
looking at a picture book together. Other such situations are *object interaction* in which mother and child work together with an
object (for example, the mother builds a tower and the child
knocks it down) and *social interaction*, such as greeting and
parting ceremonies or "pretending episodes," in which, for example, mother and child pretend together that one wood block is
chasing the other.

In these unitary dynamic sequences of events, then, a division develops into pure acts and sound acts.

For the adult who is taking part in it, usually the mother, a
requirement for the developing communication with the baby is
that she believe in the communicative intentions of the child and
that she *interpret* all utterances—and all nonutterances—of the
child. She has, as Bruner calls it, her "unavoidable theory of what

the child intends" (1978: 205). All actions of the child carry intent for her, all utterances at least an attempt at communication. Her line of vision follows the baby's line of sight with only short interruptions (Collis and Schaffer 1975). And perhaps even more important: from the fourth month on the baby follows the glance of the mother into the environment with his own glance (Scaife and Bruner 1975): the joint-attend situation is thus so tightly closed that one of the two participants can take part in the activity and thereby share in determining the activity of the other. Each can do so because there seems to be, on both sides, the assumption that the partner's activity (be it motor or vocal) is not random, but intentional. What the child (or the adult) does points to something, refers to something, represents something—a thing, an object or an action.

MacNamara's Theory

Starting from these points, how can we picture the acquisition of language by the small child? What is probably the most well-known theory of child language acquisition today gives us the answer, that of MacNamara (1972): "Small children learn their language by first determining what the adult means independent of language, and then by working out the relationship between what is meant and what is said" (1).

Let us make it clear what is being claimed here. Understanding is older than understanding language. The child understands what the adult means, what he prelinguistically and nonlinguistically means, and because he understands what is meant, this knowledge can be used as a key, as a means for "breaking" the linguistic code. Champollion could decipher the hieroglyphs, could grasp their meaning, because he already knew, with the Rosetta stone in his hand, what the writer meant.[3]

Communication begins, as we see, long before language.

---

[3]The Rosetta stone made the deciphering of hieroglyphics possible because it contains the same text in three languages: hieroglyphics, demotics (a later, conventionalized form of hieroglyphics), and Greek.

Where we have it begin is a question of definition. Is the crying of a baby already communication? It is not if we require for "true" communication that the sign be purposely used for the message. Is the fact that I do not sit down next to but across from my partner at a table a "true" communication of my competitive rather than cooperative attitude toward this partner?

We recognize the following: one draws conclusions as to what the other person wants and means from many different events; there is a large area of transition from a mere mark, which perhaps stands for nothing more specific than "I here," to the consciously used, precisely coded, sign. The place at which we drive in the peg in this field of transition to say "at this point communication begins" is a question of terminology.

Nonverbal Communication

The field of so-called nonverbal communication, out of which grows verbal communication, and where "becoming language" takes place, has been thoroughly dealt with in recent times.

This so-called nonverbal communication not only includes glances, gestures, and the like, but also turning the body, holding one's breath, and other physiological events which accompany the activities of two people with each other, without being seen, however, in the communication between these two people as a *sign.* We find ourselves in an area *before* coding in the proper sense of the word.

Wittgenstein (1958) presents such an original moment in the history of the development of language as follows: Two people are working with each other to build a house out of prepared material. The more exactly the helper himself understands the process of building, the less language is needed by the two to work together. If the helper does not know the building process exactly, the master carpenter will call "Board!" at a certain point and indicate the piece that is meant with a glance or a movement of his head. The helper will know immediately what is meant, even if he has never before heard that this piece is called a board. Indeed, he will take the piece that is intended and give it to the carpenter, even if he has never heard an imperative, because from this common process of building, from this nonverbal context, from the common desire to build, from the empty hands of the carpenter, from the empty space in the building, and from the glance and the sound of the carpenter results—what does result here? The result is not that this piece is called a "board," but rather that the helper should give this piece to the carpenter. The linguistic utterance is not yet a means "of symbolic denotation but rather for achieving a purpose" (Ogden and Richards 1923). The carpenter could also have said "that there" or "bring it here" or "you dummy."

What can we learn from Wittgenstein? That meaning in language, in any case, originally builds on a relationship between two active people with their intentions and their information and the world of objects and events around them. We can only explain what words and sentences mean by viewing "the whole: the language and the action, with which it is interwoven." Wittgenstein calls this whole a "language game" (1958).

Very similarly, Höpp (1970) maintains that language develops out of what he calls the *Einerspruch,* the "one-dictum," that is, the acoustic utterance functioning as the imperative tool with which the contributions of bystanders are summoned to action in shared work.[4]

Language is learned when the child first grasps, independent of language, what the speaking adult means and construes from what he understands, from the intentions of the adult speaker, what the utterance could mean: "He wants me to look over there," "He wants this object." Schlesinger says (1971) that the child

[4]In modern linguistics, which is heavily influenced by predominantly logical considerations, there is a widespread tendency to see the "starting point" of language in predication. Holenstein (1980) cogently argues against this position. [As noted in the introduction, the language theories developed by Wegener and Gardiner offer a different, more psychologically oriented account of predication which does not suffer under the logistically induced problems of many psychological treatments of language. For them, predication is fundamentally articulation of novelty against a background of shared fields, situations, and presuppositions. These are grounds to the predication's figure. Predication for them is simply the originary act of saying something about something, no matter what the linguistic or syntactic form of the utterance might be. See the bibliographical references to these materials listed after the introduction.—Ed.]

grasps an entire situation as an all-inclusive structure of intentional marking.

If this is true, the goal of learning to use language can be outlined as follows: to learn the rules according to which the intentional structure of a situation is represented in the structure of the language utterance. If we want to base the language acquisition of the child on the development of the intentional structure in this manner, a structure which the child construes or grasps in the specific situation, then this should be true not only for the case in which the adult means something (and says something about it) but also for the case in which the child utters sounds and (more or less clearly) means something by them.

Let us imagine a child in his play pen, whose teddy bear has fallen outside and cannot be reached. The child reaches his hand through the bars in the direction of the teddy bear and whimpers. The adult, whose attention is drawn to the scene by the whimpering, "understands" what the child "means": I want my teddy bear back. The adult "understands" because he takes it for granted that the child's behavior is goal-directed; he "sees through" the intentional structure of the situation. The child does very little toward the active development of the intentional structure; he reaches through the bars to the bear and whimpers. The whimpering gives the hand movement a specific, recognizable intention for the adult. In order to understand what the child means here, the adult needs certain nonlanguage knowledge: he needs to know that this is the child's teddy bear, that the child would rather have the bear than not have it, that the child cannot yet say, "Please put my teddy bear back into my play pen," that whimpering is usually coupled with an unpleasant situation, and so on. That is, the adult must, in order to grasp the intentional structure of the situation and then to be able to act accordingly if necessary, have this "theory of the child" which we described above.

What must the child know, though, who wants to understand what the adult speaker means? We said earlier, along with MacNamara (1972), that the child first grasps what the adult "means" independently of language and construes from this the meaning of the utterance that the adult makes in this act of meaning. What is required for this? (See Pylyshyn 1977.)

The requirements are of several different kinds. The sense impressions of the child must be organized, structured. The world may no longer be chaotic, may not be "blooming, buzzing confusion," as William James said, but it must be organized into objects which appear *perceptually* (thus independent from language) as units and are thus grasped by the child. Gestalt psychology has said much to this point, with its figure–ground differentiation and with its emphasis on gestalt-closing factors (especially the factor of "common fate"), and Piaget (1954) has added the concept of "sensory-motor intelligence" which encompasses action and knowledge-oriented perception. The child learns that *one* object is that which can be seen and touched at the same time and which disappears all at once. Experimental treatment of something begins to divide itself into the object and the (self-initiated) action *through* the treatment of it. Play has, as Bruner (1972) emphasizes, the function for man and for primates in this phase of organizing the undifferentiated events into (integrated) perceptions and acts. "The initial acts are then systematically changed to fit the further requirements of the situation. These acts reward themselves.[5] They are systematically varied, almost as if in play the limits of a new skill are to be tried out" (27). The idea of "not yet separated" ability and knowledge implied in the word *skill,* of being able to roll a ball and being acquainted with a ball, is the essential element in the vast network that must be available for language to arise. Nelson (1974) writes that from the interaction

            (in the living room, in the hall
            (mother throws, picks up, holds it
   Ball₁   (I throw, pick up, hold it
            (rolls, bounces
            (on the floor, under the table

[5]Forty years earlier Karl Bühler called this *Funktionslust,* function pleasure. [That is, the pleasure that comes from performing a function itself. The reference here is to Bühler's book, *Die Krise der Psychologie,* published in 1927, which dealt with the foundations of psychology. Bühler wanted to distinguish this type of pleasure from the type of pleasure that comes from creation, which he called *Schaffensfreude.* The whole discussion took place in the context of a general theory of play and of Freud's psychoanalytic theory of pleasure.—Ed.]

the concept of "this ball" develops, a kind of preconcept to which not only the mere appearance of the specific object belongs, but also what a person can do with it, and how a person feels or what he perceives when doing that. From the action develops what Tolman (1948) has called a "cognitive map," a network of relationships between what gradually becomes an independent and isolated object *and* the child himself *and* the adults who take part in the situation. A cognitive map says, when you do this and this with this object, that will happen. When you bump the ball, it will roll away; when it bounces, it will sound like "plopp."

Concepts as Cognitive Maps

The great achievement of the child consists in filtering out with the strength of his intellect what is permanent, what stays the same, the constant from the steady flow of events and aspects. The tendency toward making things constant (Hörmann 1967) is certainly a biological process which is very widespread; even in the animal kingdom we find this kind of recognition which ignores what is unimportant and only recognizes what is constantly important, even in different circumstances: the ape recognizes the tiger's stripes in the green light of the jungle *and* in the silver moonlight; a dog that has learned to salivate at a tone of 1000 cycles/sec will also react to a tone of 800 cycles/sec, will recognize it as *the* tone, so to speak, which concerns him.

Such *generalizations* occur on different levels. For the ape that perceives the stripes of the tiger, for the dog that reacts to a similar tone, it is a biologically "built-in" generalization which functions without any experience, because the processing of visual stimuli is regulated in this way for the ape and the processing of acoustic signals is thus regulated for the dog. Such "natural" generalizations also certainly occur in man, but other, functional generalizations are more important here. "What *functions* the same way is assumed to be 'the same'." Let us assume with Nelson a second situation:

(on the playground
Ball$_2$ (boy throws, catches

(rolls, bounces
(over the ground, under the fence

Here appears a different ball in a situation different from but similar to the first situation, with similar series of events and similar connections between events. This ball also bounces, when we let go of it; it also makes a sound when it bounces; it also rolls. The common features of the (perhaps small, green) ball₁ and of the (perhaps large, red) ball₂, that is, of "ball," the *concept* "ball," begin to crystallize, the concept which, in the structure of the adult's knowledge, then, stands "behind" the single instance. The concept is bound to the concrete instance by a peculiar, difficult-to-describe relationship which "instantiates" it. It should be clear to us what kind of task the child learns to accomplish by recognizing every ball as a ball, as falling under the concept of ball. Concepts of the kind have a functional core which consists of the different relationships and acts in which the concept has a part (Nelson 1974: 278).

When we discuss what a child must bring along to the business of language acquisition and thus present the organization of the world into objects and concepts, it is still not language acquisition itself; we are still not at the point at which the child calls this ball (not to mention every ball!) "ball." We are in the process of describing the development of what is later the "inside" of language.

To these relationships and acts, which come together in and overlap in concepts, certainly belong such relationships as "agent of the action" or "object of the action" or "direction of the action" or "owner of the object"—that is, relations for which everyday language often has no words of its own. We assume that such concepts come into being because the child who has advanced somewhat in his language uses it so that this kind of class division becomes recognizable in the grammar: living objects, which can initiate an action themselves, will later be treated differently in language (in fact in syntax) from nonliving objects, which can only be the passive object of an action. In a next step, the child will have to learn, however, to treat agent *and* patient *and* very often instrument syntactically alike, that is, as nouns functioning as subject of a sentence. The necessary convergence of semantically different categories into one and the same word class is still a rather obscure process; Schlesinger (1979) calls it "semantic assimilation."

Cognitive Structures

> There is a definite and necessary structure or *gestalt* of sensitivity within the organism, which determines selectively and relatively the character of the external object it perceives. What we term consciousness needs to be brought inside just this relation between an organism and its environment.
>
> G. H. Mead

If we pause here for a moment and take our bearings, we see that the question about the cognitive inventory which the child must bring with him to learn his language leads us into an interesting area of study in both psychology and in linguistics. We have formulated our considerations, up to this point, in a straightforward (and nonanticipatory) manner as follows: "objects, concepts, and constant relations must develop"—but what do we know *exactly* about this process of development? Does it begin, so to speak, at zero, with the famous *tabula rasa,* or are there inborn, genetically laid-out crystallization cores, so to speak, already available, around which, then, the organization of the world proceeds? And if the latter is the case, how much is laid out and thus determined, how much is free for the influence of concrete, individual experience? What cognitive knowledge does the child have *before* language? With this question we touch on the question of prelanguage *universals,* questions about the cognitive equipment that *man* has, before and without having had experience with language. To this certainly belongs the ability to be moved, the ability to move.

A tiny look into such a prelanguage cognitive structure is granted us in Gardner and Gardner's (1969) observations of their chimpanzee Washoe. Washoe began to learn American Sign Language (ASL) in daily contact with her guardians. One day she learned the sign for "open" with a particular door. After that she used this sign immediately, and without any further learning, for a different door, but also for a Coke bottle from which she wanted a drink, for a bag which she thought had food in it, for a refrigerator, and finally for a water faucet.

What is happening here? Washoe had learned an expression in language by bringing a particular gesture into relation with a particular cognitive structure. The use of the gesture shows us how far the structure reaches: open/door, open/bottle, open/bag, open/faucet—from where does Washoe "have" this structure? She did not learn it by means of language, as we presumably learned, by means of language, to bring a St. Bernard and a Dachshund together into the concept "dog." For Washoe—and for the child—the world *is* apparently organized already in a specific manner, before the organizing function of language can have an effect.

But we do not need to go to Washoe in order to find such prelanguage cognitive structures: we find them also in the overextensions which are shown in the first use of words by the child: who first says "mooi" for the moon, then for round cookies, then for round drawings on a window, round letters in a book—here "round" seems to be such a general structure which leads the act of naming but then also leads it astray.

We will have to return to this later; we must now return to the point from which we started this train of thought: What kind of knowledge and ability must the child bring with him to the business of learning language? He must bring with him, as we have described, a first—and certainly not a final—organization or structuring of the world. Second, he must bring with him or be able to accomplish a primarily temporal organization or structuring of the nonlanguage (and then also of the language) acts and kinds of behavior, with the help of which the adult means what he says. Meumann's small son, who is asked as his father holds him, "Where is the window?" must recognize, in order to understand what his father means, that the utterance "Where is the window?" is *one* coherent, organized thing, that it is an act aimed at the child himself, that its purpose is to reach the child and that a reaction from the child is expected. What do we know about the possibilities the child has for organizing the running nonverbal flow of behavior between the two people into individual, coherent acts, so that later, possibly, a verbal act can be precisely assigned to such a nonverbal one?

Let us begin very early, say with a three-day-old infant that the mother lying in her arms and that she is feeding with a bottle. The bottle is empty, the mother accentuates the end of the act and the transition into a new one by saying "so," putting the infant into a different position, and thereby also turning her hips. (Turning the hips thus into a different position can often be seen in the conversation of two adults when a change in topic occurs.) The infant thus learns to recognize the limits of a completely organized and structured total event very early. We remember here what we said a few pages earlier about the mutual turn taking of the sucking infant and the bottle-jiggling mother. Turn taking and pauses are signals to structurally important points in the sequence of events. Maternal vocalization addressed to an infant is highly rhythmic, rhythmic enough to maintain interest (to allow for the formation of expectancy), but yet with a limited or at least lawful variability (to avoid habituation). As Jaffe *et al.* (1979) say:

> One of the most important early functions of maternal speech may
> have little to do with speech *per se* but rather functions as an ideally
> suited serial stimulus to "teach" the infant the temporal patterning of
> *all* human communicative behaviors. (424)

The child must learn to make use of (verbal and nonverbal) signals to initiate, maintain, or terminate a focussed interaction—this is one of the cornerstones of the developing framework of communication.

Learning to attend to and make use of the time pattern of events is, however, important not only for the infant learning his language.

Kinesics

Such highly structured organizations of the total event shape the behavior of the adult, too. Condon and Ogston (1966) have shown that for the adult the individual parts of an utterance are fit into the series of movements in a very specific way. Eye contact plays a specific role here. The closer the speaker comes to the end of his utterance, the more he looks at his partner. If the speaker makes a prescribed syntactic pause (e.g., before a relative clause), he is more likely to look at his partner than if he pauses to think. Even with kindergarten children a general change in posture can be seen as a visual sign of readiness for a verbal utterance, whereas the end of an utterance is signaled by an increase in kinesic activity (head, arm, hand, and finger movements).

The fact that such synchronization between certain body movements and language utterances do not exist from the beginning, but that it is perceived by the very young infant and has an effect on the infant's behavior, is suggested by an observation by Condon and Sander (1974), wherein so-called interactional synchronization already revealed itself in infants who are one or two days old, that is, a synchronization of the body movements of the listening infant with the time pattern of an utterance which is intended for him.

This time structure of the utterance, the awareness of which we just discussed as a second requirement for the acquisition of language (grasping structuredness of the world was the first requirement), is accentuated and signaled not only by accompanying nonverbal movements and events but also, naturally, from within the verbal continuum of action itself. Here there are above all two means of assistance which make the time structure of the utterance clear: pauses and stresses.

The exact point in time in which a syllable is uttered is not only determined by the part of the utterance which has already been spoken, but *also* by the parts which the speaker has only planned. The same is also more or less the case for stress.

The studies of Martin (1972) have shown that the distribution of accent in the series of units which follow one another, for example, of syllables of a sentence, correspond to the structural diagram of the sentence (the tree diagram), which we have already discussed in the preceding chapter. Conclusions can thus be drawn about the structure of the sentence from the distribution of stress.

When the adult can quickly learn to perceive the structural

components of a language that is unknown to him simply by listening for a very short time to this language (see studies by Wakefield, Doughtie, and Yomb 1974), we may also assume this ability in the child: he learns to grasp the organizational units of the language he hears before he knows what these units mean and what exactly the structural relationships to each other are.

We may now summarize what we said about the second requirement for the acquisition of language: the child must learn to recognize and to realize the temporal organization of human activity, including the organization of speech activity, in more or less inclusive units.

How Is Language Learned?

What must next be added is the act of bringing these two structured worlds into relation, the world of objects and events and the world of sound and gestural activity. How can we imagine this act of bringing into relation? How can we imagine that the sequence of sounds "Come here" is learned by the child as a symbol for a very specific series of movements which is wished for by the adult? How can we imagine that the child learns to understand the utterance "Look, there goes a dog" when he hears it, learns that this black thing is called a "dog"—and that it is also called a dog later when it is small and brown and does not run but sits and barks?

The answer to this question seemed to be clear for a long time: the linguistic relationship is "tacked on" to the intended object by means of an act of learning, that is, by a simultaneity more or less of seeing the dog and hearing the sound series "dog" and possibly by an additional reinforcement, that is, some kind of reward. This *associationist* conception of language acquisition has long been held by the different schools of learning theoreticians (Pavlov, Thorndike, Skinner). This conception, however, meets with difficulties if it is analyzed. The difficulties all have primarily to do with the concept of reinforcement. Reinforcement is usually understood, in orthodox psychology of learning, as a pleasant stimulus which follows the performance of the reaction to be learned. When the child sees the dog, then says "dog" and is immediately rewarded for this utterance, the probability that the child will again say "dog" on the next sighting of a dog should increase.

It is very probable that such processes indeed take place in language acquisition, but it is extremely improbable that they are the backbone, the basic direction of this process. Three points speak against this.

(a) The child is seldom and unsystematically rewarded in the above way for an utterance of the right name for an object or event; childhood is much too short for language to be learned in this way. The adult does indeed overtly approve or disapprove of the child's utterance, but not on the basis of linguistic correctness. Ungrammatical utterances are approved of when they are factually accurate (Brown and Hanlon 1970). "Her curl my hair" was approved of by mother (by "Uh-huh") because mother was in fact curling the child's hair.

(b) Learned designations in language do not disappear again by nonreinforcement (non reward), which should be the case according to an orthodox theory of learning (extinction).

(c) The child at first understands much more of the language of the adults than he can produce himself; reinforcement, however, applies to what is *produced* by the child.

This last argument, however, must be examined more carefully. Learning to name things by means of reward has so far been seen under the aspect that the child utters the "right" name and is rewarded for this. Can a similar reinforcement occur on the side of understanding? The adult says something and rewards the child when the child reacts correctly to the name heard in a nonverbal way: "Give me the ball"—the child gives it to him— "You do that very well." Here we also remain within the behavioristic scheme of learning: what is learned is that which is worthwhile, and this is what is rewarded. Also here, on the comprehension side, the sequence of "simultaneous occurrence of perceived object, perceived label, and correct nonverbal reaction of the child," cannot carry the whole load of language acquisition. In most cases by far it is not "rewarding" for the child to show understanding for the language utterances of the adult.

This is a point for further consideration. Human communication apparently does not arise because of, or at least not primarily because of, a biological necessity. A baby has all it needs to live, without bringing its intentions, precisely coded, to the attention of the adult and without precisely perceiving the intentions of the adult or allowing his behavior to be directed by these intentions. However, if it is not the satisfaction of a biological necessity which established the connection between the two sets of conceptual units, the visually perceived and the sounds, what is it then? How can we explain that such an endless amount of learning takes place here, when the general axiom of the theory of learning, "learning through reinforcement," is not sufficient?

Must we resort for this explanation to a tendency which is, if not biological, then indeed human, toward making the events in the world understandable, more clear, toward creating order in what happens around us, with us, and in us? The world becomes a little bit more understandable, more clear, when I as an adult hear "The table is made of wood" and with that know a little bit more about what can be done with the object that I see before me—things can be laid on it, in order to have them at a better height above the ground, to have them more easily reachable; if it is cold, I can also chop it up and burn it and warm myself by the fire, which I could not do if the table were made of plastic. I learn how heavy it probably is and what kind of sound it would make if I knocked on the top, which liquids would probably leave rings on the finish and which would not. "The table is made of wood" places this piece of the world into my cognitive order—and *this* function of language must be the one which allows the flow of language events first to be set off from the process of common action: the message, that the table is made of wood, allows a richness of experience—stored in language—to become apparent behind the concrete thing, a richness which the language community has already gathered through centuries. The child does not learn language because he could not live without it, but because he could otherwise not live as a truly human being, as belonging to the species *homo sapiens*, and as a member of our society.

For man, then, is language for the sake of language? It belongs to the "essence" of man always to be able to switch over to the representative medium of language from the flow of concrete acts, to plan acts ahead, to criticize them in retrospect, and, from the difference between planning and retrospect—and this difference exists in the medium of language!—to plan again for something new.

This "anthropological" ability to bring the structured world and the structured utterance into relation, which we view as the third requirement for the child's language acquisition, may not let us forget that we are usually not dealing here with the building of a unit by associating two parts of completely different origin. Learning to speak is accomplished, as we have seen, by two people joining in a common activity; the structured verbal utterance *emerges* as part of or "on the edge" of that comn on action which intends the object or the event designated. Schatz (1978) has shown that the first indication that the child understands the adult utterance is the fact that he or she is brought to action by it: language first functions as the releaser of an action which is otherwise determined, at this stage of development, by other, nonverbal factors. It is at later stages of language development that the adult utterance is taken by the child as a specification of the action which is now "proper" in relation to this social interaction.

The inclusion of anthropological considerations allows us to recognize even further requirements for language acquisition. Terrace and Bever (1977) have contributed the interesting observation that only the human child, but not one of the five or six chimpanzees that have until now learned to use parts of language, asks about the names of things, even if he is not immediately interested in the thing itself. The chimpanzee Lana once asked her computer, "What name of this" about a box, but only because the box had candy in it, and she could only get some candy if she typed the correct name into the computer.

Man is also himself part of the world which he strives to order and by ordering to understand. He must not only bring the structured sound events into a regular relation with the ordered events around him, but also with the events inside himself. He must have the opportunity for a "conversation of the soul with itself," of which Plato spoke, the opportunity to have his inner situation,

his feelings, desires and fears, symbolized, for himself, and thus
to be able to think about what is happening inside himself. In the
final analysis, memory, with the help of which we store our
knowledge about ourselves, our possibilities for reaction, our attitudes, and so forth is largely verbal. "I, self, mine" must thus be
available as concepts in the child in order for him to be able to
operate with symbols in language. Terrace and Bever (1977) have
expressed the supposition that the ability to grasp the individual
ego symbolically, to operate with a symbol for "I" ("I'll come tomor-
row," "John is standing behind me"), is basic for the acquisition
of later syntactic abilities.

The acquisition of syntactic orderings assumes the sym-
bolical ability for the localization of "I"; chimpanzees do not have
this ability and can thus produce word chains but not an utterance that is syntactically organized and anchored in the ego.

The Grammar of Action

The last prerequisite for language acquisition in the child we
must mention is connected with the fact that human language is
"creative": a person can form utterances by new combinations of
signs, combinations that did not exist before.

We have only a specific and finite reservoir of signs, but an
infinite number of possibilities for combining these signs is available to us—of which we also make great use—because we can
structure these combinations according to rules. Knowing the
rules for an activity means being in a certain way bound, but in
another way free. Whoever knows the rules of chess knows that he
may only move the pawn in a certain manner, but this rule does
not prescribe for him the point at which he must use such a
move. To know a rule and to follow it thus means to take a very
specific limitation of the possibilities for activity upon oneself,
voluntarily, so to speak, without direct external or internal com-
pulsion. It is part of the knowledge of the rules of the English
language to forego the utterance "She good beer is."

The child who wants to acquire the use of language must
therefore bring with him as a requirement the ability to subject

his activities to rules. What do we know about this? Is there evidence for ruled behavior in this sense in the child before language?

Greenfield *et al.* (1972) gave children of different ages cups that fit inside each other to play with. First the researcher placed five different-sized cups in front of the child, then put them into each other according to a particular sequence rule ("strategy"). The child was then allowed to play with the cups after they had been taken back apart. It was found that all of the children repeatedly put the cups back together according to a specific strategy, not necessarily that which was shown them by the researcher, but according to one that was typical for a child of that age. It made no difference what sequence the researcher used to place the cups in front of the child—over and over again the child put them back together according to *his own* rule.

Even at 11 to 36 months of age (the children in Greenfield's research were of this age) the child acts according to rules, that is, already at the pre- and extralinguistic level. This prelinguistic activity also has a grammar, as Bruner says—even when it is not necessary for the success of the activity (the child could have put the cups together in a different order each time).

Once again we notice that remarkable atmosphere of the not-completely-necessary which surrounds language in its beginnings. The child takes over the communicative function of language, even though he gets enough to eat and drink and gets his diapers changed without communication. He subjects himself to rules of behavior, even though this does not do him any immediate good. How does the child "know" that he must use such rules later, years later, in order to exhaust all the possibilities of being human? Is it possible that man is a being "made for" language?

CHAPTER 4

The Phenomenology of Language Acquisition

Children confronted with a problem that is slightly too complicated for them exhibit a complex variety of responses including direct attempts at attaining the goal, the use of tools, speech directed toward the person conducting the experiment or speech that simply accompanies the action, and direct, verbal appeals to the object of attention itself.

L. Vygotsky

The relation between thought and word is a living process; thought is born through words. A word devoid of thought is a dead thing, and a thought unembodied in words remains a shadow. The connection between them, however, is not a preformed and constant one. It emerges in the course of development, and itself evolves. To the Biblical "In the beginning was the Word," Goethe makes Faust reply, "In the beginning was the deed." The intent here is to detract from the value of the word, but we can accept this version if we emphasize it differently: In the *beginning* was the deed.

The word was not the beginning—action was there first; it is the end of development, crowning the deed.

L. Vygotsky

Language as such is simply a process by means of which the individual who is engaged in co-operative activity can get the attitude of others involved in the same activity.

G. H. Mead

In the preceding chapters the point of departure for language acquisition by the child was described psychologically, and the intuitive knowledge of the (adult) user of language, which is built up by acquiring language, was also partially described linguistically. We now want to present the steps and intermediate stages by means of which development proceeds from the starting point to the end (which the linguist rather unclearly calls linguistic competence) and to discuss the theoretical explanation for this progress from the infant without language to the child who is capable of using his language.

Imitation

The first and most widespread theory of the child's language acquisition, though disregarded by most experts, is the theory of imitation: the child learns to speak by imitating what he or she hears adults saying. A series of serious objections can be raised against this theory in this simple form:

- If imitation were the decisive factor, then the words and structures that occur especially frequently in the language of adults would have to be imitated earliest and acquired earliest. This is not the case (Brown 1973).

- The recognizable imitations of a child (the mother says something, the child repeats it) are almost without exception much more primitive than that which was first said. Sometimes a new word is repeated, but seldom is a new sentence structure imitated.
- The child often produces expressions which he could not have heard: *two dogses, come/comed, the mouses*—the child thus uses incorrectly rules that are correct in other instances! This means, though, that the child does not imitate what he has heard but rather forms hypotheses about the way one speaks correctly and then tries out these hypotheses. We will come back to this later.

If it is not plain imitation that is the vehicle of language acquisition, we have to look to other possible explanations. One of them was already prepared for in the preceding chapter: language develops when parts of the flow of activity which binds two people to each other are raised to a representative medium, to language. The initial use of this medium becomes apparent in two ways: in the control of the child's behavior through verbal utterances by the adult and in the control of the adult's behavior (or consciousness) through utterances by the child. This first type of manifestation involves the child as the listener, the second as the speaker.

MacNamara's theory of language acquisition, which was introduced in Chapter 3, suggests that the abilities of the child as listener precede in time those of the child as speaker: according to this theory, the child learns to make out, from an understanding of what the adult *means*, the sense of what he *says* about or in accompaniment to something. The child's own speech, his own production of an utterance, thus presupposes the understanding of utterances in language when they are made by adults—or at least a tendency toward this.[1]

---

[1]Recently R. Clark (1977) has proposed a modified model of an imitation theory. According to it, the child's understanding of language is not better developed

Any understanding of what the adult means when he says this or that must be preceded by the child's ability to turn his attention to the human voice—and not to other events of a situation. This ability begins very early; just a few weeks after birth, the baby can differentiate language sounds from other sounds; this can be seen both in the baby's focus of attention and by means of electroencephalogram. Molfese (Freeman 1973) showed that the left hemisphere of the brain reacts differently to language, even in babies. From Eimas's research (1975) we know that the ability to differentiate among speech sounds has, even in small children in the prelanguage stage, that categorical character which is typical for the differentiation ability of the adult.

Thus certain sound contrasts which are important for language could presumably already be perceived *before* the child has an idea of meanings that could be differentiated by these sounds. Later a child learns a sound contrast mainly when a difference in meaning is signaled—for a command of his mother tongue, the child must acquire, after all, the knowledge of which differences in sound make a difference in meaning (that is, are phonemes) and which ones are only variations of one and the same "intended" sound (allophones)—as we learned in Chapter 2.

The child learns to perceive contrasts in sounds when difference in meaning is connected with them, but he acquires certain sound contrasts before others. The difference between nasal and stop consonants (*m/b*) is generally acquired earlier, for example, than the difference between stops and fricatives (*b/v*). A specific order is also shown in sound production (Jakobson 1941).

Babbling

A very special prestage of a child's language production (and one that brings special problems with it) is babbling. At a few months

---

than his speech production; both are handicapped by certain limitations of processing capacity, especially in comprehending adult speech. The child grasps and stores individual utterance fragments, e.g., endings of sentences, which he (re-) produces himself at an opportunity he thinks fitting.

of age, children begin to babble—a production, relatively similar to language, of more or less long sequences of different sounds. This babbling stage extends sometimes, but not always, to the production of the "first word." Is babbling a preform of speaking—and if so, in what way can it be viewed as such?

The view has been represented that all possible sounds are practiced during babbling, and of these sounds those would later disappear which are not represented in the particular language. A major objection to this continuity hypothesis is, however, that certain sounds appear very frequently in babbling (e.g., *l* and *r*), but then disappear completely from the repertoire of the child who is actually learning to speak and then only many months later must be rediscovered as producible. However, this representation of the discontinuity hypothesis encounters certain difficulties. We will not go further into them here. The safest way to distinguish babble from "genuine" words is furnished by behavioral and situational cues which permit the listener to pick out those vocalizations which have referential meaning and communicative intent (Braunwald 1978: 491).

The development which leads from this to later stages is sustained, as we have seen, by what we called predialogic and dialogic activities. As Bruner, certainly an expert in this field, says:

> The opening months of an infant's life reveal a transformation in the infant's crying from what may be called a demand mode—the standard biological cry, upped when untended to a very wide sound spectrum . . . —to a request mode in which energy is concentrated in a fundamental frequency, with the cry stopped for moments at a time in anticipation of response. Request crying gradually achieves stylization and differentiates to match the context—hunger fretting, wet fretting, and so on. By responding to these cries . . . the mother recruits the child's vocalizations from demand and request into more subtle communicative patterns later in the opening year of life (Ainsworth and Bell 1974). In mood, then, initial crying is transformed from an exigent demand into anticipatory request, with the infant leaving slots for the mother's response. What follows is the beginning of exchange and turn-taking, first in vocalization and, then, with the growth of manipulative skill, in the exchange of objects—forerunners of dialogue. (1979: 277)

In this way, the first formulation of the child's vocalizations is done by a process of shaping. This certainly is one factor in the modeling of utterances. A second factor is the adoption of language sounds and language structures heard in the environment of the child.

Dialogue with the Child

In order for the child to learn to recognize sounds, language sounds, and structures, they must be offered to him; the adult plays a role in this—but what kind of role? Until recently it was believed that the child is surrounded by an abundance of grammatically more or less poorly constructed sentences; this brought with it the problem of how a child could ever acquire correct grammar when there was always such incorrect speech in his environment. The way adults really speak to children has been more closely researched for only about five or six years, and it has been discovered that *this* language is different from that among adults. "Motherese" has become a subject of research for psychology.

Here it has been shown, among other things, that the beginning of an utterance addressed to a child by an adult is usually signaled in a special way to the child: the adult calls the child by name, or says "Look at this," or touches the child—all are aids in making the about-to-begin (verbal) behavior of the adult stand out as something special compared to the general flow of behavior, and to let it appear as something intended for the child: this assists the child in the structural synthesis he must undertake.

Let us not forget that this goes on against a background of joint activity; an important instance of such activity is reaching. Up to seven or eight months of age, the child reaches for the desired object with arm and hand extended, hand closing to a fist and opening again, body bent towards and eyes fixed upon the object. This kind of reaching has not yet any communicative coloring, but mother deals with it *as if* it were meant communicatively; we remember that the mother has an "unavoidable theory" of the child's intentions. As the next stage, the child's reach changes; he or she begins to look toward the mother during the act of reaching for the object.

> The gesture is changing from an instrumental reach to something
> more like an indicator—a semi-extended arm, hand held somewhat
> angled upward, fingers no longer in grasp position. . . . His gaze
> shifts from object to mother and back. He can now reach for real and
> reach for signal. (Bruner 1979: 272–273)

From this develops, in a still later stage, the pure pointing
act.

Interestingly, the change in the child's behavior is accompanied by a corresponding change in the mother's behavior:
whereas during the first stage she very frequently gives the object
to the child, in later stages she reacts, to an increasing extent,
verbally: she interprets the child's indicative reaching as pointing
and *speaks* to the child accordingly.

This social interaction is, of course, also determined by extra-
neous stimuli. Pointing, for instance, was observed by Bruner in
a 14-month-old boy to:

- objects more than 1 m distant, which were either in an
  unusual context or completely novel
- pictures of familiar objects
- "imaginary" or "hypothetical" objects, e.g., pointing to the
  ceiling and saying "bird."

As we see, language is learned in the context of a two-sided
communication, between mother (or other adult) and child. This
context is partially constructed by the mother's interpretation of
the utterances, as well as verbal and nonverbal activities, so that a
sensible text, a sensible total activity, thus evolves (see Snow
1978, Shugar 1978). It is often amazing how large is the span of
variation of the utterances which the adult accepts as the child's
side of the dialogue (Ninio and Bruner 1978). Such a mainte-
nance of the dialogue is necessary because the acquisition of reference, the relation between the sign and what it points to, is
dependent on the fact that the social roles are understood among
which these relationships can be realized.

Here is an example of a dialogue of this stage (sometimes this
kind of dialogue is called a protodialogue):

Father: Well, don't we want to laugh at all?
Child: (*Makes a face*)

Father: Oh, we're impatient today.
Child: (*Looks at the door*)
Father: Yes, Mommy is coming right away.
Child: Wawawa.
Father: You mean you think it's time to eat?
Child: Wawa.
Father: Yes, you're right, we'll wait for Mama!

We can see that the father *plays* out a mutually directed complete series of behavior with the child in which he demonstrates and practices, so to speak, the connection and exchange between verbal and nonverbal portions of the activity. By putting each act of the child's into a context, so that it fits, he enhances the child's ability to be interpreted—he also thus makes it possible for the child to interpret and to understand the adult utterance.

> Because the adult is matching what he says to what the child intends to say, the child is provided with a chance to match semantic intention to correct adult realizations . . . this match . . . is crucial to the child's learning the arbitrary rules of syntax and morphology. (Snow 1978: 254)

In a dialogue with the child the adult tries to give the child the opportunity to act as a partner in communication. To this belongs, for example, the fact that he asks such ridiculously redundant questions of the child as "Ooo, where is he then?" Just because these questions carry almost no information, because they occur in situations wherein the information is already available, the child can learn the means of information transfer, language; such routine questions also make sure that the joint-attend situation is maintained, which was discussed in the previous chapter.

Motherese has some other characteristics, all supporting the child's labor to experience and to recognize the connection between what mother means and what she says. The mother (or any adult speaker used to talking to babies) makes the grasping of this connection easier through a series of (presumably unintentionally used) aids:

- The adult talks about what he is doing at the moment. He thus creates a real "Rosetta stone" situation which is necessary for breaking the verbal code.

- He uses exaggerated intonation to make the organization of the utterance recognizable for the small child.
- He speaks only half as quickly as to adults.

The adult formulates what he tells the child on a level of abstraction which he believes to be appropriate for the cognitive abilities and requirements of the child. She does not say, "Look, here comes a 1976 Peugeot with a fuel injection engine," but rather, "Here comes a car!" She uses much simpler constructions compared with those produced for other adults; she thus leaves certain endings off words (Snow 1972); she makes sure of identification by not using pronouns which could be misunderstood, but by repeating names, and so on.

Mother not only offers utterances to be perceived, learned from or taken over by the child. At the same time, using the well-established (say at a year and a half) dialogue routine, she tightens her control over the child's speech; not all forms of pronouncing a word are now acceptable to her. Whereas during the previous months, she had supplied a correct interpretation for every utterance of the child, she now pointedly says, "What's that?" or "What do you mean?" or "I can't understand you" until the child's pronunciation falls within generally acceptable limits. As Bruner convincingly shows, the content of the mother's teaching role changes with the developmental stage the child has reached.

Again and again we have stressed MacNamara's theoretical statement: from what the adult means (and what is "communicated" to the child by nonverbal action and situational constraints) the child deciphers what the verbal utterance means which the adult produces at that time.

If we now ask what the child "knows" at this stage about his language, the psychologist who is looking for an answer must rely on concluding from the behavior of the child as listener and the behavior of the child as speaker that the child has acquired a "piece" of language ability or competence; the conclusion is in both cases in danger of being false. If we conclude from the child's behavior that he has understood an adult's utterance, there is naturally a danger—remember what we said about the imbedding of language activity in overall activity!—that the child acts in a certain way because he understood the speaker, but not because he understood what was said: Meumann should always be kept in mind here. It should also be constantly remembered that *understanding* does not mean being conscious of *one* very specific interpretation of a certain utterance: understanding begins, as we have seen, as the trigger for and specifier of an action (and continues in the adult up to the exegetical conclusions which are drawn from an utterance after lengthy consideration).

There is also a danger, however, when the child acts as *speaker*, that we will assume too much knowledge of language in him; what does the child "know" about his language when he points to his ball and says "ba" (or did he really even say "da")?

As we see, the psychology of language development is also confronted with methodological difficulties; we will run into them frequently. These methodological and interpretative difficulties are well illustrated in the following study.

Luria (1959) placed a rubber fish in front of a child of 1.3 years and said, "Give me the fish." The child did this. Did the child know what "give" "me" and "fish" mean? Did he recognize the syntactic form of the imperative? In the next trial, Luria placed a stuffed toy cat between the fish and the child and said again, "Give me the fish." The child again moved his hand in the direction of the fish, but when his hand reached the cat he picked it up and gave it to the adult. This behavior is certainly ambiguous. On the one hand, we could say that the child could not differentiate between the *objects* of fish and cat. This is, however, as we know from nonverbal behavior (e.g., preference), extremely improbable. A second interpretive possibility: the child could not yet differentiate between the *meanings of the words* "fish" and "cat." Here the question would immediately be added: can the child not differentiate between the two words because, perhaps, both mean toy animals? Could he, however, differentiate "fish" and "shoe"? Yet another interpretation of the child's mistake (Luria's own): the child could perhaps already connect the words "fish" and "cat" with the objects they indicate—the mental operation called *mapping* could thus be possible—but he cannot yet make his own actions be determined in a differentiated manner by this understanding of the words. When the hand has arrived at the first object, the powerful "give me" controlling the act of picking up an object dominates the situation.

The exact analysis of what the child *is able* to do in this situation, and what he cannot do, again marks a basic difficulty which pervades the psychology of language, the philosophy of language, and linguistics: when can we actually say that a child— or even an adult—has understood a verbal utterance? Understanding is apparently not an act which one can either accomplish or not accomplish, but rather, understanding can have different degrees, can take place on different levels. (We will return to this problem in Chapter 8.)

Feature Analysis of Children's Utterances

We have asked whether the child is perhaps not capable of differentiating between the meanings of the words "fish" and "cat" in the necessary way. If we take this together with what we just said about understanding, it seems appropriate not to speak further about *the* meaning that is understood or not, but to remember that linguistic approach which breaks down the meaning of a word into semantic features. Does hearing the word "fish" suggest for the child only those semantic features—or, expressed differently, does the child only understand such semantic features, when hearing the word "fish"—which toy cats and toy fishes have in common? If yes, then this must be shown in the fact that the child allows himself to be *regularly* led in this behavior by these features. (When "fish" and "cat," for example, have the semantic features "stuffed animal" and "whitish," other whitish stuffed animals should also be referred to by these words.)

In this way we use the linguistic concept of semantic feature in an attempt to explain an aspect of language acquisition: the child does not at first grasp the "full" meaning of a word, but only those semantic features which for some reason are in the foreground of the situation. Such a theoretical conception can explain a series of phenomena of the child's acquisition of language, as the following research shows.

In the acquisition of dimensional designations (*long/short, more/less . . .*) the child generally seems to understand the positive term (*long, more*) earlier than the negative side of the corresponding dimension. What is behind this?

Donaldson and Balfour (1969) showed 3-year-olds toy trees on which apples hung, on one tree many apples, on the other fewer. If they ask the child, "Which one has more?" they obtain 91% correct replies; if they ask, "Which one has fewer?" they obtain only 27% correct replies—the children tended in *both* cases to choose the tree with *more apples.* The children behave as if they understood what "more" means, and as if they assume that "less" means the same as "more." *Or* do they have the hypothesis that "more" *and* "less" mean something like "amount" or "number" and have the (nonverbal) tendency always to choose *that* tree on which more apples are hanging? Here the fact (1) that not all the semantic features of "more" and "less" are already relevant for the child is bound to the fact that (2) there is a specific action preference in the nonverbal area.

In another investigation of this kind E. Clark (1973) tested how precisely small children understand the prepositions "in," "on," and "under" ("in" and "on" belong to the earliest prepositions produced by children; they should thus be understood especially early). For this test the child received a small rubber animal (A) and several larger objects (B). The researcher was convinced that the child knew the names for these things (doggie, horsie, box, truck . . .). The child was then told to "put A in/on/under B." The results showed that children over three years made few errors. Younger children (1.6 to 2.11) understood "in" correctly. For "on" the findings were more complicated: the children often acted as if it meant "in." "Under" sometimes caused the action for "in," sometimes that for "on." The deciding factor for this was whether B was a container or only had a flat surface on the upper side and no container-like interior. If B was a container, the child always put A *into* the container (and automatically carried out the "in" task correctly). If B was not a container, the child put A *on* top of B.

We can sum up the "understanding" of the child at this level in two rules, where the second is subsequent to the first:

1. If B is a container, A belongs in it.
2. If B has a horizontal surface, A belongs on top of it.

For the youngest group of children (1.6 to 2.5) we can explain over 90% of their mistakes by following these two rules. "In," "on," and "under" were all *understood* in so far as the child let them act as directions for localization. In what way, however, these words were understood as differentiated (which can be equated with the formulation: which semantic features they would activate in the child) is apparently dependent on the situation, namely, on the form of B.

This is a remarkable fact. In the linguistic conception of semantic features such a feature is *always* (by definition) attached to the word; it is part of the meaning of that word. For the linguist, the meaning of the word "cup" is not dependent on the fact that there is also a table present near the cup. For the child, this is apparently different.

From these findings, we can learn yet something else which is important: the child acts according to rules or, if we like, according to patent recipes. "First try this, and if that doesn't work, try that." This kind of patent recipe which rules behavior is called a *strategy;* we will return to this concept later.

The findings make it clear that the child prefers certain cognitive relations or organizations (A to B) even in the prelanguage phase and that this kind of preference helps to determine the sequence in which the meaning of the corresponding words crystallize. The strategies of the child make it possible for him to deal with the situation, even when he does not *completely* understand what has actually been said.

Such preferred cognitive structures are, as we have repeatedly stressed, structures of perception and action. The units for which the child hypothetically takes the words heard as designations are units which play a role for the child in perception or activity: objects and events. Specific colors, forms, and especially movements are, purely perceptually, particularly obvious: moving objects thus serve as points of reference for the child's available knowledge and for knowledge that is still to be gathered (about the function of these moving objects, the sequence or results of their movements . . .). The child who hears the word "bow-wow" accompanied by a vague hand motion by the adult, all in a new and probably complex situation, will first set up the hypothesis that "bow-wow" refers to that in the situation which was most obvious to the child anyway: something that runs, barks, wags its tail all by itself, and so forth. Moving, changing noise-making object-events will thus be the targets of the first words which the child exactly understands and produces himself. According to the degree of identity which the child's hypothesis of meaning achieves with the conception of meaning which the adult has for the particular word, the child will then make either a too narrow or too broad use of this word.

Generalization and Overgeneralization

Although too narrow a use of a word by a small child is seldom obvious, overgeneralizations are very often reported. What is obvious as an overgeneralization is the excess of a process which is a major aspect of the construction of concepts in language.

When "tick tock" is used by the child not only for the designation of this clock but of all clocks, the tachometer in the car, a scale with a round face, but also for a fire hose wound around a circular spool, we can explain this overgeneralization by saying that the designation is determined by the semantic feature, "round with marks around the edge," while the additionally necessary semantic feature needed for the limitation of "tick tock" to clocks, "is used to measure time," has not yet been added to the determination of the meaning.

Although our theoretical approach still functions quite well (the child overgeneralizes because he allows the designation to be guided by only one or a few of those semantic features which define the word semantically for adults), we will soon encounter difficulties with it. "Bow-wow" can not only name this dog, but all animals, even the cloth zebra, the furry slippers, and the picture of an old man dressed in fur (Clark 1975). If we start to analyze the generalization in this example with the help of the term *semantic feature*, then "bow-wow" apparently designates something living, which moves by itself; all animals should be called "bow-wow." But when the cloth zebra and the furry slippers are also called "bow-wow," we *can* say that the designation follows the semantic features of soft, fluffy. Is the child inconsistent? Did he change the semantic features, so to speak, which were serving as a criterion? Or does our attempt encounter difficulties here generally in using the concept of semantic feature as an explanation? Does the operation with semantic features assume a complete analysis, a stable differentiation in the internal lexicon, which is just not present in the child? As adults we can indeed *describe* the overgeneralization of "bow-wow" by saying that the child sometimes follows one, sometimes the other semantic feature; but we may not convince ourselves that this description reveals what is happening "psychologically" in the child.

This scepticism about the use of semantic features in a theory of language acquisition makes it suitable for us to place overgeneralization in the child's language usage in the framework of a completely different theoretical approach, the construction of classes around a prototype. More will be said about this in Chapter 5.

A slightly different picture of these overgeneralizations presents itself, however, when we remember that they in fact very rarely endanger effective communication. As we know from Olson's (1970) theory of semantics, one of the foremost goals of a speaker's utterance is to disambiguate the situation for the listener. Disambiguation, however, is necessary only in rather complex situations. The small child, who has only a very limited number of words at his disposal, with which he or she is to refer to a wide range of referents, can do so because these homonymous words are used in nonoverlapping contexts: as a rule, there is only one possible referent to which "bow-wow" might apply. Because the meanings of the first words of a young child are always situated meanings (and not isolated items out of a systematic lexicon), some facets of the problem of overgeneralization might actually be artificial results of an approach which is too analytical to fit what goes on in the child's mind (cf. Braunwald 1978).

Diminishing semantic overgeneralization can be described,

under a slightly different aspect, as increasing differentiation of a semantic field. A semantic field is a field formed by concepts, or the words designating concepts, which are related to each other. In this sense, the words labeling animals constitute a semantic field, the designations for family relationships, and so on.[2] "Bow-wow"—first used for this dog here and now, then almost immediately perhaps for every dog, every horse, cat, cow, or sheep. On the next level of a developmental process (described by E. Clark 1973), "bow-wow" is still used for dogs, cats, horses, and sheep, but "moo" is added for the cow. At the next level "gee-gee" is introduced for horses, "bow-wow" only for dogs, cats, and sheep. Then the sheep is selected out with "baa," "bow-wow" or now also "doggie" for dogs and cats, until finally "kitty" appears for the latter, so that "doggie" remains only for dogs—the overgeneralization is at an end because "bow-wow" now has its place in the semantic field of animal names.

We must be careful not to create the impression—which can easily arise in this kind of description of development—that the achievement of the child consists only in putting the correct linguistic label on the corresponding object. The child must also learn to differentiate among objects at the same time; he probably has no inborn categories, like "dog," to which a St. Bernard and a dachshund belong but the cat curiously not. Not only must the semantic field be developed in the child, but also simultaneously and corresponding to this, a *cognitive* field. In the latter, certain prototypes may already exist, but the verbal structuring will lead to a detailed working out of the concepts with the help of the designations in language. Not only cognitive development, but also the linguistic input occurring at this time determine the differentiation of the (linguistic and nonlinguistic) view of the world which arises here (see Schlesinger 1977a,b).

We have been talking about the meaning of the (single) word which is uttered by the young child. We found that there are, in the applications of the word to the objects it designates, over- and undergeneralizations. The meaning of the (single) word uttered

---

[2]In German linguistics there is a more specialized definition of a language field which we will not go into here.

by the young child may, however, be also analyzed under a different and not less important aspect.

The child is sitting in its playpen, the ball has fallen out, and the child says "ball" to the adult. Here it is indeed clear to us which word the child has said, but not so clear what is meant by this. We have indicated above that meaning is always an intentional act, an act by which the child attempts to direct the action, the thinking, the consciousness of the adult. Therefore, "ball" is also meant in a particular way. But how? How can the mother draw a conclusion from what is said to what the child speaker meant? By looking not only at the utterance, but also at the situative and interpersonal sequence of events in which the utterance takes place, and at her "theory of the child."

In order for a person to mean something in language, he must place the words of the utterance into an intentionally arranged structure which gives them direction and thus force. The one word "ball" which is uttered by the child thus has a context: in order to understand what the child means, we must view the utterance as a complete sentence and not as a single word.[3] We have now arrived at the famous one-word sentence, the holophrastic utterance.

The One-Word Sentence

"Ball" in this instance, as the mother would explain, does not mean "Look at the pretty ball" or "That is my ball," but "Give me the ball." From her knowledge of the situation and from her knowledge of the child the mother thus constructs a surrounding structure which she can translate into the common linguistic form of adults, here into an imperative or a request. Naturally "ball" does not always stay in *this* structure; in a different situation an apparently similar utterance "ball" can be constructed, formulated, or amplified to the sentence, "See the pretty ball" or "The ball is bouncing" by the mother.

If we ask once again our old basic question, "What does the

[3]Linguistically more precise: as a spoken sentence or as a speech act.

child know about his language?" at this stage, we would perhaps say: at least so much that he can actively add to the accentuation of the total event in the framework of communication, and can use *one* conventionally coded unit for this. May we go so far as to propose that the child knows the meaning of the word "ball," but cannot yet encode in language the imperative sentence "Give me . . ."? The psycholinguist should indeed be wary about making an interpretation that connotes deficiency (the child cannot yet . . .) only because the level of adult language is taken as an absolute measure. It might also be the case that "ball" in the child's lexicon already means "being happy because of having a ball"; if so, the child does not need to embed this word in a syntactic structure which the adult would call an imperative or a request. As we can see, what is to be considered language ability in the child depends very much on what theory of the structure of language we adopt. If the concept of lexicon did not appear in this theory, all the preceding considerations would be irrelevant.

The so-called one-word sentence is therefore neither a word nor a sentence in the linguistic sense. It is part of a speech act. The word uttered plus the situation plus, very often, a gesture or a certain intonation of the uttered word together build the structural framework of the speech act. Can we learn something more specific about the meaning in the narrow sense, about the propositional content of the uttered word, from an analysis of this framework?

First we might say generally that the child would like to get the attention of the adult, just as the adult has tried from the child's first week of life to get the child's attention and to direct it by various means. A glance or a gesture or eventually a complex of sounds is used for communication generally, for bringing about a sharing of consciousness. "You think about this ball, too, look at it!" Here eye contact, as we already have learned, plays a major role: the child looks to see if his mother is also looking in the direction in which the object he means is lying (Bruner 1978). In addition, a second kind of "speech act" appears very early: the "request-want-to-have-something." (We call it a speech act even though perhaps no one speaks during it—whether a sound utter-

ance occurs, and whether it is conventional enough to be understood by an adult, is for a long time almost incidental.) This is
different from the speech act of pure attention-directing in many
ways; it develops from the indicative reaching we have described
at the beginning of this chapter.

The one-word sentence may be analyzed under a further aspect: according to the *roles* and their interrelations which we
discussed in the section on case grammar: agent, patient, instrument, and so forth. We now ask: do we predominantly find, in the
one-word sentence, one specific case role? Is there conformity for
all or for most children in the order of appearance of different case
relations?

Both questions can be answered in the affirmative: Greenfield and Smith (1976) first found a verbal expression for the
agent role. Somewhat later a movable object is also named; this is
mainly found in the speech act of request. The cases of location or
instrument hardly occur at all in these early phases, those of
experience or receiver only very seldom. The verb, which forms
the center of the sentence as the predicate, is relatively seldom
put into language at this point.

However, we cannot be sure that the child who says "Daddy"
when the father pushes him in the baby carriage actually mentions what might be called a *general* semantic relation (agent or
at least mover). Perhaps the case "mover" is restricted to father
and mother moving the carriage plus mother moving the high
chair.

Reflections on these problems are by no means unimportant,
because these semantic relations (mover-of, possessor-of, object-
of-some-action . . .) are probably the nucleus from which the
syntactic competence of the child develops. As the one-word sentence actually merits the label "sentence," we have to assume that
there is, in some hidden form, a structure contained in that utter-
ance-plus-situation. We assume that this structure is a semantic
one, relating the verbal utterance to some object or event. How do
knowledge and use of *syntactic linguistic structures* (i.e., structures relating words to words and phrases within the sentence
itself) develop from this initial stage?

Child Grammars

Attempts to answer this question are, again, beset by methodological and theoretical difficulties. One of the reasons for this is the fact that the syntactical regularities of the English language are not very intimately connected with those semantic-structural relations (e.g., of the agent—patient or object—experiencer type). English verbs in particular do not fall into a few uniform semantic-structural patterns.[4] As Maratsos says:

> Rather than there being a small set of uniquely general and distinct relations, there is a large set of relations varying on a continuum in generality, importance and clarity, represented in various degree and distribution among NP sentential roles. (1979: 299)

The young child will, in acquiring the rules of syntax, have to learn the grammatical privileges of distribution and combination, the slots into which a noun, any noun, may be inserted, and semantic considerations may guide him only part of this way.

The child psychologist who wants to describe what a child knows at a particular stage about which combinations are acceptable (grammatical) and which are not will be on more solid ground if he begins when the child proceeds from the one-word sentence to the two-word sentence, since we are no longer dependent on fantasizing of the unrecognizable structures in the child's one-word utterance. What kind of structures appear as two-word utterances? One way of searching for them is this: We could simply see whether any regularities in the order of the two words appear, regularities which the child uses as if they were grammatical rules. The child would have, so to speak, his own grammar, or more specifically, his own syntax. This is the approach which was introduced under the title *pivot-grammars* by Braine (1963), and which starts from a fascinating thesis: we

---

[4]For example, in the sentences

    Mary likes pictures

    Pictures please Mary

an identical semantic structure (object—experiencer) is transformed into two different syntactic structures with different order of NPs.

should view the child, when he puts two or three words together, not as someone who does not have a command of *the* grammar and therefore speaks incorrectly, but rather as someone who speaks grammatically, but according to the rules of his own grammar, which is different from child to child and from stage to stage of development. The small child does not speak by breaking the rules of adults or by lack of knowledge of them, but he follows the rules of *his own* grammar. In an attempt to describe these rules, Braine discovered that the two-word utterances do not by any means contain all possible combinations of the words produced by the child during this time.

After listing children's utterances, we notice two classes of words: the so-called pivots (*P*) and the words of what Braine calls the open class. Pivots are those words which can only appear at a certain point in the two-word sentence, either as the first *or* as the second word; there are not many of these. All other words make up the steadily growing open class. The syntax of a certain child could thus be summed up in two rules: $P_1 + X$ or $X + P_2$. One child had, for instance, among his *pivot* words the word "want"; his *open class* included "baby," "milk," "trunk," "car." He produced utterances of the type $P_1 + X$ ("want car"), but never of the type $X + X$ ("baby milk").

Braine's grammar is a purely distributional grammar: it states what class of words may be produced at what position in the utterance.

It was first assumed that this kind of pivot grammar and the different stages of its changing into adult grammar offered a good possibility for adequate presentation of the regularities of the child's use of syntax. Soon, however, important objections arose: first, it seems that not all children use this kind of pivot construction to any great extent (Bloom 1970). And second, a pivot grammar cannot explain the difference between two-word sentences which sound the same but which apparently are not meant in the same way and therefore do not have the same meaning: one child says, as his mother pulls on his sock, "Mommy sock." A few days later, he walks by one of his mother's socks that is lying around, points to it and says, "Mommy sock."

A pivot grammar cannot grasp the *difference* in structure

which is obviously contained in these two utterances, because it takes only surface order into account. Here an analysis in terms of case grammar, which takes deep (or semantic) structure into account, is to be preferred. The first utterance, "Mommy sock" would be agent—object, the second, possessor—object. How may the child have learned to use the same combination of these two words to express the obviously different facts he wants to point to? Has he stored some short formulae to deal with frequently met constellations of meaning? How did he pick up these formulae? Or rather: from what adult utterances heard in the environment have they been abstracted or reconstructed?

Strategies of Language Acquisition

The small child has a vague idea—let us remember MacNamara's theory—about what the adult means and hears an accompanying stream of sounds. If the child wants to establish a relation between what the speaker means and the flow of sounds, he must, as we have seen, first have hypotheses about the way in which this flow of sounds can be organized. The child formulates such hypotheses by proceeding according to two *strategies*, which can be expressed as follows:

1. Understand those things as belonging together which are spoken together, that is, what is not separated by pauses.
2. Pay attention to what is stressed. (For the following see Bever 1970 or Slobin 1971.)

These two strategies of the child's correspond, if we may see it this way, to several characteristics on the side of adult speech which we have already mentioned: when the adult talks with the small child, he or she speaks with an exaggerated exactness of prosodic organization and stress. In his reductions,[5] the child

---

[5]Dialogues between child and adult contain many reductions and elaborations. An example of a reduction: the mother says, "So, here comes Baby's breakfast." Child: "Baby breakfast." An example of an elaboration: Child: "Throw Daddy." Mother: "Yes, throw it to Daddy."

picks mainly the so-called content words out of the adult's utterance. This has naturally led to the question: how does the child realize that he is dealing with a content word when he repeats a word, as is sometimes the case, which he doesn't actually know yet? The answer to this question is relatively simple: this kind of word carries a heavy accent in the adult's utterance; the child follows the strategy, "Pay attention to what is stressed," and he is thereby brought to pick out primarily the content words—in fact, many content words are acquired earlier as function words. But stress is, of course, not the only factor determining the child's choice of which words to choose. Early nouns and verbs are much easier to visualize than the nouns and verbs predominantly used by adults.

Strategies may be fine for picking up the words—and perhaps some small chains of words—most useful to the child. The major problem of explaining syntactical development remains that

> of accounting for how the child can draw out information from the specific utterances he is exposed to about the general transfers of grammatical privilege that individual terms may enter into. (Maratsos 1979: 333)

That is, the child must form generalizations; he must act on the *hypothesis* that there are general rules governing the combination of verbal signs. The outward indicator that the child acts on such hypotheses is the fact that he begins to produce overgeneralizations:[6] "He breaked my car"; "there were mouses in the basement."

Interestingly enough, "breaked" usually appears only after "broke" has been produced for some time. Most of the irregular forms seem to be stored, at first, individually, as specific instances. Only when the child has stored also a sufficient number of instances of the -*ed* form verbs, the new general rule emerges, to which, then, the irregular verbs are also subjected. "Broke" disappears for some time or is used alternatively with "breaked."

---

[6]We have already discussed semantic overgeneralizations earlier, where the range of application of a newly acquired term is larger than it is in adult usage. Here we are talking about overgeneralizations of syntactical rules.

Because the child may alternately use his (still very hypothetical) knowledge of a general rule and specifically stored individual items, he appears to be inconsistent in his syntactic productions.

Syntactic overgeneralizations are frequent. We may take them—if we like using this term—as an expression of a strategy ("avoid exceptions"), but there is the problem that the child very often does *not* make an overgeneralization when the watching psycholinguist expects him to make one. Evidently the hypotheses about the range of validity of some syntactical rule are made not without regard to the semantic relations underlying the utterance to be generated. Here yet another strategy applies: understand combinations of words in such a way that it makes the most sense according to your knowledge of the world.

This strategy is a semantic one; it assumes a certain knowledge of the world and of language. Assuming that the child hears an utterance in which "eats," "bow-wow," and "cookies" appear, and further assuming that the child has a vague idea what these three words mean, then the above-mentioned strategy makes certain that the child also understands the sense of the whole sentence, because the bow-wow is the only thing that can eat; the dog can eat the cookies, but not vice versa.

By this strategy factors concerning content and semantic relations make possible the understanding of an utterance which the child is not yet capable of analyzing syntactically. This should, however, be an excellent means for assisting in the *acquisition of syntactic knowledge:* if the child already knows what the utterance means (because he knows some words and combines them according to this semantic strategy), then he can decode the syntactic signals (agent in nominative, object in accusative . . .) on just that basis.

This semantic strategy, for many different reasons, cannot remain the only one by which the child allows himself to be led: the meanings of the individual words and constituents often allow several sensible combinations. The meaning of the sentence

The girl hits the boy

cannot be gathered from the meaning of the individual words; one needs in addition a knowledge of its syntactic structure. In

order to establish who hits whom, the child who does not yet have
the possibility of using the syntactical structuring aids contained
in the utterance follows a *sequential convention strategy:* take
every noun—verb—noun sequence within one potential surface
structure unit as agent—action—object. Here word order is taken
as an indication of relations which are unequivocally signaled, in
adult utterances, by syntactic markers.

People were naturally interested in which order the child
shows various more or less complicated morphological and syntactic structures in his language production. Thus Brown (1973)
found, for example, that fourteen different suffixes and function
words (e.g., plural *s,* possessive *s,* article, auxiliary *be*) appear in
almost the same order in different children:

> present progressive-*ing*
> preposition *in*
> preposition *on*
> plural *s*
> possessive *s*
> articles
> third person past regular   (etc.)

This is not to say, however, that each of these morpheme
sets, once produced, will appear wherever it is required. It takes
months in which they are produced more and more regularly
whenever necessary. Here, too, the child's development is gradual
and not consistent. Very often, in this development, new forms
first express old functions, and new functions are first expressed
by old forms (Slobin 1973).

What determines this agreement in the sequence of appearance? In a subsequent investigation Brown concluded that
the sequence does not correspond to the frequency of the appearance in the parents' language, but probably to the semantic
complexity of the cognitive processes that are represented in it;
with this, however, appears the problem of how to measure this
simplicity or complexity.[7]

---

[7]Whether the appearance of a certain linguistic accomplishment is connected to
the frequency with which the form appears in the adult's language, especially in
"motherese," is a problem that is also very difficult to deal with methodically. See
van der Geest (1980).

Phases of Language Development

One more question should definitely be asked in this context. It concerns the starting point of all developmental-psycholinguistic divisions, from a methodological standpoint. Since these developmental stages or phases occur in a very specific order for the majority of the children investigated, can a certain stage (e.g., of the development of pluralization) therefore be assigned to a certain age? If we want to make general assertions about the development of language, which phase occurs after which other one, then we can only do this if we ignore the individual peculiarities of each particular case and summarize what is common to comparable children. But which children are in this sense comparable? All those 13 months old, 14 months old, all those who are 28 months old? It has been known for a very long time that some children begin to speak early, others much later; some learn quickly, others slowly. For example, if we summarize globally the utterances of all 28-month-old children, we would indeed throw very different stages of development together and thus obscure an ordered developmental sequence which is perhaps present. Brown, who is certainly the most experienced researcher in this area, made longitudinal studies of three children for several months: Adam, Eve, and Sarah. If he wants to do more than write three individual biographies, if he wants to say something general about *the* acquisition of language, he must generalize.

This he does by taking two scores for principles of classification: *mean length of utterance* (MLU) and *upper limit of length of utterance* (UP), both measured in number of morphemes. Both scores correlate highly. Brown views the mean length of utterance as a good index for grammatical complexity. (We can recognize here a certain prejudice of Brown's: learning to talk correlates for him very strongly with an increase in grammatical complexity.) Almost everything now that the child acquires in language is shown in a lengthening of the utterance: when the child adds an obligatory morpheme, when he enlarges the number of semantic roles that are expressed in the sentence, when he learns to express what is meant in a more clearly differentiated way: all this leads to an enlargement of the length of the utterance. On the basis of these measurements, Brown then distinguished among five stages:

		MLU	UP
Stage	I	1.75	5
	II	2.25	7
	III	2.75	9
	IV	3.00	11
	V	4.00	13

The table shows how this division into stages correlates with the age of three different children.

This procedure seems to be valuable, even though it has not yet been fully discussed whether the criterion of MLU also allows for comparisons between different languages.

Since the development of language in the child is characterized by an increase in complexity, it may often be advantageous to differentiate cognitive from formal-linguistic complexity (as for example Clark and Clark 1977 do). The differences between cognitive and formal complexity can be of different magnitude in different languages and can lead to major differences in the tempo of development of certain language abilities. English and Arab children begin to express the idea of "more than one" in language at approximately the same age (in English by "more" or " 'nother"). To proceed from this stage to the mastery of the plural system that is used by the adult, however, requires paths of very different lengths. While the English-speaking child masters the plural system at about the age of 6, the Arabic-speaking child is usually 14 or 15 years old when he masters the much more complex plural system of his language.

In all considerations of this kind about the complexity of a linguistic form, the danger of a circular argument is obvious: if within a certain language certain structures are acquired later than others, we assume that the former are more complex than the latter and presumably explain the sequence of the child's language acquisition by difference in complexity. An independent criterion of formal-linguistic complexity could only be contributed by linguistics, but there we find widely divergent views about the complexity of one and the same sentence.

Let us return from formal to cognitive complexity once again. The complexity of what is put into language, the differentiated quality of the expressed idea, is indeed no less difficult to establish exactly. Is "the car is useful" just as cognitively complex as "the car is green"?

As we can see, difficulties are encountered when we examine more closely the assumption that the development of the child's language proceeds from the simple to the more complex.

In addition to this developmental tendency from the simple to the complex which characterizes language development, there is another one which can easily be overlooked. Language events are to a great extent overdetermined. That is, what occurs at a certain point of an utterance is determined by a whole series of factors. What the child must learn when he learns a language is always to take all of these different factors into account, and in fact in convergence with one another. He must, as Brown says, learn to take into account, always and completely automatically, certain factors such as number, tense, case, and situation, even though they might not be at all necessary for understanding in a concrete case. But only because the child learns this can he finally also make himself understood when the situation is no longer a determinant of the expectations of the listener or a limitation of the interpretations possible, namely, when he as a creative human being has something new to say.

CHAPTER **5**

Problems in the Psychology of Meaning

A concept is formed, not through the interplay of associations, but through an intellectual operation in which all the elementary mental functions participate in specific combination. This operation is guided by the use of words as the means of actively centering attention, of abstracting certain traits, synthesizing them, and symbolizing them by a sign.

L. Vygotsky

The development of concepts, or word meanings, presupposes the development of many intellectual functions: deliberate attention, logical memory, abstraction, the ability to compare and to differentiate. These complex psychological processes cannot be mastered through the initial learning alone.

L. Vygotsky

Symbolization constitutes objects not constituted before, objects which would not exist except for the context of social relationships wherein symbolization occurs. Language does not simply symbolize a situation or object which is already

135

there in advance; it makes possible the existence or the appearance of that situation or object, for it is part of the mechanism whereby that situation or object is created. Meaning can be described, accounted for or stated in terms of symbols or language at its highest and complex stage of development (the stage it reaches in human experience), but language simply lifts out of the social process a situation which is logically or implicitly there already. The language symbol is simply a significant or conscious gesture.

G. H. Mead

Meaning and Semantic Structures

In the chapters about language acquisition it has been made clear that language is essentially a means of representative communication, of steering or directing consciousness between two people. The child acquires language by realizing that a person can *mean* a factual situation or object in language and that a person can *understand* language if he is able to refer back from the language medium to what the speaker refers to with his verbal utterance. Language is a means of communication because verbal utterances mean something. The child can later acquire the necessary knowledge of the language *system* because he learns very early to depend on the fact that verbal utterances always mean something and to think and act accordingly. Utterances mean something because they have relationships to objects, ideas, concepts, actions, and knowledge.

By meaning and by understanding we make use of these relationships, activating them and thereby allowing our consciousness and perhaps even our action to be determined by them.[1]

Meaning is relationship; more exactly it is the activation of a

[1]The nature of the process which is here called "activation" is not widely known psychologically or even physiologically. There is agreement only insofar as what is

relationship which extends between linguistic and nonlinguistic factual situations. Whereas syntactic relationships extend between the parts of an utterance which are spoken or will be spoken and can thus be considered a part of the language, the *semantic structures* to be discussed in this chapter are of a different kind: they extend between the utterance (or parts of the utterance) and the factual situation which is spoken about: actions, events, states of consciousness, knowledge, objects. Linguists, who always plead for a closed language system, have consequently paid much less attention to semantics than to syntax or morphology. The psychology of language, which sees language as a tool that man uses to master the world, must place the most emphasis on semantics, on the other hand, because here is centered the relationship of language to the world, that relationship which makes the tool-like character of language at all possible.

This chapter will present several of the established approaches in psychology which attempt to make the meaning of language units somewhat more precisely comprehensible and thus theoretically manageable.

Most approaches are based, either explicitly or only tacitly, on a fairly crude pattern: for the use of language, a syntax is necessary which gives the rules according to which signs (words) may be put together, and a storehouse (lexicon), in which the signs (words) are kept like the letters in an old-fashioned type case.

The approaches to be discussed now are therefore directed by the question: what is the structure of the lexicon? If we understand the lexicon very primitively as a storehouse of words, it can still not be assumed that the words in this storehouse are ordered alphabetically as they are in a dictionary. If, on the other hand, they are ordered according to their meaning, if words similar in meaning are stored in similar places (which are near to each other), then—this could be the next step of the argument—clarifying the organization of the words in the lexicon could be tantamount to finding out quite a lot about the meanings which play a role in language. If, for example, we could make it plausible that a group of words, *A, B, C,* and *D,* are used in a very similar way,

---

activated has been stored before (or will be stored after this activation) in some not-always-conscious storage, called memory or lexicon.

then we could view what these words have in common as *one* relevant dimension of meaning. The road to this discovery of the meaning of a word is thus by way of the discovery of which other words are similar to this word semantically—the formulation already reveals how dangerously close to a circular argument is all work in this area.[2]

Features and Dimensions

The first approach which we will discuss uses the concept of the semantic feature taken from linguistics. We spoke above (Chapter 2) about the breaking up of the meaning of lexical items into elements of meaning. The word "man" can, according to this view, be characterized by a list of (two-valued) features in this way:

> physical object +
> animate +
> human +
> adult +
> male +

If each word of a language is characterized by its own list of semantic features, then in accord with the above considerations the lexicon of the speaker/listener of this language would be structured according to these features: animate, adult, male, and so forth. This conception could be put into psychological terms by, for example, considering the understanding of a word that is heard or read to be an activation or a coming-into-consciousness of the list of features of this word.

On the basis of such a theory, H. H. Clark (1970) has suggested an impressive explanation for the word association experi-

[2]The vagueness of the term *meaning* should by now be evident: we talk about a speaker meaning something, words meaning something, words having meaning, meanings being relationships between words and the things to which they refer, meanings being stored in a lexicon. . . . It is important to be aware of the fact that these versions of the term *meaning* are *not* synonymous and *not* transformable one into another according to some simple algorithm. Some of the problems connected with this are more extensively discussed in Hörmann (1976/1981).

ment. When a person hears a stimulus word and has instructions to answer as quickly as possible with a word that is not identical to the stimulus word, he analyzes the stimulus word according to its semantic features, changes the sign of the last or the next-to-last of these features, and produces the word that corresponds to this minimally changed list of features. Whoever hears the word "man" will change the sign of the last feature (male + to male −) and produce the word that corresponds to the changed list, namely "woman." In rare cases, the sign of the next-to-last feature (adult +) will be changed: "man" is followed by "boy;" in even rarer cases, the signs of the last two features are changed: "girl" is produced. Clark can thus explain on the basis of this theory why, when a large group of subjects is given the stimulus word "man," the most frequent reply is "woman," less frequently "boy," and even less frequently "girl."[3]

Understanding a word is here seen as the activation of its list of features. As an explanation of the process of understanding, this does not tell us very much, but we can still begin to consider this: understanding has something to do with assigning an utterance (or parts of it) to what we might call various semantic groups or categories. The activation of the feature list representing the word "man" allocates this word in the group consisting of all words having the feature "animate+" *and* in the group consisting of all words having the feature "adult+," and so on. And it differentiates "man" from all words having the feature "adult−" or the feature "human−." Understanding has something to do with building groups (of things or words that are equal in some respect) and with processes of differentiating (e.g., words from words that are different in some respect). When someone says, "This is a table," the thing referred to is hereby admitted to the category of "physical objects," to the category "solid +," and onward. And it is excluded from categories like "liquid +."

If the process of understanding is a process of building groups and of differentiating—or at least is *also* this kind of process—then perhaps we could learn something about what be-

---

[3]Let us briefly point out the fact that Clark creates a new problem with this explanation: he needs the factor that is responsible for determining whether the last or the next-to-last feature is changed.

longs together in the lexicon, according to meaning, by having the speakers/listeners of a language undertake such processes of grouping and differentiating words. For clarification of the internal structure of the subjective lexicon, subjects usually are given a number of words and are asked to distribute them into groups of similar words, or they are asked to mark the similarity of any two words on a scale.

Up to now, we have said that words which belong close together according to their meaning—expressed linguistically—are characterized by having very similar lists of semantic features. Using a very similar terminology, we may view words as being points in a *semantic space* which is characterized by its dimensions. The locus of a word in each of these dimensions determines the meaning of that word. Two words will lie the closer together, the more numerous the dimensions within which they have similar values.

"Man" and "woman" are so similar because they differ on only one single dimension of semantic space, the dimension of sex.

The concept of a semantic space, which is defined by dimensions of meaning (just as our usual space is defined by the three dimensions of length, width, and height), opens up a series of interesting possibilities for thought. Operating in any way with the concept of a semantic space necessarily leads straight to the question of how many dimensions this space has and what they are.[4] A clear but inadequate answer to this question is given by Osgood, Suci, and Tannenbaum (1957) in their investigations of the semantic differential.

The Semantic Differential

Osgood is concerned with what he calls the affective, sometimes also the connotative,[5] meaning of a word or concept. When sub-

---

[4]It should by now be clear that the two approaches (semantic features, dimensions of semantic space) are generally very similar. One difference is that features usually are conceptualized to be binary (male +/−), whereas semantic dimensions take on an infinite number of values. The semantic space model has, therefore, in principle better possibilities of reflecting finer differences in meaning.

[5]*Connotation* refers to what is associatively suggested by the word; *denotation*, on

jects are asked what a word means, the answers usually show a
noncontrollable variation. In order to avoid this, Osgood instructs
his subjects to answer not by free association but by locating the
meaning of the word on a number of adjective dimensions. For
identifying the meaning of, for example, "nurse," he presents
"nurse" along with

good .... 0 .... bad
strong................... 0 .... weak
round................... 0 .... square

and a dozen or more adjective scales of this kind, and he requires
the subjects to place the word somewhere on each of these scales.
All the scales have a zero or neutral point in the middle. If the
word is placed on this point, this semantic dimension would be
irrelevant for it.

The main problem which Osgood encounters here is to determine which and how many such bipolar dimensions are necessary in order to differentiate semantically all or nearly all words
from each other. If we have, for example, the dimensions
"thin/fat" and "light/heavy," we would probably find that words
which are rated as "fat" (better: which call up the association
"fat") are also characterized as "heavy." "Young/old" will probably
correlate with "fresh/tired," and so forth. This may be interpreted
in this way: such correlating scales express something common
on which they are based and which is responsible for this covaria-
tion of the classification.

Having arrived at this point, the psychologist can ask the
classic question of factor analysis: *how many* dimensions, independent from one another, do we need to explain the occurrence
of the relations which are found empirically? These independent
dimensions could be viewed as the dimensions of semantic space.

Osgood did a number of factor analyses of the classifications
that many subjects gave for many words on many scales and
found repeatedly three factors:

---

the other hand, points to the object which is meant by the word. The denotation
of "moon" is "earth's natural satellite"; the connotation of "moon" would be
"cold, distant, lonely, longing. . . ."

Evaluation   (E)
Potency   (P)
Activity   (A)

What kind of dimensions are these?

According to Osgood's neobehavioristic view, words are signs which are related to the object or event they signify not directly, but *via* a mediating link. This mediating link is the *response* to the word functioning as stimulus, and it elicits in its turn the behavior which is appropriate to the sign (word). The mediating link represents the connotative, emotional meaning of the particular word. Words are differentiated according to different amounts of *E, P,* and *A,* which characterize the mediator which represents them.

Naturally, Osgood knows that he does not capture *the* meaning of a certain word with this, but *E, P,* and *A* are basic factors because they represent basic dimensions of human behavior: is something good or bad for me, is something strong or weak in comparison to me, is something active or passive?

The results of Osgood's analyses have so far been a three-dimensional semantic space in which the words that are classified according to the semantic differential each occupy one point. If his interpretation of the dimensions of this space is useful, then the position of the word thus described should have its psychological effect when the listener understands an utterance in which the word appears and shows this understanding in his behavior. Only in this way can a theoretical conception of this kind be confirmed.

We will present an example of the heuristic fruitfulness of Osgood's approach. Its point of departure is the daily observation that many misunderstandings and communication difficulties occur between people of the older and the younger generation. When young people talk about love or the future or fear, do they perhaps not mean exactly the same thing as older people do? Hörmann, Pieper, and Engelkamp (1976) tried to find an explanation for this by giving two comparable groups of subjects who were very different in age a series of words to be classified according to the semantic differential. There were some interesting results: "being friends," for example, was less exciting for older subjects, but more valuable than for the younger ones, just as "having visitors" or "making a visit." "Being alone" was placed much lower on the evaluation scale by the younger subjects than by the older ones. "Waiting for something" and "experiencing something nice and enjoying it" were more exciting for the older people, while the concepts "now," "the future," and "planning something" were more exciting for the younger people (for the older people, "earlier" is more stimulating). We can see that the semantic differential can serve as an aid in localizing the position of certain words or concepts in the semantic space of an individual or of a specific group of people.

The semantic differential was used by Osgood and his associates also for a comparison of different languages; the fact that the three factors E, P, and A were found everywhere suggests that here universal dimensions of meaning are tapped.

Of course, E, P, and A cannot be *all* the dimensions of semantic space according to which the subjective lexicon of the language user is structured. There must be many more dimensions than good/bad, strong/weak, and active/passive which play a role in the assimilation of an utterance.[6]

What other means, except word association tests of this kind, can be used to test models of this lexicon that we propose?

As we have already mentioned, there is a more direct approach: one can ask a group of subjects to indicate the similarity of the meaning of any two words on a scale. Fillenbaum and Rapoport (1971) have published a comprehensive account on pro-

---

[6]The method of factor analysis is, on principle, not a very good instrument with which to assess the dimensions of semantic space because it aims at *restricting* the number of these dimensions to what is absolutely necessary to account mathematically for the correlation empirically obtained. It answers to the question, "How many different factors *at least* do we need to explain our finding?" For the psycholinguist, however, it would be rather more interesting to find out how many factors can be *at the most* distinguished within a vocabulary. It is very fine to know that "nurse" and "hero" and "my own country" are seen as E+, but it would also be interesting to know in which (and how many) factors these three words differ.

jects of this kind. They usually find small subspaces of semantic space (e.g., a space for color terms or for kinships terms), but, like Osgood, not a satisfactory representation of *the* semantic space.

Scaling procedures and association tests for establishing dimensions of meaning were introduced with the following considerations: if the lexicon is organized according to semantic dimensions, if every single word can be seen as an intersecting point of the dimensions it characterizes, then words *similar* in meaning must lie "closer" together than words that are less similar. This notion of *proximity* is the basis for a theoretical and experimental approach of a slightly different kind, to which we will turn now. It is influenced not so much by linguistics as by general experimental psychology, specifically by the psychology of memory.

The liaison between psycholinguistics and the general psychology of memory is suggested by two facts which Miller (1972) has formulated in this way:

> It is a psychological commonplace that we do not take experience neat, but select, categorize, label, and elaborate it before we store it away in memory. Language plays a dual role in this process of packaging experience. On the one hand, we use language to characterize our experience, and store the linguistically coded version along with whatever iconic storage we can muster for the raw experience itself. And, on the other hand, the symbols of language must themselves be stored in memory, presumably also in some coded form easily retrievable for later use in producing and interpreting speech. (335)

The subjective lexicon of the individual, the storehouse of his vocabulary, is, in the approaches to be discussed now, *expressis verbis* equated with *semantic memory.*[7]

> Memory is our whole world knowledge, including what we know about robins, $7 \times 4 = 28$, what to do in a restaurant, and the history of the civil war. (Kintsch 1980: 2)

---

[7]By far the best overview of semantic memory is presented by Kintsch (1980). The comparison term to semantic memory is episodic memory, which contains temporally marked information about specific events—what I had for breakfast yesterday.

Semantic Memory

Semantic memory is the store we must make use of when we produce or comprehend verbal utterances. The question of primary importance is, again, how to conceptualize the inner structure of this storehouse in a way that fits into what we know empirically about producing, processing, remembering, comparing verbal utterances.

At this point we have to face a rather formidable theoretical problem. When we want to test and so to validate a theory about the structure of our mental lexicon (or about the structure of our knowledge of the world), we could do this by using a probing technique (perceiving, remembering, comparing, verifying . . . utterances) the functioning of which is completely clear to us. Only in this case could we hope to tap, with our technique, that conjectured structure we have designed to give a theoretical account of our lexicon or our knowledge. As long as we do not know precisely what goes on in the act of perceiving, or of remembering, or of verifying an utterance, we cannot be sure whether this process is an adequate test of the theory we want to prove. There will always be more than one theoretical structure which is compatible with the data of the experiment, so that all of these experiments prove or validate not one theory, but an unknown number of (different) theories. Therefore, we should not delude ourselves as to the power of these experimental "proofs"—nor as to the fact that some of the theories to be discussed below may be implemented by a computer program. This fact is not, in any way, to be interpreted as evidence that the human language user actually acts (e.g., when perceiving or remembering an utterance) in *this* way according to that structure which is specified by the theory at hand. This general *caveat* should be in the reader's mind as we proceed.[8]

Research on this problem has been guided, in the past dozen years, mainly by one specific working assumption: what lies fairly close by in the semantic memory of the individual can be reached quickly. And it has, therefore, relied very heavily on one specific

[8]This problem has been discussed in an excellent paper by Foppa (1980).

experimental paradigm: the sentence verification experiment, in which the subject has to answer yes or no as quickly as possible to verbal statements like

A robin is a bird

which are presented to him. The dependent variable, which furnishes the data from which the experimenter is to draw his inferences, is, above all, reaction time. Reaction time is here interpreted as the time the subject needs to assess the correctness or falseness of the statement he hears. How may we conceptualize this process of assessment?

Network Models

The first attempt to solve this theoretical problem suggests that semantic memory is a *network* in which the words (more precisely: the concepts[9]) correspond to the intersections or nodes. What could such a network look like?

If it is to be a network of *concepts*, this suggests the possibility of borrowing from the hierarchy of concepts presented in logic. This, as we know, is constructed according to the principles of superordination and subordination; the subconcept arises from the concept by the addition of a specifying characterization (the *differentia specifica*): the *dachshund* is a dog with especially short legs. Here *dachshund* is under the (superordinate) concept *dog, dog* under *mammal,* and so on.

This kind of logically proposed network has several very specific, important characteristics. If, for example, one constructs utterances with the predicate *is a* (X is a Y), with a noun first (X) and in the second part of the utterance a noun (Y), which is above X in the network, then a *true* sentence results: "A dachshund is a dog," "A dog is a mammal." Another characteristic of such a network is that the concepts which appear lower in the hierarchy are

---

[9]Usually these intersections are equated with concepts rather than with words, so that considerations from logic may be applied more easily. The concept intersections are, however, accessible only *via* the words associated with them.

redundant for those higher in it: if I hear "dog," I also know "mammal" and "animal."

If a word (a concept) can be put into a hierarchically structured network by an utterance in this way, and if certain truth values and certain redundancies concerning this word can be activated by this placement, then—obviously—one can assume that this kind of process also plays a role in understanding an utterance in which this word or concept appears. The theory of Collins and Quillian (1969, 1972) begins here. It came into being, and this is very characteristic of psycholinguistic research at that time, from the attempt to write a language memory for a computer: the line of thought "subjective lexicon of the language user— word memory or semantic memory of man—memory or storage of the computer" determined to a great extent the direction of research both in the psychology of language and in the psychology of memory of that time.

Collins and Quillian want an economical model (storage space in a computer costs money) and they therefore take not only the *is a* relation into account in their network but also the *has a* relation, that is, they also localize attributes of the concepts in their model. A *bird* has feathers, a *bird* lays eggs. A *mammal* has the attribute of bearing living young, and onward. Attributes of the concepts are brought into the network of concepts—and this is the economical aspect of Collins and Quillian's model—always with the highest concept to which it applies. "Has feathers" and "lays eggs" is not with *robin, sparrow, starling, blackbird*, and so on, but only with *bird.*

Now to the test of this model.

In a network model the distance between and the hierarchical position of the nodes should play a role psychologically. If similarity of meaning or semantic relatedness is the same as "a short distance away," then the sentence, "A *dachshund* is a *dog*," should, for example, be more quickly verified than the sentence, "A *dachshund* is a *mammal*." And when the attributes are included, the sentence, "A canary is yellow," should be more quickly verified than "A *canary* has *feathers*" because "yellow" appears directly with *canary* as an attribute, but "feathers" appears with *bird,* which has its place on a higher hierarchical plane.

According to this model, processing a linguistic input by the

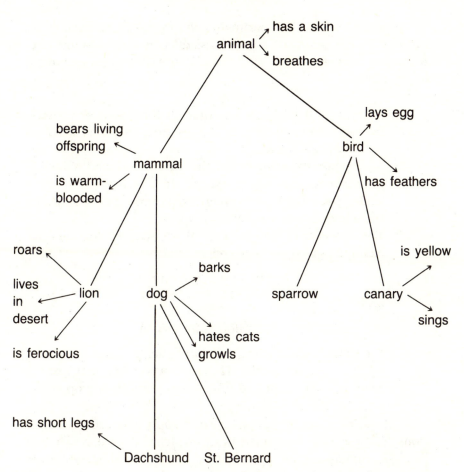

listener consists, in a first attempt toward formulation, of localizing the nodes which correspond to the words heard and of discovering the path between the nodes which represents the kind of
relation between the concepts which is expressed in the sentence.
If we give a subject the task of deciding whether the sentence, "A
canary has a skin," is true or false, the subject will seek out
whether a path leads from *canary* to "has a skin" (which probably
appears with "animal"), a path which represents the relations
which are expressed in the sentence heard.[10]

[10]The Collins and Quillian model includes only, as we recall, paths representing
(in upward direction!) the relation *is a*, and pointers representing the relations

In a long series of experiments the model has proved to do rather well; the *semantic relatedness effect* is quite a stable phenomenon. Models of this kind have, however, certain disadvantages, too:

1. It seems questionable whether all the possible relations between concepts can be represented as paths between nodes with attributes.
2. In decision experiments of the kind mentioned, falsifications always take much longer than verifications which lead to the judgment "correct"; this cannot be explained by the above model as such.
3. The model fails also for several positive verifications: for example, given the sentences

    The lion is a mammal

    and

    The lion is an animal

    the first should be verified more quickly than the second, according to the model. This is, however, not only not the case, but the empirical findings are exactly the opposite.

Let us, as a short digression, add some general considerations to these last mentioned findings: what does it mean that "lion–mammal–animal" apparently is not stored in our semantic memory in the hierarchical structure in the way that the model predicts? This can first mean that, in addition to the *position* of the conceptual nodes in the model, something like availability or familiarity of the concept plays a role in how quickly this concept can be used: *mammal* is perhaps less familiar because it is rarer than *animal.* This assumption, however, contradicts the basis of the model, to which such frequency viewpoints definitely do not belong. The determining factor in the model is structure alone and not frequency or familiarity.

---

has a. There are, of course, many more types of logical relations possible (and expressible in language), relations which are *not* covered by models of this kind (for example: contains, owns, hates, is offspring of, . . .).

A second approach toward explaining such divergent results consists in retaining the basic model (structure is the determining factor) but in changing the structure, that is, the position of the points of intersection, in the appropriate region.

We could say: what was first recorded here was a logical, or, if we will, a zoological system—who knows, then, whether the concept system that we have in our heads corresponds to his zoology? Perhaps lion also belongs closer to *animal* than to *mammal* because we already understand in *animal* something very similar to *mammal*.

An answer to this question can be attempted by using not logic for the construction of the network but the technique of similarity scaling that was mentioned above. Henley (1969) had college students classify which animals were similar to others. It was shown that the major dimensions for ordering are size and ferocity. Elephant, horse and camel are contrasted to mouse, rat, and rabbit, but also the lion and the tiger on the one hand to the cow and the rabbit on the other. It was also important whether the animals were found on a farm; cow, chicken, pig are subsumed in one category. It would now be interesting to undertake investigations of the kind done by Collins and Quillian on the basis of a network developed in *this* way, that is, empirically (and not logically or zoologically), but the technique of the sentence verification experiment ("A dachshund is a dog"—yes/no) is naturally limited to network structures in which, through strict super- and subordination, the subconcept has a redundancy relationship to the concept above it—and this is necessarily the case only for logically constructed networks.

Now back to the main line of our argument: according to the original Collins and Quillian model, processing a linguistic input is represented by a search process starting from the node representing the first noun (X) in the sentence to be verified. The model does not specify, however, how this search process gets its direction. Here a major revision of the Collins and Quillian model, the Collins and Loftus model (1975), presents a more parsimonious alternative: (active) search is replaced by (more passive) spreading activation.

We introduced network models by equating similarity of meaning with proximity in semantic memory, in which the meaning of a concept is represented as the node of a network relating this concept to others. In contrast to, say, Osgood's semantic space, the network models do not decompose the meaning of a concept into meaning elements or dimensions. From the discussion of the network models we now proceed to a different model group, which operates, again, *via* decomposition of meaning, the so-called *feature models.*[11]

Feature Models

In the network model, semantic similarity was represented by proximity in the space of semantic memory; in the feature model, semantic similarity is represented by an overlapping of the semantic features of the particular concepts. In the terminology of set theory, the similarity of two concepts would be defined by the intersection of their features. If we imagine that a concept (X) is characterized by the features a, b, c, d, and e, then it is more similar to a concept (Y) that has a, b, d, and e than to a concept (Z) that is characterized by a, b, m, n, and o.

Such a relatively primitive determination of similarity merely by the *number* of common features does not accomplish very much. It only describes a categorization, as does the network model, in which all concepts which appear under the node "bird" are connected in the same way, namely, by the same *is a* relation, to *bird.* If *bird* is completely characterized by the features a, b, c, and d, then all concepts which also have the features a, b, c, and d belong in the category *bird.*

However, we again find in empirical investigations that the sentence

The eagle is a bird

is verified faster than the sentence

The chicken is a bird.

[11]The just-mentioned differences notwithstanding, these two types of models are rather similar; there are authors who maintain that network models can be transformed into feature models and vice versa.

This cannot be explained by a simple feature model because every member of the category has—because he is characterized by the same set of features—the same "rights." "Eagle" and "chicken" belong to the category *bird* in the same way.

Do they really?

The feature model which we will present in more detail begins at this point. It originates from Smith, Shoben, and Rips (1974). The authors imagine that several features represent important, *defining* aspects of the meaning of a word, whereas others represent highly *characteristic* but actually more accidental aspects. The features representing a word are thus ordered into a series beginning with the absolutely necessary *defining* features and ending with the merely *characteristic* features. Example: if we consider the word *robin*, it occurs to us that robins have wings, hop around on two legs, have a red breast, sit on low branches, and are wild. Of these, the first three features are probably more decisive as to whether we place a bird we have just seen into the class of robins than the last two. We cannot be sure in every individual case of the point at which the sequence of features of "absolutely necessary, otherwise it's not a robin" changes to the features which are usually attributed to a robin but are not necessary. (The more abstract a word is, the smaller the number of its defining features usually is.)

What empirical indications are there for such different weighting of features? First, there are indications in the use of language. We say for example:

> A robin is a real bird. Exactly speaking,
> a chicken is bird. If we do not take it
> too literally, a bat is a kind of bird.

In such *is a* sentences, "hedges" are built in, which make certain combinations acceptable (Lakoff 1972). It would never occur to us to say

> Taken literally, a robin is a bird.

Robin as well as *chicken* fulfill the defining features of *bird*. Apparently, in addition to these defining features, there are other differences in meaning which appear only in the characteristic features. The hedge, "taken literally," is used when the defining but not the characteristic features are available. The hedge, "if you don't take it too literally," (or "some kind of . . ."), on the other hand, indicates the use of the characteristic but not all the defining features.

How does the Smith *et al.* model now explain the fact that the sentence

The eagle is a bird

is verified faster than the sentence

The chicken is a bird?

The authors assume that verification involves a comparison process which runs over several steps. In the first step, a quick overall comparison of *all* features of subject and predicate term (eagle/chicken and bird) is made. If this step indicates high similarity of the two sets of features, the response "yes" or "true" is generated; if it indicates low overall similarity, the response "no" or "false" is generated—as, for example, when the sentence is presented

A lion is a bird.

When the comparison process in step 1 results in an intermediate degree of similarity, a second step is initiated: comparison of only the defining features of subject and predicate.

In this way, the model explains quite elegantly why the sentence

The eagle is a bird

is verified faster than

The chicken is a bird.

"Eagle" has, presumably, all of the defining and most of the characteristic features of "bird"; the positive response will be generated by the first step of the model. "Chicken," on the other hand, lacks some of the characteristic features of *bird* ("flies," "lives wild" . . .); the "chicken" sentence will be verified only after executing also the second step of the model: comparison restricted to the defining features.

This model also rather neatly explains the fact that it takes longer to falsify the sentence

The butterfly is a bird

than the sentence

The lion is a bird.

In a different type of experiment, the authors gave their subjects questions of this kind: How typical is the *eagle* for the category *bird*, how typical is a *duck* for the category *bird*, and so on. From these *typicality values*, it becomes clear that an individual bird is a more typical example of the category bird the more the characteristic features of the class concept agree with those of the individual example.

Smith *et al.*'s feature model has proved itself in a whole series of different kinds of experiments. It is also quite easily amenable to mathematics.

We will stay, for a little while, with the empirical finding that different individual members (eagle, chicken, penguin) somehow do not belong to the category *bird* in the same way or to the same degree to which they would be assigned to the category according to a logical (or zoological) definition. This is rather a stumbling block for traditional (Aristotelian) logic, which decrees that membership in a category is either given or not given, *tertium non datur*, and that one can always unequivocally infer—from an inspection of the features—whether an item is a member of the category or not.

The philosopher Wittgenstein has already protested against this assumption. He showed very impressively that we can indeed say whether something is a *game* or not, but we cannot completely list all the features that define the class or category of *games* (1958). We group the *games* together because they have a certain "family resemblance" which we cannot analyze further.

Prototypes and Family Resemblances

To learn more about the role of this family resemblance in semantic memory is the goal of the next approach to be discussed here, that of Rosch (1973, 1975; Rosch *et al.*, 1976). For Rosch, categories have an "inner structure" insofar as there is something like a nucleus, a core, a prototypical center around which—at different distances—the individual members of that category are located. The smaller the distance to the *prototype*, the higher is the *typicality value* of that item. An apple is much more definitely a *fruit* than a coconut, a sparrow is much more typical for *bird* than a penguin, murder is more definitely a *crime* than stealing, a chair more typical for *furniture* than a floor lamp. The more typical a member of a category is, the more easily it can replace the category name itself.

The difference between the approaches of Rosch and of Smith *et al.* is that Rosch sees the prototype as a gestalt in the sense of gestalt psychology, whereas Smith *et al.* speak of a different weighting of individual features. Rosch says: The members of the category *fruit* belong together not because they have some feature or another in common which *defines* the category fruit, but because every individual member shows a more or less large *family resemblance* to the other members of the category.

There have been attempts to relate this concept of family resemblance again to a feature approach by relinquishing the postulate that membership in a category be defined by one and only one definite set of features. Hampton (1979), e.g., speaks of polymorphous concepts, whereby category membership is treated

> as a continuous scale, where the position of a word is defined by the number of category features it possesses; thus highly typical members would be at the top of the scale, having a large proportion of the category features. (451)

The difficulty with this argument, however, is that it presupposes that all features of the category are known. And we remember Wittgenstein persistently asking us to list *all* features *games* have—and our inability to do so.

Our discussion has now arrived at a field which is called, in mathematics, *fuzzy set* theory. With this theory, tribute is paid to the fact that often there is a transitional zone which cannot be exactly described between the area where a concept or a word fits and where it does not fit.[12] The meaning of *game* (or of *chair* or of *cup*) can be seen as a fuzzy set of semantic features. This means that a particular feature (e.g., for *game*, that "two people take part") must not be either a member or a nonmember of the defining set of features, but that it belongs to this set of features with a *degree* of membership which lies between zero and one.[13]

The psycholinguistic consequences of this theoretical view were first investigated by Labov (1973), although still without an explicit relation to the mathematical concept of fuzzy sets. He showed his subjects drawings of a cup the form of which was gradually changed in height, width, thickness, presence or absence of handles, and so forth. The subjects were asked to name the object in the drawing. It was shown that there is an area of the 100% cup, so to speak, which is surrounded by transitional areas in which some subjects called the object presented to them a *glass* or a *bowl* or a *dish* or a *vase* rather than a *cup*. It was not the case, however, that the group of drawings which were called *cup* by all subjects could be defined by *one* particular set of features. For example, even if the object's name begins to change from *cup* to *glass* as it moves beyond a certain ratio of length to width, one can still get the subjects to call it a *cup* by giving the drawn object a handle.

Different semantic features are thus of different importance for the definition of a concept; we cannot say of any subset of these features that they are necessary and sufficient for defining the concept.

Labov's investigation had a further result which is eminently important for the psychology of language: the transitional area between two terms can be moved or changed by the linguistic or imaginal context. If, for example, a container form is presented which is called a *cup* by half of the subjects and a *glass* by the

[12]Fuzziness should not be confused with uncertainty in the sense of information theory. Before the dice are thrown, there is uncertainty in relation to the result, but the result is not fuzzy or vague.
[13]A membership degree of zero would be "never and in no way a member"; a membership degree of one would be "always and completely a member of the defined set of features."

other half, the numerical relationship changes if we tell the subjects that there is coffee in it: now almost all subjects use the word
cup.

The importance of this finding can hardly be overestimated.

The meaning of a certain word has until now tacitly been
viewed as a point in a many-dimensional semantic space or as a
list of semantic features. Where this point was located, or what
this list looked like, was determined by the meaning of that particular word alone. Only because the words bring their own meanings with them can there be an interaction of these individual
meanings, and from this results the meaning of the sentence.

The findings and considerations which we have just discussed compel us, however, to doubt the basis of this whole approach. Must we abandon the view of the sentence as a configura-
tion of words because the words in daily language use are not the
same basic parts of an utterance as we dictionary-spoiled linguists view them to be? Is the utterance as a whole the primary
factor? Does the utterance determine what a word means?
Should we perhaps completely give up talking about one hard and
fast meaning of a word as if it were an easily manageable unit?
These are questions for which neither linguistics nor the psychology of language can at this time offer suitable answers.[14]

Network models, feature models, prototype models are suggested as solutions of the basic questions: what is the inner
structure—and the mode of operation—of the speaker/listener's
semantic memory?

Until now, whenever we spoke of semantic memory, we understood what was stored in this memory to have a verbal character: words or lexemes or concepts or semantic features, themselves no longer words, but which could be thought of as quite
close to language. This leads to the following difficulty: even if it is
possible to break down words or more complex language expressions into semantic elements, these elements themselves still
remain so similar to language that the process of understanding
as a "translation" of something coded verbally into something not

---

[14]Aspects of this problem are discussed in Hörmann (1976/1981) and Kintsch
   (1980).

thus coded (as well as the opposite process of meaning something in language) is not yet explained. Do not the elements ("male," "has a skin" . . .) also have to be decoded?

Meaning as Imaginal Representation

This problem does not arise if the manner of representing language units in memory is conceived of entirely differently, namely, nonlinguistically: when the concept which we express with a word is represented in memory by an *image*. The word *car* would not be represented in the consciousness or in the memory of the speaker/listener as a list of semantic features (made of metal, four tires, expensive . . .) or as a node in a semantic network (above *VW, GM, Ford,* and below *means of transportation*), but as a *visual image* of a car.

With this we have arrived in a completely different theoretical landscape: we have given up decomposing the meaning of a word into components. The image of car is something unified, which cannot be broken up into the image of metal, the image of four tires, and so on. We have also given up the idea that the meaning of an individual word or concept is determined by its position in a semantic network.

The idea that the meaning of a word is represented as an image and that understanding this word is equivalent to the activation of this image had a number of important supporters at the beginning of this century, but it could not be maintained for a long time because there were many serious objections to it, for instance:

- Not all people have a visual image of a house when they read or hear the word "house"—and if they have one, it is often so different from those of others that communication would hardly be possible on such a basis.
- In language there are a great many words for which no one has yet postulated a visual or other image—what would be the representing image of the word "but"?

In addition, there is the difficulty of conceptualizing the interaction of the words in a sentence as the interaction of images.

Because of these difficulties the idea of "word meaning as image" was soon completely driven out of language psychology. We know today that this occurred too early and too completely. Let us look at the issue here more closely. It has been common knowledge for a long time that concrete words or sentences are understood more quickly than abstract ones. "Cows eat grass" is easier to understand and to remember than "The proletariat produces surplus value." One theoretical explanation for this superiority, that of Paivio (1971, 1977), says: concrete words and sentences are stored as images *and* as words, whereas abstract words and sentences are stored only in verbal form. This so-called dual-coding hypothesis (for concrete material two codes, for abstract material only one) can explain a series of research findings very well, but it is not uncontroversial. Several investigations have been undertaken within its circle of influence, however, which become directly relevant to our problems.

Moyer (1973) had his subjects compare from memory animals and objects according to their size. He asked: what is larger, a zebra or a lamp? Reaction time to the question was measured. It was shown that the reaction time was longer, the smaller the *actual* difference in size between the objects is. This is easiest to explain if we assume that analog representations of the named objects take part in this comparative act (and not only digital representations, as semantic features are).[15]

Paivio (1977) then went one step further with the following considerations: instead of presenting words in the comparison experiment, he presented pictures and asked his subjects again: what is larger, a zebra or a lamp? (The picture shows the zebra and the lamp in natural size relationship). The subject decides

---

[15]The difference in size between two objects can be represented *digitally*, i.e., by numbers, where the larger object has a higher number than the smaller. The difference can also be represented in *analog* fashion, for example, by presenting the larger object as bigger (or darker or louder) than the smaller. An analog representation can in principle reveal the finest differences; a digital representation can only follow a continuous change of a difference in a step-by-step way, that is, from one number to the next.

very quickly, more quickly than with the words *zebra* and *lamp*. Then Paivio gave other subjects different pictures in which the lamp was drawn larger than the zebra. The subject needed more time to decide because, as Paivio interprets it, there now arises a conflict between the size relationship in the picture and that in memory. The lengthened time span does *not* appear when the subject is shown words printed in different-sized letters rather than pictures:

LAMP ZEBRA

because these words must, according to Paivio, first be translated into the image code, and in this image code the zebra is still larger than the lamp. The conflict arises only with the pictures, because pictures are coded directly, that is, in the same code as the memory image, namely, in the visual code—which is an analog code.

The problems touched upon here have yet another aspect. In Moyer's model, for instance, judgment about the relative size of the zebra (is it larger than a lamp?) has to be computed, for it is extremely improbable that "larger than a lamp" is stored as a unitary property information with "zebra" in semantic memory. There are just too many things in the world which are "smaller than" or "larger than" to be stored as properties or features of the word "zebra." On the other hand, of course, there are absolute properties of "zebra" which might be stored as such: "black and white," "has stripes," "is a mammal." The fact that we have to assume (at least) two qualitatively different processes which relate a noun to its properties is not taken into consideration in most of the models of semantic memory.[16]

We will not go further into these problems here.

It seems to be rather well established that in many cases the meaning of a word is either completely or partially represented by an image.

Looking once again back at the different approaches to conceptualizing the structure and mode of operation of semantic

[16]Kintsch (1980) points to it; Rips and Turnbull (1980) presented an interesting series of experiments dealing with it. A thorough discussion will have to include Bierwisch (1967).

memory, we may draw the conclusion that there are probably many different ways of representing the (semantic) content of what is said or meant. Probably we have to assume analytic processes like decomposing a unitary meaning into a list of elementary semantic features, but also processes operating on a more holistic level, as the findings of Paivio and also these of Rosch show. The (sometimes heated) discussion about Paivio's theory centered on the question as to whether the representation in memory is an image *or* more likely an abstract feature or a node in a rather abstract semantic network. Paivio says that in some cases it can be both image *and* a more abstract representation. But could we not also assume that the owner of the memory, so to speak, decides in which code the representation should appear? And that he reaches this decision, for example, according to the kind of task during which he must call on his semantic memory?

Let us finally take a brief glance at the question: how could we conceive of the coming together and working together of words in a sentence when we start from the position "word meaning as image"?

As a first answer we may say that a total image representing the meaning of the sentence is *constructed* from the word images, a total image, all elements of which are simultaneously in consciousness. "The boy hit the girl" would be represented as a visual (and perhaps also acoustic and kinesthetic) image of a boy hitting a girl. The integrated total image as the substrate of the meaning of a sentence already played a major role for Wilhelm Wundt. In the last chapter we will become acquainted with the concept of a *semantic description* representing the meaning of a sentence, which includes some of Wundt's ideas, of course avoiding the commitment to the modality of imagery.

We have already pointed out the difficulties of an attempt at understanding meaning for all words and for all speakers/listeners as images of a visual or some other kind. We will now leave this approach and turn to a presently widespread type of research, the attempt to represent *meaning as proposition*. With this step, we move away, as it were, from the efforts to connect assumptions about language processing with what we know about (semantic) memory.

Meaning as Proposition

First some preliminary remarks: Until now we have often spoken about the meaning of words and have attempted to understand this meaning as a node in a semantic network, as a set of semantic features, or as an image. With word meaning thus understood, we then attempted to grasp the meaning of the sentence in a further step, whereby the meaning of the sentence was conceived of as the sum or as the gestalt-like aggregate of the word meanings.

The approach which will now be described, that of understanding the meaning or content of sentences with the help of the concept of *proposition*, does not begin with the individual word but with individual facts or events or relationships which are reported in the utterance. The old division into syntax and lexicon, which has until now pervaded all these theories, is here no longer valid.[17]

One of the reasons for proceeding in this manner is as follows: if we ask people who have heard a few sentences what they still know about them after a short time, they very seldom produce a word-for-word copy (unless they were told ahead of time to remember the sentences word for word), but they remember what could be loosely called the "content of what was said." If they heard "and then the dog was petted by Paula," they might remember "Paula petted the dog." If they heard "The sailor was not dead," they might remember "The sailor was alive," etc. (See Sachs 1967.)

Apparently the words heard are often not remembered exactly, but rather the important contents and units of statement. Whether the dog was petted by Paula or Paula petted the dog, the difference between active and passive formulations of the statement is relatively unimportant. It is important that Paula *petted* rather than struck the dog, that *Paula* and not *John* petted the dog, that Paula petted the *dog* and not the *cat*.

This unit of statement which usually centers around the predicate

---

[17]We will see later that the approach which operates with propositions cannot in fact get along without the word-lexicon, no matter how this might be conceptualized; the proposition theorists simply do not talk about it.

pet (Paula, dog)

is called a proposition or also a predicate-argument structure. (For more on the following see Engelkamp 1976.) We became acquainted with them in Chapter 2.

It is obvious that we proceed basically in a different way here than in the other approaches that we have discussed in order to understand meaning systematically. There we mainly spoke about word meaning and it was an additional problem how to conceive of the connections of the individual words for the meaning of the sentence. The items from which we started occurred in a structure which ran perpendicular to the sentence, so to speak (dog–mammal–animal). The longitudinal structure was mainly a problem for syntax, with all the disadvantages which resulted from this, as we have seen.

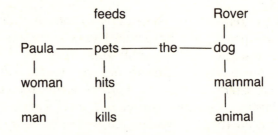

The propositional approach begins with larger units, namely, with the elementary structures of *sentence* meaning:

Paula_____pets_____dog

It should be made clear that this propositional or predicate-argument structure is a deep structure. The surface structure of a sentence otherwise constructed

The dog was petted by Paula

has the same propositional structure as

Paula petted the dog.

A proposition has as its center a predicate, on which depend a number of arguments. (Predicate and argument are, by the way, concepts from logic, not primarily from linguistics.) The predicate opens up, as we say, empty spaces around it, which can be filled in by arguments.

These arguments are seen by Fillmore (1968) as categorical ideas or judgments which man can have in relation to his environment: who did something, what happened, who or what was affected, where did it happen, and so on. One argument is thus reserved in many utterances for the person active in an action (for the *agent*), another for the passive recipient of an action (called the *patient*), a third often for the means by which the action was accomplished (the *instrument*). In our sample sentence "Paula" would be the agent, "dog" the patient argument of the predicate "pet."

The roles which the individual arguments play in the drama of the sentence are, as we see, conceived of in decidedly psychological terms by Fillmore. They are for him the basic ways of understanding the events of the world. (We have already indicated in earlier chapters that the linguistics of Fillmore has many points of contact with developmental psychology, especially that of Piaget.)

As we have said, propositions should be considered a part of the deep structure. They do not consist of words, even though we must of course use words when we want to talk about them. If propositions belong to the deep structure, the question is raised as to how they are realized or represented in surface structure.

This can be achieved in two ways: first, *via* the lexical characteristics of the words which are used for the representation of the proposition, and, secondly, *via* certain syntactic indications. To the first: the feature "living," "can act independently" must be characteristic of a noun that could be used as the argument "agent." This is corroborated by an experiment of Blumenthal (1967). He found that for subjects to whom sentences like

Gloves are made by tailors

or

Gloves are made by hand

were presented for later recall, the word "tailors" was a much more effective prompting to recall than the word "hand." This can only be a result of the fact that in understanding the word "tailor" the ability to function as an agent-argument is activated, whereas "hand" only brings with it a more exact adverbial description. It is clear already from the difference in the lexical meaning of "tailor" and "hand" which roles these words can play in the representation of the proposition in every case.

This is, however, not always the case; often lexical knowledge is not enough. In the sentence

The boy hit the girl

it cannot be seen from the lexical meaning of the two nouns which of them should be seen in the role of agent and which in the role of patient. This must be signaled here by syntactic indications. The surface structure must reveal that one of the nouns functions as an agent; this is signaled by the surface structure nominative case.

We came to the concept of the proposition or the predicate-argument structure in our search for possibilities for systematically understanding the meaning of sentences. We became acquainted with the proposition as an overall unit of meaning which has its own structure. It should have become clear that the propositional approach does not represent an alternative to those approaches which deal with understanding the elementary meaning of words. If we can view the sentence

The dog bites the rabbit

as the proposition *bite* (agent: dog, patient: rabbit), it still tells us nothing about what a dog is—at the most, that it is something with the ability to be an agent, so to speak. What the word "dog" means must also be taken from a kind of subjective lexicon; we must locate it in a semantic network or retrieve it as an image from our semantic memory.

The propositional approach does achieve at one decisive point more than the previously discussed attempts: it allows us to recognize and to represent meaning structures which pervade the sentence and which are responsible for the fact that a sentence means more and different things than do its individual words or the sum of these words. [18]

We have now become acquainted with the most important of those approaches which try to put some order into the problems of what meaning means psychologically. We should now be able to investigate the events and processes that occur in an utterance.

[18]An interesting integration of a subjective-lexicon approach with the more comprehensive propositional approach is attempted by Miller and Johnson-Laird (1976). So far, however, this lacks empirical support. [See now P. N. Johnson-Laird, *Mental Models: Toward a Cognitive Science of Language, Inference, and Consciousness* (Cambridge, Mass.: Harvard University Press, 1983) for a full and systematic development of this position.—Ed.]

CHAPTER 6

The Structure of Utterances

Even the expression at the sensory level and the combination of expressions into higher linguistic configurations are governed by certain regularities which are distinct from the freely intended meaning and yet are of greatest importance for the expressive possibilities of meanings through language.

J. Stenzel

Man's thought is 'relative' with respect to the possibilities of expression afforded by the available language systems and their semantic structures insofar as it can only take on form by complying with these given conditions. But if human thought becomes objectified in relation to the available language it does not mean that it is also mentally determined in this manner. Relativity does not imply determinism. The human spirit has the freedom to put to infinite use the finite means of the available language. However, whatever it may be able to express verbally it will never be able to achieve total independence and absoluteness. Only in this restricted sense can one speak of a linguistic relativity principle.

H. Gipper

In the preceding chapters we have indicated that language utterances

- are themselves structured, on many levels
- are in most cases part of a larger language and/or non-language structure.

Utterances are organized hierarchically as such and are part of a situation or of a context which also has an organizational structure. In this chapter, we will present examples of the way in which this fact of structuredness and the embeddedness-in-structure of an utterance is *psychologically effective*, and which psychological phenomena can accompany it—without any attempt to present a complete overview of up-to-date research and findings in this area.

We will start by recalling that the structures inherent in or surrounding a verbal utterance may be of very different qualities: social structures, linguistic structures, emotional structures, and so forth. Let us exemplify what we are looking for by this question: is it possible to show a dependable relation between a particular linguistic structure (e.g., the distinction between an independent and dependent clause) and a characteristic of producing or processing an utterance containing that linguistic

171

structure (e.g., that a pause is always put before pronouncing a dependent clause)?

In the years of early psycholinguistic enthusiasm the fact of finding such a relation was interpreted as proving the "psychological reality" of the (linguistic) structural characteristic in question (e.g., Fodor and Bever 1965).

Today interpretations are rather more cautious, because there is no cast-iron proof that the psychological phenomenon observed (in our example, the pause) is brought about by the occurrence of that particular linguistic structure (in our example, by the speaker producing an independent and a dependent clause). Other structures, other factors, could have the very same effect. (And, moreover, what precisely is psychological reality?)

Nonetheless, finding psychological relations and dependencies within an utterance and between (parts of) the utterance and its situational, social, or other context is certainly a necessary way to learn more about what goes on when we use language.

Utterances occur in different contexts or situations. For our purposes a division into dialogue (or conversation), text (or monologue), and sentence will be adequate.

Determinants of the Dialogue

Our first question is thus: does the dialogue reveal an "inner structure" in the sense that the shape or quality of any part of it is determined by the fact that it is located at this particular position in that structure? Does this assumed dialogue structure have any psychological consequences?

A first structural characteristic of the dialogue is shown in the rules which determine who may begin and in what way. These rules are very different from language to language—or should we say from culture to culture? The conversation between two American students begins with "hi" and ends with " 'bye," whereas in a Japanese conversation, the speaker must first decide between two levels of language (normal or polite) which are signaled by corresponding suffixes on the verbs. The Japanese speaker must then take a so-called reference axis into account, upon which he must locate himself, the listener, and the person about whom he is speaking. Such factors as age, sex, and social position play a role in the process of location on this axis. The style which is chosen in this way has an effect, for example, even on the different verbal forms, according to whether one is talking about oneself, one's younger brother, or one's boss. (There are similar differences in Javanese).

In most European languages (and in American English) we find less strict prescriptions following from the social constellation of the two members of a dialogue group, but there are, of course, comparable effects; we need only think of the different forms of address. Brown and Gilman (1960) found mainly two factors which were responsible for person *A* being on a first name basis with person *B* or not: power and solidarity. However, the decision about which form of address to use is influenced not only by factors inherent in the social structure of the dialogue group, as we see in present-day German, where there has been a general inflation of the *Du*-form, especially among young people and people of leftist orientation who want to draw attention to their progressive ideology. It would be next to impossible to find a clear-cut structural basis for this inflation.

Let us therefore proceed from these considerations belonging more to the sociolinguistic than to the psycholinguistic realm to psychological phenomena in dialogue in a narrower sense. Conversation demands a kind of formal agreement between the two partners: each wants to reach the goal that he has before him at the beginning of the dialogue—he wants to direct the consciousness of the partner to something specific, or he wants to get information for himself, or something similar. And each partner knows that the other also has intentions. Thus both must—in an alternating manner as equably as possible—be able to say something; there must be rules for this game.

The conversation usually begins (see Sacks, Schegloff, and Jefferson 1974) with a summons—answer sequence (a request for a conversation and a reply to it). Whoever wants to begin a conversation must get his prospective partner's attention (we remember the child who establishes eye contact before entering into a communication situation). This can occur *via* verbal or nonverbal means: one can tap the prospective partner on the shoulder or call him by name, or, if one does not know the name, with "hey" or "old man" or "good morning."

Whoever is approached in this way and has a mastery of the English language (and to this belongs also the knowledge of the division of roles in the language game of beginning a conversation) knows that he must react in a certain way if he is spoken to thus: he would probably also say, "Good morning" (perhaps with a rising tone, or signal that he now expects something further from the partner), or he will turn to the speaker and make eye contact, or something similar. He will not, however, say "Good-bye," nor himself ask a question such as "What time is it?"

There are similar structure rules for the opening of a telephone conversation: the one who is called must say the first word, usually "hello" (in America) and/or identify himself. Thus we can see that successful communication rests on some kind of preunderstanding, the establishment of a common basis for the verbal activity. Part of this preunderstanding is furnished by the fact that each and every speaker/listener takes for granted that he himself as well as his partner will adhere to some very general communicative rules, e.g.:

- Make your contribution as informative as is required.
- Do not say anything you believe or know to be false.
- Make your contribution relevant to the aim of the present dialogue.
- Be clear, try to avoid ambiguity, obscurity, disorderliness in your contribution.

These rules have been noted by Grice (1975). In each dialogue, so much attention is instinctively paid to them that we are usually unaware of their importance. However, observing these conversational postulates is not enough. The common basis for the dialogue must be more specific, must adapt to the twists and turns of the discourse. Thus, apart from the sharing of certain knowledge, there is also during conversation a signaling by verbal and nonverbal means as to how the speaker structures or would like to structure the situation. If someone is polite or wants to be polite, he will express his intentions with more words than if he does not particularly want to make such an impression (Schönbach 1974). Terbuyken (1975) analyzed telephone interviews which students held with interviewees belonging to the following categories: friend, unknown student, professor, administrator, minister. It was shown that a whole number of formal linguistic characteristics (length of utterance, number of relative clauses, etc.) were specific and typical for the particular social structure in which the dialogue took place. The course of a conversation depends to a great extent on the fact that the listener learns in time that he is soon to take over the role of the speaker. Only then is it certain that he will have planned his utterance to the extent that no uneconomical pause arises when the previous speaker has finished his utterance. We have already discussed (in Chapter 3, on the nonverbal basis of the verbal utterance) the role of eye contact in the control of this turn-taking. The function of eye contact is also important for differentiating between a "request" for speaker change and a mere pause to think or plan by A: if A pauses *without* looking at B, a change of turn will much less frequently take place.

We realize how very accustomed we are to paying attention to the visually supported way of directing the dialogue, when we listen to a telephone conversation between two people; it is full of "false starts," that is, of segments in which B begins to speak, but A has not yet completely finished. In the usual face-to-face situation, for the listener B, his readiness to begin speaking soon is usually signaled by a change in position in relation to A, who is still speaking. If we analyze in this way the structure of the discourse situation and the course of the conversation, the important role of nonverbal signals (kinesics) becomes evident at many choice points.

Conversations also have an end. The partner who wants to begin to do this, for example, in a telephone dialogue, must do it according to very specific rules; otherwise he creates confusion, perhaps seems impolite. Schegloff and Sacks differentiate between two stages: (1) A and B agree to end the conversation; (2) they actually end it. When someone, for example, wants to initiate (1), he will either pause when he would otherwise have his turn to speak and/or say an extended "yeah" or "well" or a slow "so." Then *B* must take the next step, namely, to take the preparations for ending further or to begin a new topic.

In face-to-face conversations and on the telephone, reduction of syllable rate is often used to bridge the end of one sentence and the beginning of another; it tells the listener that the speaker still wants to hold the floor. The more preplanned a discourse is, the more capacity there is for the shaping of surface sentences, and this is shown not only in a reduction of false starts and repetitions, but also in a greater number of pauses used for the deliberate choice of words (Deese 1980).

Structure of Texts

There is still a considerable amount to say about the psychological effects of the structure of conversations. Let us show now, however, that there is also a structure active in a monologue which a speaker gives before a listener, a structure that can be recognized and taken into account if one wants to clarify in psychological terms the production or the understanding of a larger section of connected utterances, that is, a text. Until rather recently, linguistics recognized the sentence as the largest unit of speech; it was thought that only stylistic or rhetorical considerations governed the global or sequential organization of sentences in a speech, a description, a story, or a text. Psychological investigations, on the one hand, and a rather new branch of linguistics (text linguistics) on the other, have, however, shown in recent years that texts are pervaded by a variety of structures which have very tangible effects on the processing of the texts in production and comprehension. In contradistinction to the grammatical structures governing the sentence, however, text structures do not claim attention by appearing "right" or "wrong"; there are no "ungrammatical texts." Violation of the optimal (or usual, or normal) text structures has more subtle effects, as we will see: effects on comprehension, memory or the aesthetic impression the text makes on the listener.

Let us begin with a particularly instructive investigation:

Linde and Labov (1975) had about one hundred New Yorkers describe their own apartments. From the resulting descriptions, which were to a great extent formally similar, the authors found indications as to how a verbal description is planned, structured, and carried out, with a text or monologue which is certainly not difficult for the speaker to produce but which he has not learned by heart before. He must make it up on the spot and the experimenter can observe what factors are at work (Figure 3).

Of those asked, 97 percent organize their description according to a certain scheme: they take the listener along on a verbal tour of the apartment (the other 3 percent describe it by verbally drawing a blueprint: "Imagine a rectangle with a square. . .").

The tour begins at the entrance of the apartment and lists the main rooms in the order that they could be reached from the entrance. If the imaginary visitor comes to a room which has no other room behind it, then he does not "enter" the room but only "looks" into it.

The kitchen, the dining room, the living room, and the bedroom are described in full (by the way, here the effects of the text organization extend into the individual sentence—it begins with the definite article), while storage rooms and such are only mentioned briefly (and with an indefinite article—"a small closet").

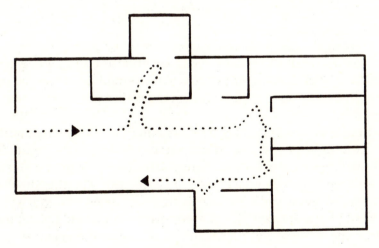

Figure 3

Something important is made clear in this example: if we ask for a description of an apartment, a structure is activated which controls the sequence in which the individual rooms are mentioned in the text.

However, the structure touched upon here reaches down one level further, namely, into the syntax of the sentence which is used to mention the particular room, as we have seen. Thus, the speech act of describing is organized on at least three or four levels, and the determination of part of the syntax of the sentences to be produced has, of course, consequences right down to the process of articulation.

D   (Speech act of describing)

↓

Sequence of the
utterances

↓

Structure of the
individual sentence

↓

Speaking

Here again, as is usual when one is investigating the structured character of a linguistic event, we find the event guided and organized by many different factors acting simultaneously and on different levels. Certain factors affect only one level, others several levels.

In many cases it has become customary in the description of the structure of texts also to use the terms deep structure (DS) and surface structure (SS). Conversations, descriptions, texts have a deep structure which in itself is sometimes further divided into several levels and a surface structure, namely, what is actually said by the speaker. Thus, to return to Linde and Labov, not only is the sequence of rooms in the description determined by the DS of the speech act "describe your apartment," but also the description occurs in so-called vector-space units (whereby a *static* vector describes the direction statically—"left, straight ahead, on the right"—and a *mobile* vector describes the path: "If you turn left now," "now walk straight ahead"). The description in vector-space units has a further influence in determining the point at which one sentence is to end and a new one begin—a property of SS—but many other factors are naturally involved in this decision also.

Linde and Labov have shown us the regular structured character of the description of an apartment: the regularities at work here can be described in some twenty rules. Thus the competent speaker of American English must master some rules and follow them in order to make the usual description of an apartment. (He must, of course, follow many more rules of American English, namely, the rules of sentence syntax, semantics—he must choose the right words—of articulation, and so on—but twenty rules are necessary to answer the single, simple request, "Describe your apartment."

Series of events stretched over time are also usually described according to certain rules; one of the most important of these is that what happened earlier in time is also reported before what happened later in time. It takes special constructions (which are harder to understand and to remember) if the speaker wants to deviate from this natural sequential structure.

This natural structure of a text obviously plays some role for the listener or reader. When he processes the text adequately, the structure of the *text* (and not merely the structure of the individual sentences which make up the text) is in some way extracted and stored as a representation of that text. How does he do this abstracting? Which cues does he use?

As we know, texts differ from a simple collection of sentences by a number of relatively obvious characteristics. Such characteristic features of the surface structure of texts are, for example, title, repetition of arguments from earlier propositions in later ones, pronominalization, the use of the definite article when a certain object is mentioned for the second or subsequent time, and so forth. We will now discuss a first model of text structure.

It was developed by Kintsch (1974, 1976; Kintsch and van

Dijk 1978) and operates with propositions as units, that is, with *semantic* structures, in which a predicate usually connects two or more arguments with each other. This propositional deep structure usually corresponds to a verb in the surface structure for the predicate and to a noun for the argument. The structural coherence of the *text* results, according to Kintsch, from the overlapping of the arguments in subsequent propositions and from their hierarchical organization. This will be made clear with an example:

(6.1) The Greeks loved beautiful works of art. When the Romans conquered the Greeks, they imitated the Greeks and thus learned to make beautiful works of art.

This text has, according to Kintsch, the following propositional structure:

1. love (Agent: Greeks, Patient: works of art)
2. beautiful (Patient: works of art)
3. conquer (Agent: Romans, Patient: Greeks)
4. imitate (Agent: Romans, Patient: Greeks)
5. when (3; 4)
6. learn (Agent: Romans, Patient: 8)
7. consequence (3; 6)
8. make (Agent: Romans, Patients: 2)

These propositions are not equal to one another but are organized hierarchically. Those propositions occurring earlier are superior to those occurring later. In our example, 1 has the highest level; 2, 3, and 4 are dependent on it, because "work of art" is used again in 2 as an argument, and the argument "Greeks" is used again in 3 and 4. The propositions 2, 3, and 4 thus make up the second level in Kintsch's hierarchical system. All further propositions refer to arguments in the second level and therefore make up the third level.

What evidence can Kintsch now present for the claim that his model actually describes psychologically relevant dimensions of texts?

We can first refer to an investigation by Kintsch and Keenan

(1973) for the theoretical fruitfulness of the organization of a text into propositions. Here subjects were given texts to read which contained different numbers of propositions but the same number of words. It was found that a text is read more slowly the more propositions it has. The reading rate is thus apparently adjusted according to the number of units of meaning of this kind (propositions are of course units of meaning) packed into a text.

More to the point is an investigation by Kintsch *et al.* (1975) which showed that the hierarchical order of the propositions is also effective. Subjects read a text and were asked to reproduce what they could remember of it afterwards. It was shown that propositions of the higher level in the hierarchy were remembered with a much higher frequency than those on lower levels. Further investigations by Kintsch make it seem probable that superordinate propositions are remembered better because of the further propositions processed after them, in which the same arguments are repeated, and are thus connected to the superordinate propositions already available. The more unified the manner in which a whole text focuses on *one* superordinate proposition, the fewer propositions it has which cannot be subordinated to the dominant one, the easier it is for the listener or reader to grasp the intended inner connection of the text.

This (first) model by Kintsch evaluates mainly the number of "inner connections" in a text; the recurrence of arguments is one of its main characteristics. More sophisticated models were presented by Kintsch and van Dijk (1978) and by Kintsch and Vipond (1979). These later models specify the meaning of a text at two levels:

- at the level of microstructure, where an ordered list of micropropositions represents the individual "ideas" contained in the text
- at the level of macrostructure, where a list of macropropositions represents a kind of abstract of the text.

Both micro- and macropropositions contain a predicate relating to one or more arguments.

The model assumes that the listener or reader cannot comprehend the whole text at once, because of limitations in the capacity of his "processing apparatus." Instead, a memory representation of the text is established in cycles. A microproposition is related by argument overlap to micropropositions that are retained from previous cycles. Thus, a network representation of the text is gradually established. In addition to comprehending the microstructure of a text, listeners or readers understand the macrostructure. In macroprocessing, the comprehension cycle comprises a whole paragraph, not only a sentence. Macropropositions are constructed from micropropositions under the control of a schema.

A *schema* is, in this context, a knowledge structure that all or most people have concerning the usual organization of a text of a certain kind. We know how a fairy tale is organized; we know how a recipe is organized, or a weather report, or a report on a marriage ceremony. (We will have to take up this aspect—knowledge of conventional text forms and use of this knowledge in processing texts—later on.)

In the Kintsch model, individual micropropositions are scrutinized as to their relevance to the schema. If they are relevant, they may be adopted directly as a macroproposition, or they may be constructed or expanded or generalized into macropropositions.

As to the heuristic value of this model, which is actually far more detailed than our description of it, one of the first questions should concern its postulate of two (separate, connected, interdependent?) levels in the processing of a text. Vipond (1980) has actually published some preliminary experimental evidence of two levels of recall. He notes that the relative importance of each of these structures will probably depend on the task required in the experiment: macrostructure might be especially important for long-term retention, microstructures for question answering or recognition tests.

Buschke and Schaier have published (1979), not yet within the scope of the Kintsch model, however, an interesting experiment showing that recall of a story involves distinct memory units (in Kintsch's terms, micropropositions) which are sequentially ordered according to what Kintsch would call macropropositions and what Buschke and Schaier call a *story grammar*.

Story Grammar

With this term we have arrived at a conception of text structure which is slightly different from that of Kintsch. The proponents of story grammars (Mandler and Johnson 1977; Rumelhart 1975; Thorndyke 1977) draw heavily on the observations of Bartlett (1932) in the investigation of long-term memory. Bartlett read his subjects fairy tales and then had them retell the stories after a period of time. The retellings were different from the originals in very characteristic ways: they were more schematic, more ordered; they left unusual elements out; they added other things which could have been expected at certain points. Bartlett's conclusion from this was his famous theory of memory: remembering is a process of reconstructing according to a schema. We have in us a pattern which tells us how stories, how fairy tales should go, and this model guides each individual act of remembering the particular story.

When we consider that for centuries fairy tales, sagas, and stories could only be passed on orally, we cannot be surprised that their structure reflects in a very clear way certain organizing and structuring processes which occur in the speaker/listener during the assimilation of these fairy tales and sagas. These fairy-tale or story patterns are based both on our knowledge of the causes and connections of events in the world and on the repeated hearing of stories and fairy tales.

Story grammars attempt to describe, in a formal way, the internal organization or structure of a story as it is usually, or generally (or should we say normally?), encountered.[1] Nearly all of them divide a story first into two constituents: setting and plot. The plot is further divided into a series of episodes. Episode is defined as a subgoal, the actions that attempt to attain that subgoal, and the outcome of these actions. We will exemplify this general pattern with Thorndyke's (slightly more sophisticated) version of 1977:

[1]Problems like "Where does this structure come from?" "Is it universal for all mankind or are there different structures in different cultures?" "How are we to conceptualize the mechanism by which this schematic structure directs any narration of a new story, or my recall of an old one?" are as yet hardly discussed anywhere.

Grammar rules for simple stories

Rule number			Rule
1	story	→	setting + theme + plot + resolution
2	setting	→	characters + location + time
3	theme	→	(event)* + goal
4	plot	→	episode*
5	episode	→	subgoal + attempt* + outcome
6	attempt	→	{ event* / episode }
7	outcome	→	{ event* / state }
8	resolution	→	{ event / state }
9	subgoal / goal	→	desired state
10	characters / location / time	→	state

As we see, a generative grammar for stories is here presented. According to this, the symbol "story" can be translated into setting + theme + plot + resolution, and so on. The successive use of these rules in generating a story leads to the development of a story with a hierarchical structure which includes several levels and which has as its surface structure the actual propositions which occur in the concrete story.

Setting contains some information about the time, place, and main character. The *theme* presents the central core, so to speak, of the whole story, often the goal of those primarily involved. In a fairy tale, the setting and the theme would be something like: "once upon a time there was a kingdom with an old king who had a beautiful daughter who did not want to marry." By *plot* we understand a number of episodes, each of which presents a group of actions contributing toward the achievement of a goal or partial goal. The *resolution* is the final result of the story in relation to the theme. Parentheses show optional elements, the asterisks recurrent ones.

Now to analyze a story according to this grammar:

(6.2) (1) Circle Island is located in the middle of the Atlantic Ocean (2) north of Ronald Island. (3) The main occupations on the island are farming and ranching. (4) Circle Island has good soil, (5) but few rivers and (6) hence a shortage of water. (7) The island is run democratically. (8) All issues are decided by a majority vote of the islanders. (9) The governing body is a senate, (10) whose job is to carry out the will of the majority. (11) Recently, an island scientist discovered a cheap method (12) of converting salt water into fresh water. (13) As a result, the island farmers wanted (14) to build a canal across the island (15) so that they could use water from the canal (16) to cultivate the island's central region. (17) Therefore, the farmers formed an association in favor of the canal (18) and persuaded a few senators (19) to join. (20) The association brought the construction idea to a vote. (21) All the islanders voted. (22) The majority voted in favor of construction. (23) The senate, however, decided that (24) the farmers' proposed canal was ecologically unsound. (25) The senators agreed (26) to build a smaller canal (27) that was two feet wide and one foot deep. (28) After starting construction on the smaller canal, (29) the islanders discovered that (30) no water would flow into it. (31) Thus the project was abandoned. (32) The farmers were angry (33) because of the failure of the canal project. (34) Civil war appeared inevitable.

Application of the rules of the story grammar to this particular story shows us (Figure 4) a deep structure underlying the sequence of thirty-four sentences. After this description of the functioning of a story grammar we may now turn to the question which is of paramount importance for the psycholinguist: do these structures affect the psychological processing or understanding of the story by the language user?

Thorndyke (1977) manipulated the underlying structure of several stories by giving the texts to a first group of subjects in a form corresponding to the one above, to a second group in a form which introduced the theme gradually and successively; a third group heard the whole story without the proposition belonging to

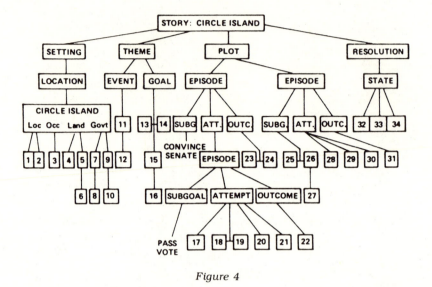

Figure 4

the theme; a fourth group heard the sentences without any reference to time or causal sequences.

A memory test showed that the more inner structure a story has, the more of the story is remembered. The probability that a certain individual fact from the story will be remembered depends on how central the passage which contains this fact is in relation to the whole story. When the subjects were asked to write a summary of the story afterwards, the subjects of the first group (those who had heard the story in its original structure) remembered only the most important of all the facts, whereas the subjects of the other groups emphasized the details or events which were not structurally central to the story. The subject can thus only summarize what is organized according to this kind of story grammar.

In more recent experiments, it has been found that goal-oriented episodes in stories are stored as separate chunks in memory. Recall of the actions in an episode is affected by the length of that episode but hardly at all by the length of other episodes. The probability of recalling a general superordinate action in a story increases with the number of subordinate actions that further specify it (Black, Turner, and Bower 1979). Careful analysis of the data obtained shows that establishing the macropropositions which constitute a text involves, in many cases, not only extraction of these propositions as they are "hidden" in the text, but also processes of integration and of inferential construction as well. Separately acquired facts are put together to form a new, more general idea. (The theoretical model for conceptualizing this is very often a memory network with nodes and labeled connections.) This integration is facilitated by (a) the proximity of the facts to be related in the sequence of the text and (b) the degree of correspondence in wording of the information common to these related facts (Hayes-Roth and Thorndyke 1979). The "height" of a given piece of information in the content structure of a text affects the probability that this information will be integrated and retained in memory (Walker and Meyer, 1980).

Leaving now the discussion of story grammars, we still have something to say about the integration processes going on whenever two or more utterances are produced about the same topic. In one approach to these integration processes, a distinction is made between presupposed and focal information: a presupposition is that part of a sentence which the speaker assumes the listener to know about or to take for granted. The focus, on the other hand, is meant by the speaker to convey new information (and is, therefore, usually stressed in pronunciation). An example which contains presupposed and focal information within *one* sentence is:

(6.3) It was John who killed Mary.

Here the speaker obviously presupposes that the listener knows that Mary has been killed; the focal (new) information is that John was the killer.

The question is now, which cues does the speaker use to signal to the listener what he should take as presupposed and what as focal information? There are, as far as we know, several of these cues in our example. The relative clause signals presupposed information, and "it was" is used to point out focal information. When we now look at the integration of two sentences, we will find that the listener identifies a focus in the first sentence because this part is more heavily marked (and stressed) than the presupposition. This focusing evokes in the listener some kind of expectation that subsequent sentences should contain more information about this focus. A second sentence is accordingly analysed as to whether it contains an element which might relate (as focal) to what now becomes presupposed information contained in the first sentence. An example: First sentence:

(6.4) John started a row by insulting Mary.

Second sentence:

(6.5) The row soon spread to all participants.

In the first sentence, "a row" is introduced as focal information (it is new and therefore the indeterminate article is used). The second sentence takes up what was focal and uses it now as presupposed information (*the* row). The repetition of the element which changes from focal to presupposed is apt to facilitate the integration of the two sentences.

This integration would be more difficult if the first sentence were followed by this *second sentence:*

(6.6) Insults may be dangerous even to long-standing friendship.

Here the second sentence takes up something which has not been focal in the first sentence; the expectations generated by the first sentence in the listener are not satisfied by the second sentence (Cf. Yekovich, Walker, and Blackman 1979).

A slightly different facet of these integration processes is discussed under the heading of foregrounding (Chafe 1973). A concept is foregrounded if the conventions of the language community allow a speaker to assume that the listener now has this concept or idea, first introduced at some earlier point, actively in mind. How are we to conceptualize this reactivation of concepts introduced earlier (when presumably they were dominant)? What is the status of such concepts or ideas during the interval between first and second "activation"?

Lesgold, Roth, and Curtis (1979) have shown that sentences take longer to comprehend when the information they refer to is not foregrounded. A concept may remain foregrounded, after it has been first mentioned, as long as it can be integrated with concepts in subsequent sentences.

When the propositions inherent in a portion of the text are

not directly linked to the antecedent (e.g., by overlap of arguments), some time-consuming restatement may be necessary for comprehension. If no antecedents are to be found in a preliminary cycle of search, inferential bridges must be constructed by the listener.

As we see, analysis of the structures responsible for text cohesion and text comprehension brings us very close to one of the central problems of the psychology of language: the problem of understanding; we shall return to this problem in Chapter 8.

Before closing our discussion of the psycholinguistic structures of texts, we have to consider a specific characteristic of many texts: the headline. What influence has the headline on the processing of the text which follows it?

Kintsch's early model already accorded a highly influential role to the first proposition of a text, and the headline is, in a manner of speaking, the first proposition the listener/reader encounters in hearing or reading the text. Especially when the early propositions of a text contain an argument (or arguments) introduced in the headline, these propositions are localized on a high level of the text hierarchy. In his experimental investigations Bock (1978) found ample evidence for the fact that the quality of the headline influences the emerging structure of the text and so, for instance, also the recall of this text after an interval.

Sentence Structures

Up to now we have spoken about the structures of the dialogue, of texts, stories, and fairy tales. We are here concerned, almost without exception, with deep structures of which we are not immediately conscious, which belong to our tacit knowledge, and we are only vaguely aware of it if the rules of this knowledge are not followed or are broken. So we must make use of a special indicator process, for example, a memory test, in order to discover their psychological effect. If we now continue our search for structures proceeding from the dialogue and the text to the next smallest unit, the sentence, there is a fundamental change. Some (or most?) of the structures pervading a sentence are of such a kind that we may not stray from them without setting off an alarm which says "That is incorrect." The sentence is a country in which strict laws are in force, the rules of grammar.

Because this is the case, we can guide our somewhat vaguely directed search more precisely toward its goal. We now ask: what are the indications that the structures of grammar, with which feelings of correctness or incorrectness guide us to comply, determine, beyond this feeling, the psychological processing of a sentence, that is, the perception, remembrance, reproduction, and judgment of a sentence?

We want to begin the presentation of the psychological effects of grammatical structures with an experiment which in certain respects can serve as a model example (and in fact has served as such). According to phrase structure grammar, a sentence consists of subunits (the phrases), which show close connections among themselves. The sentence

(6.7) That he was happy was evident from the way he smiled

shows the deepest structural division between "happy" and the following "was," smaller, less deep divisions also between "that" and "he" and between "evident" and "from." Fodor and Bever (1965) have suggested the following considerations about this: whatever makes up a psychological unit is more resistant to interference from outside than what is not closely unified; this is a well known finding from perceptual psychology. If the phrases which are worked out by the linguist are also units in a *psychological* sense, then additional stimuli from outside should be able to force their way *into* such units with more difficulty than *between* them. Based on this hypothesis, Fodor and Bever presented their subjects in the experiment with sentences of the above kind on a tape recording; there was a short, easily heard click at a certain point in the sentence. The subjects were to say at which point in the sentence they had heard the click. Result: if the click was exactly between "happy" and "was," it was located correctly. If the click occurred shortly before or after this point, though, the subject heard the click between "happy" and "was" anyway; that is, it was subjectively moved to the division point between the phrases. Phrases are apparently structures which have an effect on perception.

When we talk about a sentence's being structured in phrases, the difference between deep structure and surface structure is not yet taken into account. As we recall, Chomsky's generative grammar laid stress on the fact that the listener must recognize the (different) deep structures contained in

(6.8) John was eager to please

and

(6.9) John was easy to please

in order to understand these two sentences. The fact that we *experience* these two sentences quite intuitively as different structures already points to the idea that the psychological analysis which the listener carries out must advance from the surface to the deep structure. This and a series of other considerations lead us to expect that the deep structure could prove to be especially psychologically effective. Corresponding experiments have above all been done by Blumenthal. If subjects are asked to learn sentences like (6.8) and (6.9) and then are given the word "John" as an aid to memory in a subsequent memory test, it is shown that one can more easily reproduce ". . . is eager to please" from this than ". . . is easy to please." Apparently the logical subject of a sentence is a more effective memory prompt than the logical object (Blumenthal and Boakes 1967), even though the word "John" has the same position in the surface structure of the two sentences.

This interpretation makes syntactical factors responsible for the effects we find. In a similar experiment, however, we have to accept semantic structures as well: in sentences such as

(6.10) Gloves are made by tailors
(6.11) Gloves are made by hand

the logical subject (tailors) is a better aid to memory than the adverbial (hand). However, the fact that "tailors" is the subject in the DS can only be recognized by the listener on the basis of his semantic knowledge.

In fact, we may interpret the above mentioned findings of Blumenthal also in terms of a grammar which is closer to semantics: the agent of a sentence is a more effective memory prompt than the experiencer.

We see that there are, obviously, structures which determine what goes on in the psychological processing of sentences, but we are hard put to say precisely what kinds of structures these are.

Similarly, we have talked in a rather vague manner of structures having psychological effects, being accompanied by certain psychological phenomena like pausing or recalling, because these structures in some way or other determine the processing of the utterance.

Is it possible to be a bit more specific about how these effects are brought about?

Johnson's Model

An attempt in this direction is offered by Johnson (1965). He assumes that processing of an utterance involves what Miller (1956) has called recoding. According to Miller, in the processing of information stimuli of a certain modality (e.g., visual) are translated, recoded into a different modality (e.g., articulatory); signs or signals are translated from one code into another code. This is usually done because in the second code the stimuli are more condensed (take less room in memory) or are less prone to deteriorate quickly. Recoding is thus an instrument to make optimal use of the limited capacity of memory: in a highly condensed "chunk" more information may be stored than in a chunk existing in a less parsimonious code.

Johnson now takes the linguistic-logical concept of generating (a sentence) over into Miller's psychological theory: the psychological process of sentence production begins with the most condensed unit (chunk) S, which contains, *in nuce* or in an embryonic form, the entire sentence to be generated. This highest and most condensed unit is, in a first step, decoded into *NP + VP*, just as the rules of generative grammar require—only now these units are conceived of not linguistically as phrases, but psychologically as chunks, that is, memory units, containing or representing these phrases. *VP* remains as a unit (chunk) in short-term or working memory, while NP is further decoded into article plus adjective plus noun. Look at this example:

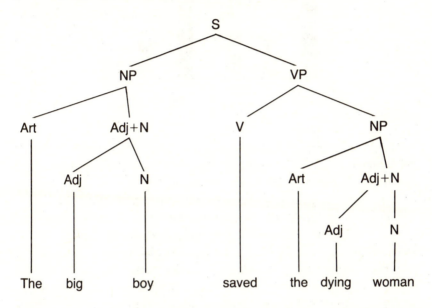

Adjective plus noun are still in storage while the article is being recoded into the final lexical unit "the." In the next step, the unit adjective plus N is further decoded, and so on. All the while the unit VP is held in storage, until it too is decoded down to the word level.

Johnson's theory thus attempts to reflect the "from left to right and from top to bottom" process of sentence generating, prescribed in Chomsky's grammar, as a series of storage and decoding steps which run throughout the sentence or parts of the sentence while they are being produced or processed.

We will not be further detained by the fact that this model has taken over not only the strengths, but also the greatest weaknesses of Chomsky's model, namely, the postulate—psychologically quite improbable—that the words, which carry meaning, are only chosen in the last step of sentence development. Let us ask what this model achieves; let us ask whether and to what extent it can reflect a structure which will prove to be of heuristic value. It should in fact be effective in just the sector from which Johnson

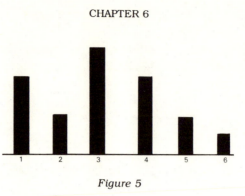

Figure 5

took his coding theory, memory. Code units of this kind, *chunks*, as Miller calls them (1956), are thought to be units of memory, especially those of short-term memory.

Johnson begins with the following consideration: the higher the level on which a coded unit lies, the more steps are necessary for "coding down" this unit to the word level (see Figure 5). The greater the number of steps, the greater also is the susceptibility to error. With the psychologically very sensible postulate that fewer errors should occur *within* a unit than between two units, Johnson creates the possibility of testing his theory experimentally. In an investigation of retention fewer errors can be expected in the transition from "big" to "boy" than in the transition from "boy" to "saved." In other words, the probability of a transitional error at point (2) would be much smaller than the probability of a transitional error at point (3) or at point (1).[2]

Johnson had his subjects learn a great number of differently constructed sentences and then tested recall. He could establish a significant correlation between the "height" in the hierarchy of a sentence constituent, as we have just shown them, and the rank order of the transitional error probabilities (TEP) found in the experiment. With this, Johnson achieved something rather important: according to this model we can imagine how the plan for a specific activity (how to produce or recall this sentence) is

---

[2] A "transitional error" is scored when the first word (say, "big") is recalled by the subject, but not the following word ("boy"). We give here an abbreviated account of Johnson's theory, without going into some of the details responsible, e.g., for the actual rank order of the expected TEPs.

realized.[3] But, again, we must remember that the fact of a correlation between the height of a unit in the coding hierarchy and the probability of a transitional error occurring in its reproduction does *not prove* that the model is correct. There are an infinite number of other, different models, from which the same rank order of the error probabilities might be predicted. Nevertheless, here we have, as it seemed at that time, a manner of visualizing how the processing of an utterance might be dependent on the (linguistic) structure of that utterance: a manner of visualizing, and so explaining, as long as our hypotheses about the working of this apparatus (e.g., that there are chunks, which are decoded one after the other and so on) are found acceptable.

Semantic Structures in the Sentence

However, the main criticism against Johnson's approach was based not on these arguments but on the fact that the correlation found, although significant, was rather low. The role, then, which syntactic structure plays in sentence processing, according to Johnson, is at best not a very important one. To find a reason for this is not very difficult: the structure Johnson talks about is a purely syntactic one (NP, Adj, V. . .), and, to begin with, it is not very likely that the processing of a sentence (and thus what we remember of an utterance heard) could fail to depend to a rather large extent on the *content* of that utterance. Therefore, we

---

[3]Let us indicate here parenthetically that the problem "What does it mean to plan something and to carry out a plan" is an old problem in psychology. Neither the behavioristic stimulus–response theory nor holistic or Gestalt psychology can explain adequately why the correct subaction is carried out at the correct point in the total activity. What is behind the fact that we must (and can) already begin a certain movement in playing the piano before the previous ones are finished? These are questions formulated by K. Lashley (1951) to which Miller, Galanter, and Pribram (1960) have attempted preliminary and still rather formal answers. [A rich description of a concrete instance of such problems is to be found in D. Sudnow, *Ways of the Hand* (Cambridge, Mass.: Harvard University Press, 1978). His account of learning to play the jazz piano, as a paradigmatic form of improvised behavior, is generalizable to other domains. It gives us the beginnings of a microphenomenology of performance.—Ed.]

should find some way similar to Johnson's to look for effects of the *semantic structures* contained in the utterance.

That the effects of semantic structures may override those of the syntactic structures broached by Johnson was shown by Engelkamp (1973).

Engelkamp presented his subjects with sentences like

(6.12) The fisherman with the glasses kept time.
(6.13) The fisherman with the rod kept time.
(6.14) The fisherman with the watch kept time.

These three sentences have exactly the same syntactic structure and so let us anticipate the same rank order of transitional error probabilities. The rank orders actually found in the experiment, however, are very different from each other. The reason for this must be some semantic factor.

How does Engelkamp now explain his findings? He sticks to the conception of recoding of memory units (chunks), but he defines chunks semantically; they are those miniature semantic structures we have encountered earlier, the propositions. A proposition is centered on a predicate which implies (or allows or demands) one or more arguments to complete it.

Now if the predicate implies the nouns serving as its arguments (but not vice versa), probability of recall for those nouns should be high if the predicate is recalled, higher than for nouns which do not serve as arguments of the predicate. In

The fisherman with the watch kept time

the noun "watch" is instrumental argument to the predicate "keep time." In

The fisherman with the glasses kept time

the noun "glasses" is *not* an argument of the predicate "keep time." Therefore probability of recall for "watch" should be higher than for "glasses," given that "keep time" is remembered. And this is what Engelkamp actually finds. In addition, he finds something about the "inner dynamics" of the propositional structure: the predicate implies its arguments, but arguments do not imply the predicate. If we take a group of subjects recalling "glasses" and a group recalling "watch," these groups do not differ in their recall of "keep time." The structure connecting the predicate with its argument(s) is obviously not symmetrical.

The better retention of coherent predicate–argument structures, which Engelkamp reports, again shows something which we pointed out earlier: the processing of an utterance means imposing structure on the utterance, and giving structure to an utterance means, among other things, constructing a hierarchy of more or less comprehensive units. The dynamics of this structuring is widely one of drawing together and joining this with that, and, correspondingly, of separating that from yet another subunit.[4] We have encountered this process of structuring by connecting and separating before. We find its effects in neighboring sentences when the listener is expressly commanded by a (usually syntactic) signal to bring the sentences into relation with each other. One of the most effective "connecting" signals is the pronoun.

(6.15) The cat was yellow and the dog chased the cat

is more difficult to retain than

(6.16) The dog chased the cat which was yellow.

The sentence (6.16) forms a more condensed unit; it takes less storage room and is therefore more easily recalled than (6.15).

Affective and Action Structures

The effects of this process of structuring by forming units are, however, not restricted to memory. We will now turn to effects of a more emotional or affective quality. What happens when, within one utterance about one and the same person, contradictory statements are connected with each other? What effects does this inconsistent structure have upon the listener?

Merdian (1977) approaches an answer to this question by

[4]The wide applicability of this principle in text comprehension and memory dynamics has been stressed by Bock (1978).

presenting, to his subjects, utterances consisting of two parts which contain information about my attitude toward a person and about my actions. In a first example, the two parts of the utterance are to a certain extent contradictory:

(6.17) Fritz is a nice guy.
       I visit him rarely.

In another utterance, there is more correspondence:

(6.18) Fritz is a nice guy.
       I visit him often.

Or in

(6.19) Fritz is not a nice guy.
       I visit him rarely.

Here my attitude, expressed in the first sentence of the pair, is consistent with my action, expressed in the second sentence. What effects, if any, does an inconsistency of affective-actional structure have on the listener? Merdian tries to answer this question by having his subjects rate on a scale *how often* the speaker actually visits Fritz. It was found that the numerical meaning of *often* with respect to *rarely* is adjusted in such a way to be more consistent. *Often* in the combination *nice/often* is rated more frequent ("more often") than *often* in the combination *not nice/often*.

Between the two parts of such an utterance exist, as we see, highly dynamic structures influencing what goes on in the listener. The elements entering into the new emerging unitary structure do not remain what they may have been in isolation or in other comprehensive units. Merdian's findings give us a first hint that these processes of structuring by forming units probably are goal-directed. Part of that goal is certainly that the outcome of the processing should make sense. This tendency toward making sense is, of course, not something which automatically occurs from the amalgamation or connection of the parts or elements of the structure; it is something actively sought by the listener. In Chapter 8 we will discuss this tendency to make an utterance, at nearly all costs, sensible, because it is a characteristic of the act of understanding.

In this chapter we have been concerned with the psychological effects of structures inherent in verbal utterances. We have spoken about linguistic structures, social structures, and cognitive structures, and we have seen that structures of different specificity have their psychological effects. There are indications that in the use of language very general structures are also effective which are at first sight rather distant from language. Thus Ertel (Ertel and Bloemer 1975) showed that analogous structures of activity pervade both language and nonlanguage processes and can thus influence each other. Ertel was interested in the difference between affirmative and negative utterances. In affirmation, he says, the agreement between two cognitive units is emphasized ("the sheep is big" refers to the agreement between "sheep" and "big"), whereas negation separates two cognitive units because they do not agree. If in an affirmative utterance two cognitive units are brought together, and in the negating utterance two cognitive units are separated, then the structures of activity lying beneath these utterances might be influenced by a simultaneous occurrence of nonverbal structures of activity. Ertel thus had a group of subjects learn affirmative sentences along with a simultaneous putting together and negative sentences along with a simultaneous taking apart of a cut-up paper square; another group of subjects learned affirmative sentences while taking apart the squares, the negative ones while putting them together. In the first group, the structure of the verbal activity agrees with the nonverbal activity; in the second group the structures are contradictory. The subjects in the first group learned the sentences significantly better than those in the second group.

Analogous structures in language and in nonlanguage action—we have arrived at a kind of structure which is more general than the affective and semantic and syntactic structures with which we have so far become acquainted in this chapter. At some point between the very general structures described by Ertel and the linguistic structures spoken of earlier we will probably have to localize structures in man's cognition of the world which are reflected, as it were, in the structures of the verbal utterance. According to Osgood (1979), there are two basic types of subject–verb–object cognitions:

1. expressing *action* relations, where actor–action–recipient is the natural ordering in cognizing, because the animateness of the actor against the (relative) passivity of the recipient favors this order
2. expressing *stative* relations, where figure–state–ground dominates because of the gestalt-like characteristics of both figure and ground.[5]

> Thus . . . one would expect prelinguistic cognizings like Man Kick Dog (action) and Dog On Floor (stative) to be more natural than Dog Kicked By Man or Floor Under Dog. If the underlying naturalness principle is valid, then one would expect the earliest sentencings—by contemporary child and by now extinct man–ape—to be active (rather than passive) and figurative (rather than ground-active). (224)

Without going further into Osgood's speculations on the primitive stages of language in general, we will take this as a last example of how utterances are pervaded by structures of very different kinds. The psychological effects of these structures are correspondingly different.

---

[5]Gestalt psychology has shown that figures are prominent (e.g., in speed and ease of perception, in recall, etc.) before an undifferentiated ground. The figure is in the focus of attention, while the ground is not attended to. These relationships hold for visual as well as for auditory stimuli.

CHAPTER 7

The Production of Utterances

The relation of thought to word is not a thing but a process, a continual movement back and forth from thought to word and from word to thought. In that process the relation of thought to word undergoes changes which themselves may be regarded as development in the functional sense. Thought is not merely expressed in words; it comes into existence through them. Every thought tends to connect something with something else, to establish a relationship between things. Every thought moves, grows and develops, fulfills a function, solves a problem. This flow of thought occurs as an inner movement through a series of planes. An analysis of the interaction of thought and word must begin with an investigation of the different phases and planes a thought traverses before it is embodied in words.

L. Vygotsky

It is the subjective activity of thinking which creates an object. For there is no single kind of idea which can be regarded as a purely receptive contemplation of an object previously given. The activity of the senses must be combined into a synthesis with the inner activity of the mind. . . . To do this language is essential.

W. von Humboldt

Gestalt psychology holds [that] sensory units have acquired names, have become richly symbolic, and are now known to have certain practical uses, while nevertheless they have existed before any of these further facts were added. Gestalt psychology claims that it is precisely the original segregation of circumscribed wholes which makes it possible for the sensory world to appear so utterly imbued with meaning to the adult; for in its gradual entrance into the sensory field, meaning follows the lines drawn by natural organization; it usually enters into segregated wholes.

W. Köhler

The grammar of the linguist describes, as we have already said, the structure of sentences in the form of a system of rules. The linguist looks at language as such, that is to say, neither under the aspect of producing or speaking nor under the aspect of understanding the particular sentence. Grammar and lexicon are valid for the linguist in the same way for both production and for reception. Therefore, psycholinguistics has also tried for a long time to describe speaking and understanding in one unitary model.

The development of a unitary model for speaking and understanding, however, was impeded by two facts: transformational generative grammar (TGG), dominating linguistics with its emphasis on the *generating* of sentences, was more congenial for a model of *production,* whereas the experimental method dominating psycholinguistics could more easily be used for the process of *understanding,* since this is more easily treated as a dependent variable than is the spontaneous utterance.[1]

[1]The situation was different—this must be mentioned here—in Russian psychology of language, which was guided to a much lesser extent by one dominating linguistic theory than Western psycholinguistics has been. In Russian psychology of language, a production model of speaking was close to the basic conception of "language as activity." This approach is discussed more thoroughly in Hörmann (1976/1981).

However, with the bond between generative linguistics and psychology of language gradually loosening, psycholinguists found that a unitary performance model for the acts of speaking *and* of understanding could be developed only by ignoring many facts which had become known in the meantime. Understanding an utterance is certainly not a generation process in reverse. A whole series of facts and theoretical conclusions speaks for a separate theoretical treatment of these two acts (see Straight 1976):

- In young children, understanding precedes the ability to produce speech.
- The production of an utterance is determined to a much greater extent by the social situation than the understanding of an utterance.
- For the listener, sentences are often ambiguous, for the speaker practically never.
- The "linearization" of an utterance (that is, its transition into a series of words) cannot be a perfect reflection of its delinearization in the process of understanding.
- In understanding, one can almost completely disregard phonological errors in the utterance heard; it is hardly possible to produce such errors intentionally as a speaker, and the same is the case for differences in dialect.
- From aphasia research two major groups of difficulties are known: patients with difficulties in understanding (from damage to the Wernicke center) and those with formulation and pronunciation difficulties (from damage to the Broca center).

When we now try to sketch a model of the production of verbal utterances, we will have to remember some phenomena which confront us daily and with which this model should agree.

Planning of Utterances

First there is the experience that utterances can be planned more or less far ahead. Whoever has to give a talk about a certain theme will consider beforehand in what order he will touch on certain aspects. In this drawn-out planning (which can assume different degrees of concreteness up to and including memorization), factors of briefer time span can also be included. In other cases these are the only determining factors: when we give an answer to a colleague's comment in a discussion, or when I interrupt someone else's utterance in order to change it into a joke by twisting the meaning. Here the speaker did not clearly "know" at the beginning of his utterance what he would say; he must thus conceive the plan in fractions of a second and carry it through. The fact that plans exist even for short, spontaneous utterances (according to Deese [1978] about half of 20,000 sentences were shorter than 3 or 4 seconds) becomes clearest to us in cases wherein we notice *during* the utterance that we are not going to "arrive" in the intended way and that we must therefore make a change. Apparently we have available not only what was already said, but also, in some form, what ought to be: the plan according to which an utterance is constructed is in different stages of realization at this point in time.

Where and how does a plan develop? What is its starting point? Let us first put it vaguely: it starts with the speaker's intended message. Let us ignore the problems arising from the question of what a message in the condition of being intended actually is, and ask further how this intention is formed with the help of the grammatical rule system and the lexicon; and how, perhaps with yet further help, it is formed into that sequence of sounds which the speaker finally sends on the way to the ear of the listener.

This development is a process in time and so we may conceptualize it as something taking place in different phases or stages. If we do this, we can further ask, what happens at what point in this process—when is the syntactic structure determined, when are the words to be used chosen, when is it decided that a certain formula for politeness will be used, when is the main accent of the utterance produced?

The structure of an utterance, as we know from the preceding chapters, must be located on different levels; the planning of an utterance will also probably occur on several levels. In complete agreement with such a model is the attempt to explain certain *errors* in utterances and *pauses* by relating them to specific points in the structure of the model. This line of thought will be taken up later.

A complete model of the development of an individual utterance would have to begin with accounting for *why* at this point in the flow of events something is said by the speaker, and *how* the utterance which is to be produced now is determined and formed by being embedded in this stream of events.

Presuppositions of the Utterance

No utterance stands alone. Even the first sentence of a dialogue has at least a situative context and takes into account what is yet to come in the form of language or of activity. A speaker addressing a listener has, in each and every speech situation, a general aim: to change the consciousness of the listener. In order to do this effectively, the speaker must connect his utterance to what is already present in the listener.

An example of this (after Osgood): During the time of the miniskirt fad, two male students are walking across the campus; they meet a woman student going the other way. When she has passed them, one student turns to the other and says, "And her hair is dyed, too."

The utterance occurs here probably because the speaker assumes a similar interest in such things in the listener. The utterance is constructed in this way because the speaker calculates that it hits upon a very particular (not only determined by the view of the miniskirt) condition of consciousness of the listener. He does not need to ask, "Did you see that girl" and he can begin with "and her hair" without first identifying which hair he means. He says "is dyed, *too*" and thus continues the thought which he assumes the listener has also.

The speaker wants by means of his utterance to direct the consciousness of the listener and therefore constructs the utterance in such a way that it fits the supposed position of this consciousness and takes it into account.

This general speaker's strategy can of course use different means. Olson (1970) has shown that the choice of the name of a specific object is determined by this strategy. In a playful experiment, a small paper star is hidden under a round white block. A child is brought in, and the adult is supposed to direct the child's search by telling him under what block the star is. The round white block is shown next to one or two other blocks: a square white one and/or a round black one. If it lies beside the square white one, the adult will indicate the hiding-place of the paper star by saying,

"It's under the round one";

if it lies beside the round black block, the adult will say,

"It's under the white one";

and only when all three blocks are visible together, will he use

"It's under the round white one."

For pointing out one and the same block three different utterances are used in three different situations. The utterance is chosen in such a way that it eliminates the uncertainty of the child who is looking for the correct block. There is no mention of searching, because the speaker assumes that the child is playing along; there is no mention of blocks, because the listener knows that the child knows that the star can only be under a block.

Knowing what the listener wants in a situation and what he knows about the situation—this is the assumption and the basis for the genesis of most of a speaker's utterances. The speaker builds his utterance, as we say, on *presuppositions.* The planning of the utterance must take this basis into account. From this basis the instrument for changing the listener's consciousness, the utterance, is to be constructed.

It is rather difficult to determine, in a concrete situation, what the presuppositions of an utterance are. Asking the speaker, after he has pronounced the utterance, what he knew or assumed about the listener's state of consciousness will reveal only some of the more superficial and/or specific presuppositions. Some of the presuppositions forming the basis of an utterance,

on the other hand, are rather tacit agreements between *every*
speaker and *every* listener: that the utterance does make sense—
its occurrence and its content. It fits into a contract, albeit vague,
to which everybody who uses language subscribes.[2] As is often
the case with things which seem to be obvious, the existence of
this contract becomes noticeable chiefly when it is violated or
ignored. The utterance

(7.1) It's raining, but I don't believe it

is not so much a linguistic as an anthropological monstrosity,
against which we must secure ourselves by a membership contract, so to speak, in human society. When someone who is looking around under a streetlamp says that he lost his key a hundred
yards away but that there is more light for looking under the
lamp, he *must* be at least drunk for us to accept the utterance.

The disastrous effect of this—syntactically and semantically
completely well formed—sentence (7.1) shows that the content of
a sentence cannot be separated from the fact that it is uttered
here and now. In order for an utterance to have its intended effect, the speaker must take the entire speech act into account.[3]

Utterances build on presuppositions. To guarantee that the
utterance "makes contact" with the presuppositions the speaker
assumes in the listener, the utterance is frequently so constructed
that it is easy for the listener to connect the "new" information
coming in with the "given" information to which it relates; we have
discussed in Chapter 6 some of the cues signaling how and with
which "givens" contact is to be made.

Presuppositions are basic to every utterance; they are, however, not the whole basis. Presuppositions determine only partially what the speaker is going to say. How far down must (and
can) we probe to find more about the beginnings of an utterance?

Schlesinger's Model

Language is the thought-forming instrument. Intellectual
activity—entirely mental, completely inward, proceeding, one

---

[2]We have talked about these conversation postulates (Grice) above; we will come
back to them in Chapter 8.

[3]The speech act theory of Austin and Searle was discussed in Chapter 2.

might say, without a trace—manifests itself in the sounds of
speech and thus can be perceived by the senses.

W. von Humboldt

An answer to the question above will eventually come up in
the discussion, which we are about to begin, of an actual production model of the utterance. Our description starts, however, not
with the basis but with the central part of this model, which was
published by Schlesinger (1977a,b).

The model is very psychological, i.e., relatively distant from
the generating concept of TGG, even though its author's manner
of discussion is undoubtedly shaped by this school.

The central part of Schlesinger's model is a component which
represents the content of the utterance to be created, that is, a
semantic component. He calls this the *input marker* or *I-marker*
because it functions as input for the next components.[4]

I-markers are a formalization of what the speaker is going to
express. They are semantic structures, small, but not atomic
units of meaning. They may be best understood as similar to
propositions, but not necessarily centered around a predicate. As
an example, Schlesinger uses the sentence

(7.2) Mary had a little lamb

in which "Mary" is the owner of the "lamb" and "little" the attribute of the "lamb." The I-marker underlying this sentence
could be presented as follows:

(Owner—property: *Mary*, (attribute *little*) *lamb*)

I-markers thus contain elements and the relations between
elements; *Mary, little, lamb*, are such elements. These elements
are not yet words, but still concepts; words first appear in the
utterance itself. As evidence for the fact that we are dealing with
protoverbal (prelanguage) *elements*, Schlesinger brings in two
observations: (1) we often begin a sentence without knowing exactly which words we are going to use and must then look for the

[4]The term I-marker is chosen by Schlesinger in analogy to the phrase-markers (P-
markers) used in TGG; we have met them in the tree diagrams in Chapter 2. A
second meaning of I-marker is intention-marker.

fitting word for a moment. And (2): a chain of I-markers can in principle be realized in different ways, that is, in utterances that are different in surface structure. The I-markers contain only what is in the final analysis linguistically relevant for the utterance, but they contain all that is linguistically relevant.

The I-markers are the central component of the production process and make up the input for the next stage of the model. This consists of the application of the *realization rules.* In this stage what was until now "purely semantic" becomes more concrete. The realization rules must make certain that an appropriate linguistic form is found for the relations contained in the I-markers and for the (until now still protoverbal) elements of the I-markers. There are several classes of realization rules:

1. The *relation rules* assign the protoverbal elements to a grammatical category, prescribe the relative position of the elements, bring in affixes, prepare an appropriate contour of intonation and the actual phonological form.
2. The *lexicalization rules* choose a word in the lexicon for every protoverbal element, a word through which this element can be expressed. The expression "little sheep" could also have been used for the protoverbal element which we call "lamb" above. Such synonyms are more exactly demarcated in the lexicon by so-called shunting markers, which determine the context in which the particular word can be used appropriately, for example, literary style, vulgar, formal. We will have something to say about this below.
3. The *rules of agreement* secure the agreement of the words in the utterance (e.g., that all are in the plural).
4. The *intonation rules* take care of the final form of pronunciation of the whole utterance.

The lexicalization rules are, as we have just seen, sensitive to context and social situation. With this Schlesinger takes account of a well-studied question: what effect does the social-psychological relationship between speaker and listener have on the form of the utterance which the speaker makes to the listener? Olson had asked earlier what effects the cognitive aspects of the situation have; now we are talking about the social-psychological or the sociological aspects. This aspect has been studied by above all Herrmann and his colleagues. (Herrmann 1979; Herrmann and Deutsch 1976; Herrmann and Laucht 1977). He follows Olson and views first the alternatives for naming which avoid confusion, but he adds that the adequate choice of the correct or fitting word is dependent on the flexibility of the speaker in naming things, which is in turn specific to the personality. A word is fitting not only when it refers unequivocally to what the speaker wants to convey to the listener; the fittingness of a word depends also on its adequacy in the social context in which the utterance is produced. The I-marker

Father—owns—much—money

may in one social situation be lexicalized to

(7.3) My old man is rolling in dough,

in a different situation to

(7.4) Father is rather well-to-do.

Herrmann has shown that if the "naming flexibility" of a speaker is high, he will, for example, choose a name from the lower level of vocabulary if the social distance between himself and the listener is short and if the emotional relevance of the object to be named is large for the speaker. A less flexible speaker will not be able to vary his vocabulary according to the social-psychological aspects of the situation.

The decision how verbally to encode an object referred to in the utterance is, of course, subject not only to social criteria, and/or the naming flexibility of the speaker. Pursuing Olson's initiative, Herrmann has found in his investigations that in distinguishing one object from similar ones, those discriminating features are used which most easily and safely guarantee that the listener attends to the object meant by the speaker; the speaker verbalizes (only) those components which, *pars pro toto*, guide the listener's comprehension process to where the speaker wants it to be (cf. Herrmann 1979).

To return to Schlesinger's model: If, as we have just seen, a specific group of I-markers can be realized, *via* qualitatively different realization rules as quite different utterances, then Schlesinger needs some factor to determine whether the present I-marker should be realized by the realization rules *a, b, c* or by the rules *e, f, g*. Schlesinger sees this factor in *communicative considerations*. They direct the choice of the realization rules. This component thus not only has an effect on the lexicalization of the protoverbal elements but is also responsible for decisions which choose among utterances such as

(7.5) The logs were cut up with an axe.
(7.6) There were logs that were cut up with the axe.
(7.7) The axe cut up the logs.
(7.8) It was the axe with which the logs were cut up.

Thus the focus of the utterance is established here (what is in the foreground), the presuppositions are taken into account by making connections to what has already been said, and so on.

Figure 6 shows what the model looks like.

The model still requires completion on two sides. So far it ends with a program for an utterance but does not contain any more about how this program will actually be put into language sounds, that is, how it will be articulated. Schlesinger does not want to say anything about this because it is of no interest to him. Much more important and more interesting is the other side which is still missing. Are the I-markers the beginning, or can we and must we consider, within the framework of the model, where they come from and how they are developed?

It should be clear that with this question we have arrived at an important point. The I-markers are, as we heard, of a semantic nature, that is, they are already very close to language. Their elements are indeed not words, but protoverbal concepts; their relations assume a categorization (example: owner/property). Is there a nonlanguage level before or beneath this level? If yes, how can we imagine it?

With this question we touch on an old problem, the relationship of thinking and speaking. To what extent is thinking dependent on language? There has been a long and in no way conclusive discussion on this point. Rather than go into it here,

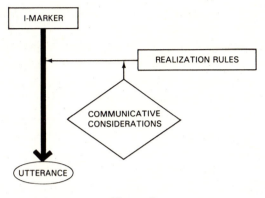

Figure 6

we will merely indicate the range of this discussion by highlighting two extreme positions which have been taken.

The first is rather well known everywhere under the key words *linguistic relativity hypothesis* or Whorf hypothesis (1956). Whorf, a student of American Indian languages, had extreme difficulties in finding translation equivalents in these languages for concepts used in the European languages. One of the languages studied makes no clear distinction between nouns and verbs, others have no clear-cut present, past, and future tense, the Navajo equivalents for "to pick up" or "to hold in the hand" require different forms depending upon the nature of the object being handled. The Eskimo has 18 different names for falling, blowing, wet . . . snow, but *no* unitary term for snow. So Whorf asks, does the world look different to the Eskimo than it does to us? For the Eskimo, what melts in spring is not the same thing (snow) that fell during winter. For Whorf every language determines and controls the possibilities which are available to the speaker of this language for *thinking about the world.* For instance, we understand miserliness as a real, actual, and enduring trait of a person because it is a noun and nouns have something like a lasting substantial character. Miserliness is also there, albeit hidden, even when its possessor is not acting miserly at the moment. Our conception of miserliness is formed by the fact that in our language this trait is represented as a noun. Or: because we have the word *weed* in our language, we see the world around us perhaps differently from people who cannot differentiate on the basis of their language between plants (useful ones) and weeds. There are indications resulting from experiments for the fact that one can *perceive* or recall certain colors better when there is a precise name for them. For Whorf, man's view of the world and his thoughts about the world are shaped and restricted by the words (and word classes) which are placed at his disposal by the particular language he speaks. There is no clear-cut division between thinking and speaking.

Opposed to this view is the one that refers back to a situation which we have all experienced, in which we in fact "know what we mean, but just can't find the right words to express it." Here, contrary to Whorf, a sharp division is made between nonlanguage thinking on the one hand (that is, a nonverbal code form, which is today sometimes called "mentalese") and *language* or verbal coding of thoughts.[5]

Schlesinger's view is close to this second position. He thinks there are nonlanguage levels underneath the level of the I-markers, those of the cognitive structure. The *cognitive structure* is prelinguistic and directs the construction of an I-marker. He gives three reasons for this postulate of a separate nonlanguage basic level:

1. Usually only a part of what is seen, known, or thought is formulated in language. We say, "There comes a car," even though we simultaneously perceive that the car is a red Volkswagen. This choice must be made *before* the I-marker component in Schlesinger's model because he has postulated for this component that all that is contained in it must be linguistically, that is, for the content of the utterance, relevant and must appear there.

2. We often change what we want to say in the middle of a running utterance. How can we imagine this within Schlesinger's model? There are two possibilities: (a) It can happen because different realization rules come between the I-marker and the ut-

---

[5]Most linguists advocate a sharp division of this kind because they believe that in this way they could conceptualize a process of production and comprehension "as such," free from all psychological requirements and from intrusions or interferences by factors which are outside of linguistics proper.

terance (e.g., a different choice of words). Then the existing I-marker which is behind the utterance is not changed; a relatively close paraphrase occurs. Instead of

(7.9) One engine is working on this plane

one might say

(7.10) One motor is o.k. on this aircraft.

(b) Or the speaker can change from one I-marker to another. If, for example, someone says

(7.9) One engine is working on this airplane

he could also say instead

(7.11) Three engines are not working on this airplane.

He *could* say this *if* there are two I-markers which are not identical but are based on the common cognitive structure: four-engine airplane with three engines not working. Here we find a further paraphrase (7.11) which is farther away from (7.9) than is (7.10).

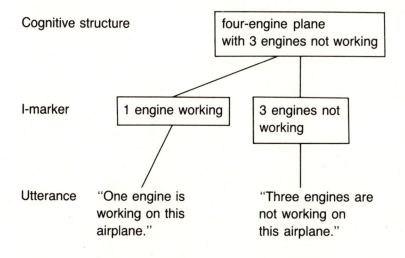

As we can see, Schlesinger concludes from the fact of paraphrases differing in distance that he must assume yet another level below the level of the I-marker, that of cognitive structure.

3. A third reason which speaks for a differentiation between I-

markers and cognitive structures: we often feel that we are having difficulties putting a thought into language. These difficulties can be of different kinds. If they are very general and themselves difficult to formulate, then they can probably be localized in the genesis of the I-marker out of the cognitive structure (Schlesinger calls this *coagulation*). A different kind of difficulty occurs when I know what I want to say, but the fitting word does not occur to me. This tip-of-the-tongue phenomenon occurs in lexicalization, that is, in the process of realizing the I-marker as an utterance.

About coagulation, that is, about the choice or construction of one I-marker out of the several possible I-markers inherent in a given cognitive structure, little is said in Schlesinger's model.

Thus, in its final form, Schlesinger's model of utterance production describes a two-step process (Figure 7). Cognitive structures develop one or more I-markers by means of coagulation controlled by an I-marker selector. The I-markers, which contain the meaning of the utterance to be produced, are transformed, by the application of realization rules (controlled by cognitive considerations), into an utterance program which is the immediate basis for articulation.

The Genesis of Sentences

With this, our presentation of the Schlesinger model is complete.[6] When we now turn to empirical investigations of utterance production, we will certainly not be successful, in each case, in localizing the particular investigations at a specific point of Schlesinger's model; these investigations are conceived in other and often very different theoretical languages. We will attempt, however, at least occasionally, to give the approximate location in a model to which the findings are relevant.

---

[6]Some aspects of this model correspond to ideas prevalent in Russian psychology of language. There the development of an utterance is described as proceeding from a stage of "inner programming" *via* "inner speech" to the stage of "outer language" or "outer speech." Inner speech is here conceived—and this goes far beyond Schlesinger—as the activation of the motor aspects of words.

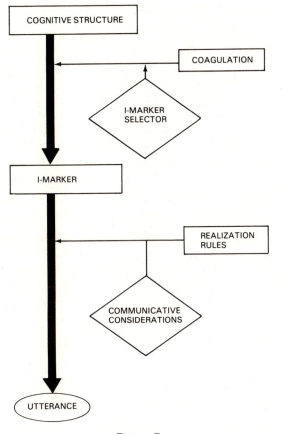

Figure 7

Let us begin with what Schlesinger calls the coagulation of a cognitive structure into an I-marker, that is, the selection of that about which one is going to speak, out of what one thinks, perceives, and feels. This can follow a broad prestructuring which is already available. The speaker thus differentiates, apparently, with respect to what seems worth reporting. In what way are these differences determined?

A preliminary answer might be: according to the phenomenal laws of perception. Whatever is chosen out of the cognitive structure—out of what is perceived—as the basis of the utterance usually corresponds to what we call the *figure in front of a ground* in the psychology of perception. When there is a cup on a table and we are to describe it, we will say

(7.12) A cup is on the table

but not

(7.13) A table is under the cup.[7]

The perceptual organization of what we see contains in and of itself determinants of the form of the verbal account a speaker is going to produce about that visual scene. Gestalt psychology has collected a wide range of perceptual principles which take effect here; Flores d'Arcais (1973 and in Levelt and d'Arcais 1978) has followed the traces left by these principles in the verbal utterances which describe these perceptions:

- It is easier (takes less time) to begin a sentence by starting with a word referring to the larger rather than to the smaller of two objects.
- It is easier to produce an active sentence when the surface object of the sentence refers to an object on the left of the scene.
- It takes less time to start uttering a sentence describing an event in which the direction of the action is from left to right than *vice versa.*

In another experiment, his subjects were shown pictures which were to be described by simple sentences, for example, a picture in which a man was carrying either a large suitcase or a small bag. When the subjects produced active sentences, the agent of the visible action became the subject of the sentence:

(7.14) A man is carrying a trunk

or

(7.15) A man is carrying a bag

---

[7]It is interesting to speculate what perceptual (or other) conditions would induce a speaker to produce 7.13.

were produced with about equal frequency. If, however, the subjects were asked to produce passive sentences,

(7.16) A trunk is being carried by a man

was produced much more frequently than

(7.17) A bag is being carried by a man.

In the investigations of Flores d'Arcais, a number of different perceptual factors: size, direction, animateness, for instance, influence the form of the utterance produced, and this influence interacts with the linguistic constraints imposed on the speaker (whether he is instructed to produce an active or a passive sentence).

The figure/ground dynamics and similar vectors we have just found to be inherent in verbal utterances describing visual scenes are also at work when we speak not about visible objects but about happenings. (The stream of consciousness of a speaker has its figure/ground relations, too.) Let us take for this another example, the utterance

(7.18) First the boy was hanging around; then he ran away.

In planning and executing this utterance, the speaker also had to organize what was to go into that utterance and in what form and sequence. He had to screen what he reports about the events, choose variable screen sizes, summarize what is similar, and contrast it to what is different: hanging around versus running away. "Hanging around" is here a whole class of movements and situations, naturally, just as "running away" characterizes a class. On the way from the cognitive structure to the basis of the utterance (the I-marker) a process of choice and a classifying summary (coagulation) takes place whereby the organization into figure and ground plays an important role. What becomes the figure and thereby the candidate for being taken into the I-marker and then into the utterance is, however, determined not only by perceptual dynamics, but also to a rather large degree by the speaker's effort to help the listener connect the "new" information with what he already knows or is supposed to assume. Osgood has given some fine examples of these dynamics in a very well known essay

(1971), "Where Do Sentences Come From?" In an experiment he shows his subjects a few simple situations and gives them the task of describing them in such a way that a six-year-old who is standing outside the door would know what is happening.

First situation: the investigator is holding a small black rubber ball in his hand. The subject describes this accordingly:

(7.19) The man is holding a black ball.[8]

In the second situation, which follows immediately, the same ball is lying on the table. The subjects say:

(7.20) The ball is on the table.

To begin with, let us look only at the article. We see that in the first situation, where *ball* first occurs, it is an indefinite article, whereas in the second this is exchanged for the definite article; apparently the acquaintance with the object is important here. Use of the definite article signals the listener that "this refers to something you have already heard about." This, however, is obviously not the whole story; why is the *table* referred to with the definite article when it is mentioned for the first time: Does the speaker uttering (7.20) try to link it up not with his first utterance (7.19), but with the cognitive structure basic to it? The table, although unmentioned, has always been visible in the room.

Third situation: a red ball is lying on the table. The subjects say:

(7.21) A red ball is on the table

or

(7.22) The ball on the table is (now) red.

Let us again notice the kind of article: if the ball is viewed as a new one, then the indefinite article is used; if the situation is, however, so conceived that the ball (just mentioned) "only" changed its color, then one can use the definite article.

---

[8]Osgood's subjects are instructed to refer to the experimenter always as "the man."

Fourth situation: the ball rolls across the table. The subjects say:

(7.23) The ball is rolling across the table

but not

(7.24) Across the table the ball is now rolling

even though the table has already been present more often than the ball; the ball is the figure because it moves, and so it is mentioned first.

In this first demonstration of movement practically nothing is ever said about the speed of rolling; this happens in a following instance, however, very frequently, *if* the speed is different from the first time: something like a norm of expectation has been established in the speaker; what deviates from the ground of the expectation is put into language as the figure. The speaker starts from a common frame of expectation (and the listener expects him to do this).

Our utterances are, as we see, formed to a certain degree by the *frame* in which they are embedded. As Neisser puts it:

> Sentences involve extended anticipations in their own right. . . . Like plans for looking, they are rarely specific in advance. We "know what we are going to say" before saying it, but only in the rather general way that we know what we are going to see before seeing it. (1976: 170)

Being a holistic schema, a frame creates expectations, in the speaker and conversely in the listener, about what is to come next once this whole frame has been activated.

The frame, or the expectation of the speaker, helps determine not only *what* will be included cognitively and what proceeds from the cognitive structure to the utterance, but also (our next example) *how* the utterance is constructed. This construction can be manipulated by changing what we might call the center of gravity of such a frame. Prentice (1967) gave her subjects the task of describing pictures in a short sentence. They could see a small scene in the picture which was describable by means of an agent–predicate–object sentence. Before the picture to be described was presented, another was shown briefly which consisted of either the agent or the object of the scene from the main picture. If the agent was shown beforehand, then the word sequence agent–object was used in the sentence produced more frequently than the sequence object–agent; the situation was reversed if the object was shown beforehand.

In a similar experiment Tannenbaum and Williams (1968), by means of a few sentences, directed the attention of their subjects either to the agent or to the object in a picture which was viewed afterwards and then required the subjects to describe the picture in either an active or a passive sentence. Response time was measured up to the beginning of the utterance. There is a large difference in this response lag between the two kinds of sentences when the attention is turned to the agent, but only a minimal difference when the subject's attention had been focused on the object of the action shown. As we see, the verbal description of a perceived scene varies with how the speaker is "tuned" for processing the visual scene. The tuning is brought about by some sentences the speaker hears or a picture he sees beforehand, and it has its effects, on the other hand, on the utterance produced by the speaker. Speech production is part of an ongoing, integrated activity.

What "Springs Out"?

A figure stands out from the ground; the utterance produced is centered on "what leaps out" for some reason. In this connection, the concept of *salience* is frequently used today; we will now discuss what is considered one of the main effects of salience: the order of the surface constituents in an utterance, and the causes and effects of deviations from the (usual) order.

Osgood (1980) mentions several factors of salience. The first is the *natural* organization of our cognitions according to figure before ground, moving above stationary, large before small, animate before inanimate. This is based on perception (and would thus be located in Schlesinger's model below the level of the I-markers) and corresponds to a natural ordering of the constituents of an utterance: agent before action, action before object: S–

V–O. This sequence is, at the same time, a rank order of salience: the agent (usually represented by the subject) is the most salient constituent of a sentence.

Osgood goes one step further: the more salient a constituent of a particular utterance for a particular speaker, the further to the left will it be located. "Unnatural" sequences (deviations from the usual S–V–O ordering) will, as we see, result from additional salience factors. One of the salience factors possibly competing with the natural ones is *vividness*, that is, for Osgood, the affective loadings[9] of the words to be used in the utterance: the higher the E, P, or A loadings of the words, the more likely they are to be located early in the utterance.

If grammar or convention or other factors prohibit early production, the component having high salience will be *stressed*. For example, when we are talking about the adventures of Mary, our next sentence may take the form

(7.25) Saturday morning, while dusting the hall, she saw a vám-
     pire.

Assuming the early position of "Saturday morning" and so on is needed for connection with the information given in previous parts of the text, the highly vivid (and therefore highly salient) word "vampire" receives the major stress of the sentence.

Whereas vividness is an intrinsic property of the words used, *motivation* of the speaker is a type of salience that is *attributed* to the speaker as a result of his personal interest, his involvement, and the like.

And a third factor competing, eventually, with the natural order of constituents is *topicality*. The cognitive entities which constitute the theme or topic of, say, a conversation, or which are in the center of my perceptual activities will tend to be localized

---

[9]See our previous discussion of Osgood's theory of the affective meaning of words. [Hörmann cites in his (1979): 168–169 the following text from J. Stenzel: "'Fundamental meaning' often lies in the emotional stratum which maintains a certain tension between the conceptual parts. From the emotional stratum different meanings derive a more precise conceptual content. But orienting impulse or emotive gesture is primary."—Ed.]

early in the utterance to be produced: if I see from the window my own little dog assailed by a big dog, the utterance

(7.26) That ugly mutt belongs to the Smiths down the street

is much more probable than

(7.27) The Smiths down the street own that ugly mutt.

As we see, the salience of the cognitions going into an utterance form a resultant dynamic of sometimes converging, sometimes competing, forces. The effects of this dynamic interplay are reflected in the utterance by word order on the one hand, by the allocation of major and minor stress on the other, and, presumably, by a special pattern of pauses as well.

For Osgood, the order of the constituents in an utterance is determined by syntax and salience, and salience is, for him, mainly (emotional) importance. Determination of the order in which the constituents are going to appear in an utterance can be seen, however, under a slightly different aspect. The beliefs, attitudes and communicative intentions of the speaker play an important role. Clark and Haviland (1977) discussed what they call a *given–new contract* tacitly assumed to be valid between speaker and listener. Take, for instance, Ann trying to tell Ed she has just seen John hit Bill. She will do so in different ways

(7.28) John hit BILL.
(7.29) Bill was hit by JOHN.
(7.30) It was JOHN who hit Bill.
(7.31) John HIT Bill.   (etc.)

Each of these sentences expresses, linguistically, the same proposition, but Ann would use (7.28) when she assumed that the listener, Ed, already knew that John had hit somebody. She would use (7.29) or (7.30) when she assumed that the listener already knew that Bill had been hit by somebody.

As we see, (7.29) and (7.30) are used in exactly the same way, but the compliance with the given–new contract is implemented by different means: stress, word order, using a cleft sentence.

In honoring this given–new contract, in "decoding" the different salience signals, the listener can process the input utterance to that point in his stream of consciousness which the speaker intends, and he is most likely to use this utterance in the way the speaker wants him to use it.

Ertel's Investigations

Sequence of the constituents and emphasis are, however, not the only effects of the speaker's affective predilections, of the "objective" structuring of his perception, and of his allegiance to the given—new contract. The whole structure of the utterance reflects the cognitive and emotional position the speaker takes in relation to the utterance. Ertel (1977) points this out in an approach which is influenced by Gestalt psychology. His argument runs as follows: For the sentence

(7.32) Paul is meeting Mary

an asymmetrical structure is usually assumed, either in the form of a tree diagram or in a division, following Fillmore, into agent and patient.

Both are actually inappropriate here, because when Paul meets Mary, then Mary also meets Paul to the same degree; both are agent and patient in the same way. We should thus ask what is really responsible for the speaker's using (7.32) or

(7.33) Mary is meeting Paul.

Ertel's answer: a sentence is the result of an active mental construction which is accomplished in the phenomenal field of the speaker. The speaker's ego also belongs to this phenomenal field, even if it does not appear in the sentence itself. In sentence (7.32) Paul is mentioned at the beginning (Paul is the grammatical subject), because Paul is closer to the speaker's ego than Mary. If the opposite were the case, then the utterance would take the form of (7.33). If the ego were the same distance from both, the sentence would be

(7.34) Paul and Mary are meeting.

What is at work here is a basic psychic operation which Ertel calls *nominal seizing:* the speaker seizes one and only one of the cognitive units which are available candidates for the utterance and makes it the primary point of orientation of the sentence which is to be constructed. Usually the noun representing this orientation point is in the position of the sentence subject. This noun becomes the *point nearest to the ego.*

What evidence can Ertel give for this thesis? He gives his subjects pictures in which there are several people, some in front of and some behind a fence, and each of whom has a name (Figure 8). The speaker who is most in the foreground says the sentence (in a balloon as in the comics), for example

(7.35) I like the girl who is standing in front of the fence

or

(7.36) Hans likes the girl who is standing in front of the fence.

Figure 8

The subject is to tell which girl the sentence is referring to. It was shown that for sentence (7.35) Ann was always mentioned, whereas for sentence (7.36) Mary was chosen as often as Ann. If the ego and the speaker coincide, then the identification is easier and less ambiguous than when the speaker is talking about someone else (Hans).

Almost all the investigations of word-sequence factors in sentences so far mentioned share a tacit assumption: that the speaker who determines the sequence of the articulation no longer has much freedom in this phase. He can perhaps decide between Paul meeting Mary or Mary meeting Paul, but he must be happy with what is already prepared for the utterance, so to speak. This corresponds exactly to Schlesinger's postulate for I-markers: everything is determined in them that will be expressed in language afterwards. The speaker can rearrange things slightly, but nothing more.

This is not the whole picture, certainly. Take, for instance, those basic *frames* we have already talked about. The effects of these structures are not restricted to constituent sequence or stress; they have an influence also on the choice of lexical realizations going into the utterance. The frame of commercial transaction (containing "buy," "sell," "money," "pay," "cost," "property," etc. and the relations connecting these terms) is brought into use by the speaker with a particular "direction":

(7.37) (a) He sold her the car for $500.
     (b) She bought the car for $500.
     (c) The car cost her $500.

In every case, we move within that frame (known to the speaker and the listener) to which belongs, for example, the knowledge that the exchange of goods for money implies a change in ownership. But by turning the frame to a particular perspective, the speaker presents the listener with different points of view far beyond the mere information about the fact of the transaction.[10]

In the last few pages we have discussed some of the structural

---

[10]Schlesinger would probably maintain that the choice between (a), (b), and (c) is controlled by what he calls communicative considerations and that all three sentences come from one and the same I-marker. This is in my opinion not correct: the differences already exist in the cognitive structures.

factors determining the form of the utterance to be produced. While doing so, we have of course been aware that there are still other large and important sets of factors of that kind: the rules of syntax, of morphology, and of phonology. The effects of these factors are "visible" in each and every well-formed and well-pronounced utterance. What we now must discuss is *how* and *when* these different factors become operative in the temporal course of the production of the utterance.

It is important to see that this question leads beyond the scope of a production model like Schlesinger's. Schlesinger merely points out that factors like lexicalization rules and rules of agreement ought to be considered but says nothing about how and when such rules take effect.

The first problem we encounter along this path is a methodological one: how are we to learn which parts of the plan are realized first? How to discover which parts of the utterance are produced in the same stage, which determined early, which late, that is, only milliseconds before they are pronounced? There is evidence for the fact that planning (or realizing a plan) in a dialogue differs from planning (or realizing a plan) in a monologue (see Beattie 1978, 1979). The speaker often averts his gaze during planning periods to reduce potential interference between such cognitive planning and the processing of incoming visual information.

If we want to go beyond this rather unspecific observation, we need indicators for the important points in the temporal course of producing an utterance. There are mainly three such indicators: pauses, slips of the tongue, and accompanying gestures.[11]

Pauses, Slips, and Gestures

Let us begin with the question: from the pauses that a speaker makes what can we find out about the process of production in language utterance?

[11]The analysis of different types of gestures as indicators of the temporal course of planning and executing verbal utterances is of relatively recent origin. We will therefore discuss mainly the other two indicators. Readers interested in this analysis of gestures are referred to Butterworth and Beattie (1978) and to McNeill (1979).

First, it is interesting to note that pauses take up almost half of total speech time and that the speed of speech is varied mainly by means of pauses, rather than by changes in the speed of articulation. Generally, one distinguishes between unfilled and filled pauses (uh . . .); the latter seem also to be connected more with national than with linguistic habits in a narrower sense, because they seem to be more frequent for Americans, for example, than for Englishmen.

Now as to pauses serving as indicators of segmentations in the production of an utterance: if a new thought appears within a chain of utterances, the speaker makes a pause before pronouncing it, or pronounces it more slowly. Goldman-Eisler (1968), who carried out important experiments in this field, interpreted this as an indication of the fact that these points are especially important for planning or for carrying out a plan. They are points at which information is generated. Such planning pauses very often occur at grammatical border lines, for example, between the noun and the verb phrase of a sentence or between the verb and the object ("the shoemaker cut . . . the leather to fit").

We will not go into the details of "pausology," as O'Connell (1980) calls this subdiscipline of the psychology of language but just mention two interesting investigations. Grosjean (1980) found that pausing is affected both by the relative importance of constituent breaks and by the relative length of the constituents. When these are of unequal length, speakers will displace the pause to a point midway between the beginning of the first constituent and the end of the second if at that point there occurs an important syntactic boundary. Thus the speaker tries to obey two (sometimes conflicting) needs: to respect the linguistic structure of the utterance and to balance the length of the constituents in the output.

In an investigation which can be placed somewhere between psycholinguistics proper and patholinguistics Klatt (1980) found that the length of pauses between words in a sentence read by aphasic subjects[12] is dependent upon the grammatical complex-

---

[12]Reading aloud is, of course, not equivalent to free production of utterances, and aphasic subjects are not normal subjects. But, on the other hand, it may be that aphasic subjects, because they have much more difficulty in speaking, show the

ity of the following word; grammatical complexity is here the number of "empty slots" a verb opens up in its vicinity (see Chapter 2). The more of these valences a certain grammatical category has, the more information must be retrieved from memory and the more time is required before articulation. A surprise in this investigation was the fact that the longest pause was made in general before the second article.[13] Klatt interprets this as a hesitation not *before* the second article but *after* the verb; the subject is still busy monitoring what he has just pronounced.

If this is correct, the simple interpretation (pauses indicate points at which information is generated) is no longer tenable: pauses may also be caused not in the line of production but by the subsequent process of controlling production.

Filled pauses frequently occur before the first content word of a phrase: the speaker has presumably already planned to a high degree the form of the utterance but cannot find the fitting word; we remember what was said in Schlesinger's model at that point. So we find

(7.38) The . . . uh . . . uncle of my sister-in-law.

The pause is (at least in the United States) filled probably as a paralinguistic signal to the listener that the speaker will continue immediately.

Distribution and length of pauses are taken as indications of the temporal pattern of the utterance to be produced. In a similar way, the distribution of stressed and unstressed syllables tells us something about the production of the utterance. As we learned earlier, stress, together with or *in lieu* of word order, has the function of guiding the listener's attention to what is given and what is new information. For van der Geest (1980), stress, gesturing, and probably all other nonverbal signals accompanying speech are restricted to the comment part or the psychological predicate of the message. He assumes, therefore, that the nonver-

---

effects of structuring processes which go unnoticed in the highly automatic speech of normal subjects.

[13]Klatt had his subjects read sentences of this general form: The lanky farmer wore the sloppy clothes.

bal aspects precede the verbal aspects of sentence production in one way or another. According to Halliday (1967), "tone groups" (larger units containing several phonemes and characterized by a unitary course of intonation) are signals for the "mood" of the speaker, that is, his attitude toward the content of what he says; in this sense, too, there is an affirmative, an interrogative, an imperative . . . mood.

As we see, prosody, intonation, and stress form a system comprising several layers or levels. An analysis of these structures might therefore reveal something about which parts of an utterance are determined on the same level (in the same phase) of planning or converting the plan into the "reality" of spoken utterance.

As Martin (1972) finds in his experimental investigations, the elements to be stressed are probably *planned* before those not to be stressed; thus at a certain stage a *rhythmical* plan exists for the sentence which is to be spoken, a plan which predicts the distances (in time) between the units which are to be produced.[14] What are these units of production, these prearticulation units which exist, for a fleeting moment of time, during the emergence of the utterance? We will come back to this question after discussing the second means of analyzing the time sequence of production: slips of the tongue.

Errors in language are known to all of us; especially well known in English are spoonerisms, named after the Reverend William A. Spooner, an Oxford don, whose pronouncements included the beautiful:

(7.39) It is easier for a camel to go through the knee of an idol (the eye of a needle). . . .

The whole area of such research is sometimes called haplology. We will analyse a sentence here as an example. The teacher comes into the room and says,

(7.40) When I come in through the window, you must close those doors.

[14]In Russian psychology of language the motor aspects of these rhythmical plans are emphasized.

What happened here? We can first say that the speaker mixed up "doors" and "window," saying "window" where "doors" was intended. But what does "intended" mean? There must have been a plan as a basis of the utterance which had determined at a particular stage at which point a noun was to occur, without having yet chosen what noun. Since, on the other hand, the planning of the utterance cannot have a purely syntactic basis—the speaker certainly has an idea of the content of the utterance he is going to produce—the error must have occurred in the integration of the syntactic plan with the semantic one. (Here we may recall Schlesinger's lexicalization rules, although these do *not* fit into an explanation of our example.) Syntactic planning seems to result in a structured sequence of *slots*, as it were, which are filled in lexically in a later phase of the plan's completion.

The analysis of this kind of slip of the tongue shows something else, too (see mainly Fromkin 1971 and 1973). In exchanges (doors, window), positions are almost without exception exchanged which should receive similar stress; an exchange of a stressed for an unstressed syllable rarely occurs. Above all, the total contour of intonation of the entire utterance remains the same. The intonation contour of the utterance, that is, the temporal fixation of the main and secondary stresses and of the tone group seems to be established at a relatively early stage of the genesis of the sentence. (This intonation contour plays an especially important role for the understanding of sentences.)

The lexicalization occurs, as we have said, after the establishment of the sequence of the elements. But this must be corrected. The old teacher said

(7.40) When I come in *through the window*, you must close *those doors.*

Thus not only *slots* for the nouns must be established syntactically at an early stage, but also the fact that the first noun is to be singular, the second plural. This is *not* exchanged along with the nouns in the error, even though this room only had one door but many windows.[15]

---

[15]In the German original it is still more complicated. In "Wenn ich zum Fenster hereinkomme," the ending of *zum* agrees with *Fenster* but would not agree with

We see that the realization of the plan of the utterance obviously goes through several phases or stages, with different kinds of words materializing at different points along that temporal course.

Thus Fromkin arrives at the following four-step model of the planning of an utterance:

1. The syntactic outline of the constituents is established as word slots with a supersegmental pattern of stress.
2. The nouns, verbs, adjectives, and so forth are chosen and put into the fitting slots.
3. The function words are placed in the slots and given the appropriate affixes.
4. The exact phonetic form is established, as is the speed of pronunciation.

This model is quite different from Schlesinger's; the basic cognitive structure is missing, but the syntactic planning is presented in a differentiated manner instead. Mistakes, it must be added, can occur at different stages; the well-known Freudian slip can usually be understood on the level of lexicalization: the "position" in the lexicon is correct, but then a word is chosen which differs from the correct one in one feature—"love" instead of "hate," for example.

Problems and Questions

So far, all the production models and theories we have discussed have shared a (common) tacit assumption: what the speaker produces is sequences of words. It may start with an I-marker containing protoverbal elements, but the unit of analysis of the final product is the word. Some years ago a slightly different approach was presented by McNeill (1979). Here the meaning unit (called the *syntagma*) is also the unit of production and articulation.

Tür. That is, the final form of the preposition can have been determined only *after* the (wrong) noun was inserted.

> The organization of utterances apparently takes the following form.
> There is a structure of concepts and relations that corresponds to the
> speaker's meaning. This structure falls into one or another gener-
> alized category of ideas, such as the idea of event, action, state, loca-
> tion, property, entity, or person. The speaker organizes and moves
> from one of these generalized ideas to another, for example, from the
> idea of an event to the idea of a location, and in so doing is guided in
> coordinating the articulation of speech output. The unit of produc-
> tion . . . is based on the structure of concepts, and within this con-
> ceptual structure there are processes for coordinating speech output.
> (1979: 241)

These syntagmata are units of meaning pronounced as single
outputs. The syntagma *may* coincide with one of the usual linguistic units (phrase, sentence), but what is important is that it
is *a functional* unit for the articulation of a meaningful unit. For
McNeill, part of the meaning of any utterance can be represented
on a sensory-motor level, and this level is fundamental for the
programming of the utterance. Sensory-motor representations
are simultaneously part of meaning and part of action.

If this conception is heuristically useful, a careful analysis of
the pronunciation of an utterance should reveal that it is structured according to the syntagmata it contains. McNeill finds, in
an empirical analysis of two-person conversation, that nearly all
phonemic clauses—sequences of phonemes bounded by silence
and/or terminal contours and containing only one primary
stress—coincide to a very high percentage with the underlying
sensory-motor ideas. That is, pauses, a unitary intonation contour, restriction to one primary stress, and rather often—as
McNeill adds—the precise temporal course of an accompanying
gesticulation all correlate with the meaning and with the articulation units in production.

McNeill does not say much about how grammatical (syntactic) determinants cooperate with these semantic ones. After all,
then, the rather disquieting conclusion we have to draw from the
foregoing discussion of different explanations or models of utterance production is this: we seem to be equipped with *two* production systems—one operating more in the domain of syntax, the

other more in the domain of intonation.[16] It is not clear, precisely, how meaning enters the picture (McNeill's statements concern only *categories* of meaning, for example, events or locations, but not what events or what location), and it is not clear how these two production systems converge in determining the actual articulatory program of the speaker.

In a similar way, Chafe (1980) says that because

> a speaker does not follow a clear, well traveled path, but must find his way through territory not traversed before, where pauses, changes of direction, and retracing of steps are quite to be expected (170)

utterances therefore resemble what William James as early as 1890 called a series of flights and perchings. Spontaneous speech is produced in well-defined spurts, because the focusing of consciousness is a sequence of discrete snapshots rather than a continuous movie film. These spurts are, according to Chafe,

> slightly less than 2 seconds in mean duration, and contain a mean of about 5 words. They tend to be single clauses syntactically. . . . They usually exhibit a "clause-final" intonation contour. I hypothesize that these spurts of language are expressions of underlying perchings of consciousness. (171)[17]

Hesitations in speech production may point to the speaker's reaching a new focus of consciousness, or to a difficulty in finding the best way to verbalize a focus. Foci of consciousness, again, cluster together to form larger units which are verbalized as sentences.

There is yet another unsolved problem in theorizing about speech production. Most production models assume tacitly that the whole utterance is to be produced from scratch. For Schlesinger, for instance, each and every utterance starts by coagulating a cognitive structure to one or more I-markers, and so on. In fact, however, as Fillmore says,

---

[16]The juxtaposition of these incomparable domains points out how thoroughly we are at a loss to find one satisfactory approach.

[17]Interestingly enough, the linguist Chafe here has to suggest to *psycho*linguists that they should pay more attention to consciousness.

an enormously large amount of natural language is formulaic, automatic and rehearsed, rather than propositional, creative, or freely
generated. (1976: 9)

Whole sentences and still more frequently parts of sentences are
pronounced which are *not* planned, constructed, and assembled
anew but are taken as a whole from some kind of store. What kind
of store is this? It is certainly not what we have called the "lexicon" of the language user. How is it organized? What are the
retrieval principles according to which it works?

This using of prefabricated (parts of) utterances is sometimes, especially in neurological literature on aphasia, discussed
under the heading of "automaticity of speech." We should, however, be aware of the fact that this term does not explain anything.
How are we to conceptualize the interaction between and convergence of what is freshly produced and what is more or less
"automatically" transferred from a store of half-finished spare
parts?

Kempen (1977) offers an interesting approach to this problem. For him, the production of utterances has three aspects
which he calls conceptualizing, formulating, and speaking. He
maintains that very frequently the conceptualization process is
strongly dependent upon the formulation process; conventional
models, like Schlesinger's, discuss only the inverse direction. Instances indicating the importance of this dependence of content
upon formulation are cases of content revision in the midst of
planning or pronouncing an utterance: the speaker notices a mismatch between conceptual intention and syntactic possibilities
and resolves the mismatch by revising the content for the remain-
ing part of the utterance. The determination of what finally comes
out as the utterance has been taken over, as it were, by what
Kempen calls a *syntactic construction.* This is a pair consisting of
a conceptual pattern and a syntactic frame. The conceptual pattern is a combination of relationships (e.g., agent, object, instrument) and concepts; the syntactic frame expresses the conceptual
pattern belonging to it: noun—finite verb—noun, for example, expresses in English the conceptual pattern agent—action—object.
There are, for Kempen, two probable sources of syntactic con-

structions: (a) repetitive speech situations and (b) situational scripts. In both cases, the speaker anticipates what he is going to say and which formulations he will use. So it can happen that the syntactic frame becomes the leading part of the whole syntactic construction and, with this, the main factor of the utterance.

Kempen's model explains the inclusion of one kind of "prefabricated" parts in an utterance, that of syntactic frames. It is highly probable that there are other sources of prefabricated parts: semantic relations taken over from the speaker's own previous utterances or from utterances he has heard recently from other people, the melody of an utterance still lingering in memory, and the like. The interplay between genuinely new productions and these more or less "revised editions" of whole old utterances is still far from clear. It is here, however, that some of the most important applications of the psychology of language are involved: teaching an aphasic patient to recover his propositional speech from some automatic relics, explaining the processes going on in simultaneous translation, or teaching a foreign language so that it will be more or less automatically available. The possibilities multiply themselves.

CHAPTER **8**

Understanding Speech, Understanding Speakers

It is thus important for the understanding of the existence and development of language to state clearly which factors and processes make it possible for us to understand language at all, and to investigate in what way these factors gain significance for the formation of language.

P. Wegener

Our capacity to endow language with meaning must be recognized as a particular instance of our sense-giving powers. We must realize that to use language is a performance of the same kind as our integration of visual clues for perceiving an object, or as the viewing of a stereo picture, or our integration of muscular contractions in walking or driving a motor car, or as the conducting of a game of chess—all of which are performed by relying on our subsidiary awareness of some things for the purpose of attending focally to a matter on which they bear. These are exercises of an integrative power which can comprehend a triad in which the person *A* sees a *B* as bearing on a *C*, or else uses a *B* for

239

the purpose C, and these integrations can be seen to be essentially tacit.

M. Polanyi

Understanding is the inward sign of the potential for reacting appropriately to what we see or hear.

J. Deese

Understanding: Beginnings and Endings

A suitable introduction to the problems of understanding language is the report of the child psychologist Meumann, which we have already mentioned briefly in Chapter 3. The father with his small boy in his arms goes to the window and asks—in German—"Where is the window?" The child points to the window and says, "Da!" (there!). Meumann senior then asks: "Où est la fenêtre?" and then in English, "Where is the window?" Both times the child points to the window and says, "Da!" And when the father finally asks (again in German), "Where is the door?" the child points to the window again and says, "Da!"

What did the child understand in this scene? Certainly not as much as we would assume after the first series of questions and answers, but we also do not want to say that he did not understand anything.

Two thoughts arise from this anecdote: understanding does not seem to be an all-or-nothing affair; perhaps there are levels or stages of understanding—we will come back to this. And second: what is actually a criterion for whether something is understood or not? When the listener can repeat the utterance he heard word for word? Or when he behaves in accordance with the utterance? (But what would "in accordance" be here?) Does the listener un-

241

derstand what the speaker says, or what the utterance means, or even what the speaker means? We do not want to and are not able to distinguish precisely between these different formulations now, but it is perhaps appropriate to recall the thesis which runs through this whole book: the speaker makes an utterance in order to change the listener's consciousness. With this thesis in mind, we see that, after all, it is not so much the question of what the *object* of our understanding is (whether the sounds, the words, the sentences . . .) and what the relationships between these objects are, but rather that these are, on different levels, all *means* to an end.

We see how difficult it is to determine where language understanding *ends.* It is just as difficult to say exactly where it *begins.* Orthodox linguistics has worked very little on this problem. This is not surprising, because linguistics is only interested in language-as-such and not in language-for-us; it uses the criterion of correctness or incorrectness for sentences but not the criterion of understood or not understood. At best, understanding is assigned to psycholinguistics as belonging to performance. Only very recently have linguists tried to supplement syntax and semantics with their own study of usage (pragmatics), but they still rely to a large extent on concepts which were introduced for completely different purposes (namely for the description of syntactic and semantic competence).

The difficulties in delineating the problem of "understanding" have led to some evasive maneuvers. Thus many linguists and psycholinguists concern themselves mainly with the understanding of *sentences* and seem to imply by this that the perception or recognition or understanding of the phonemes, the syllables, or the words of these sentences is either completely unproblematical or that it has already been worked out satisfactorily in other sciences. They are happy to have the term *perception* available in addition to that of understanding, and give to "acoustic perception" or "speech perception" the task of describing the elementary grasping or recognizing of those sounds, syllables, and words of which the sentence to be understood consists—as if any psychologist were able to say where "hear what he says" passes into "recognize what he utters" and finally to "understand what he means!"

As long as we make no attempt to avoid these difficulties, we must grapple with two facts: (a) in order to understand an utterance a person must (always?) recognize at least several of the words or lexemes or sounds produced by the speaker; (b) the recognition of individual words or lexemes, on the other hand, is highly dependent on the understanding of the entire utterance.

The process of understanding, therefore, cannot be a one-way street (like "from the elements to the whole"); whoever wants to analyze it must know that *bottom-up processes*—the input that comes from outside—interact with *top-down processes*, with whatever comes from the knowledge, ability, and expectations of the listener. (Let us make it clear right away that these two terms provide no substantial information but at best a direction for the investigator's search.)

If, in the course of understanding, these bottom-up and top-down processes work together, and if we do not want to limit understanding only to the understanding of *sentences*, then what suggests itself is that we might have a theoretical discussion of the process of understanding begin with those very units from which linguistics puts together lexemes, words, and sentences, that is, with the phonemes, the smallest units which signal meaning in language. But we are no longer so naive as to formulate our basic question thus: Is understanding based on the recognition of phonemes? We will, in a more careful way, try to find out something about the role which phonemes play in this entire process.

Phonemic Models

Two findings are important for this: one and the same phoneme can be based on quite different acoustic factors, that is, it can have a different physical basis, according to who produces it and according to the sound context in which it is produced. The second finding: in many cases it is not possible to perceive or to recognize a phoneme when it is presented to the listener's ear in isolation. For correct perception, two or three phonemes in sequence are necessary for recognizing all of them and thus also the first one, or the phoneme (this is especially true for vowels) must be produced for at least 250 milliseconds, or, when the phoneme produced is shorter, a silent period of the same length must follow it.

Every explanation of these findings must take into account the main requirement for recognition systems of this kind: such a system must be able to abstract from the huge variation in which the sound form of the individual phoneme comes to the listener. An *a* or *r* spoken by a woman from Georgia has completely different acoustic characteristics from those of an *a* or *r* spoken by a man from Brooklyn who has a cold. The recognition of a phoneme can thus not be thought of as a simple matching in the listener between the actual input and a model he has available—it is not possible to store so many models!

As we see, the acoustic differences between the Georgia *r* and the Brooklyn *r* must be ignored for perception; it is not so much an acoustic or phonetic code, but a phonological one which is basic to what goes on in comprehension, that is, a code in which only those sound differences "count" which are important for speech comprehension. For about thirty years we have known that perception of speech sounds is categorical: the listener perceives very small sound differences which mark the borderline between two different phonemes, but he does *not* perceive sound differences of the same order of magnitude when these differences lie well within the boundaries of one and the same phoneme (in our example: the differences between the Georgia *r* and the Brooklyn *r*). Discrimination within the category seems to be suppressed, this suppression being, however, not so much the effect of a (missing) capacity of the organism, but of attentional factors: the listener is set to hear *speech* sounds of his specific language (Studdert-Kennedy 1980).

Phoneme perception presupposes segmentation: the listener has to assess the boundaries of each phoneme. One of the questions posed by this task is this: is segmentation an auditory process preceding phonemic classification, or an automatic consequence of classification? Another question: how large are the functional units which the listener cuts out of the acoustic flow to operate his perceptual processes with? Take, as an example, the finding of Repp *et al.* (1978). They recorded the sentence "Did anybody see the *gray ship*" on tape and then varied

(a) the duration of the fricative noise at the beginning of *ship*, and

(b) the duration of the silent interval between *gray* and *ship*.

The duration of (b) and that of (a)—and the proportion of (b) to (a)—determined whether the subjects heard (recognized, perceived, comprehended . . .)

> gray ship
> gray chip
> great ship
> great chip

What kind of "mechanism" integrates these different cues in one or the other percept? It would seem as if the listener took together what is produced in one integral articulatory gesture. "The system follows the moment-to-moment acoustic flow, apprehending an auditory 'motion picture,' as it were, of the articulation" (Studdert-Kennedy 1980: 55).[1]

Analysis-by-Synthesis Theories

The fact that phoneme perception (or, by the way, syllable perception or word perception as well) cannot be conceptualized as a simple matching of incoming (stimulus) features with a template or model may be seen also in a slightly different theoretical aspect. When not all, and not always the same, cues or features of the acoustic stimulus may be used to perceive the phoneme *a* or the phoneme *r*, perception must be based on the assessment of a partial subset of these features. A few of the sound features of the phoneme to be perceived can probably be directly determined from the acoustic signal, while the others, not identified with certainty, are *constructed* by the listener according to what is

---

[1]This is an extremely interesting combination of two ideas: (a) that phoneme perception is related to the perception of the respective cues and features in a manner analogous to the relation between the perception of motion and the perception of twenty-four still pictures per second in a movie; and (b) that *articulatory* "togetherness" (i.e., a characteristic of production) is the basis for perceptual patterning.

called *analysis by synthesis*. An analysis-by-synthesis model assumes that the listener adopts, on the incomplete basis available to him, a hypothesis, "that could be the phonological unit X," by building up out of the features actually perceived the phonological unit complete in itself. He does so on the basis of his knowledge of his language. He completes the unit by projecting the missing characteristics. This synthesized unit is then compared to the total input. If the hypothesis "that is phoneme X" is supported, then X *is* recognized. If there is a discrepancy in the comparison between the synthesized unit and the input which is too large, then the listener must try again; that is, another phoneme or another syllable must be synthesized.

In order to test the hypotheses, not only is more phonetic information probably brought in, but also syntactic and semantic information, a point which we have not yet discussed here.

Analysis-by-synthesis theories thus make it understandable why even the perception of the smallest unit (we have spoken of phonemes until now) always functions by way of fitting into larger, more inclusive units: the hypothesis that was formed for the identification of the small unit can be tested only on something larger. We have here a first example of the way that bottom-up and top-down processes work together: what is suggested by several features of what is heard (bottom-up) must be completed from the knowledge (top-down) which the listener has of the rules and the construction of his language, and probably according to several other bits of knowledge, too. At the same time it also becomes clear here why the syllable, an aggregate of phonemes, and not so much the phoneme itself, appears as the basic unit at this level of consideration. Syllables, that is, pairs or triplets of phonemes, are far more constrained in their occurrence in language by the regularities of that language (and the expectations of the listener [see below]) than is a single phoneme; quite a number of words begin with *a*, but rather few begin with *abi*.

We may face the most serious challenge to analysis-by-synthesis theories in an argument of the following kind:[2]

---

[2]We use the plural, because there are several differing theories of this type; the differences are not to be discussed in this introductory book.

The processes postulated here take a lot of time. How can our understanding of language function so quickly when many attempts at synthesis are necessary even for the recognition of a single phoneme or a single syllable? It can be said against this objection that the synthesis of input units does not begin at zero and also does not follow the principle of trial and error, but that it is guided to a great extent by the expectations which the listener develops in the course of a text or a dialogue and in the course of the individual utterance in relation to what will probably follow immediately. He will of course always expect something, something which will be within a more or less specific framework. The listener construes expectations with differing probabilities of realization; he construes them on the basis of what has just been *and* of what he has stored as being possible in his language, in a text of this kind, in a dialogue with this person, and so on.

This brings us directly to the question of *what* stores are here made use of and *how* they are accessed. Up to now we have talked in a rather loose way about the perception of the sounds constituting a syllable or a word, and we have said that these sounds, which we call phonemes, are only partially determined by the acoustic features of the stimulus and then "synthesized" by supplementary information drawn from knowledge stored in the listener. It is also possible, as Foss and Blank (1980) suggest, that access to the two "sources" of information integrated in this analysis-by-synthesis model may be gained separately. These authors interpret their experimental findings approximately as follows: speech input is represented, in any circumstances, in a phonetic code computed directly from the acoustic stimulus information available. This is true even for utterances in a foreign language. At the same time[3] the listener is trying to gain access to the word in question in his mental lexicon. At this stage, the full phonological specification of that word becomes available to the listener; he hears and understands a form which is largely determined by his semantic (and other) knowledge.

---

[3]"At the same time" is to be taken *cum grano salis;* it is to be understood here as meaning that *both* codes are "computed" by the listener, the phonetic and the phonological.

Foss and Blank think, therefore, that two codes are "computed" by the listener. The more context and expectations facilitate access to his lexicon, the more will he rely on the phonological code.

As we see, perceiving, grasping, understanding what a speaker means seems to go on, simultaneously, *via* several different (but partially interdependent) codes. Much the same fact might be expressed in a slightly different formulation: the understanding of an utterance is determined by knowledge from several different sources, knowledge which narrows down the range of possibilities to be expected. We will distinguish, for the time being, three such sources, the prosodic, the syntactic, and the semantic, and discuss them in this order.

The Role of Prosody

One Sunday night I happened to walk for some fifteen paces next to a group of six drunken young workmen, and I suddenly realized that all thoughts, feelings, and even a whole chain of reasoning could be expressed by that one noun, which is moreover extremely short. One young fellow said it harshly and forcefully, to express his utter contempt for whatever it was they had all been talking about. Another answered with the same noun but in a quite different tone and sense—doubting that the negative attitude of the first one was warranted. A third suddenly became incensed against the first and roughly intruded on the conversation, excitedly shouting the same noun, this time as a curse and obscenity. Here the second fellow interfered again, angry at the third, the aggressor, and restraining him, in the sense of "Now why do you have to butt in, we were discussing things quietly and here you come and start swearing." And he told this whole thought in one word, the same venerable word, except that he also raised his hand and put it on the third fellow's shoulder. All at once a fourth, the youngest of the group, who had kept silent till then, probably having suddenly found a solution to the original difficulty which had started the argument, raised his hand in a transport of joy and shouted. . . Eureka, do you think? I have it? No, not eureka and not I have it; he repeated the same unprintable noun, one word, merely one word, but with ecstasy, in a

shriek of delight—which was apparently too strong, because
the sixth and the oldest, a glum-looking fellow, did not like it
and cut the infantile joy of the other one short, addressing
him in a sullen, exhortative bass and repeating . . . yes, still
the same noun, forbidden in the presence of ladies but which
this time clearly meant "What are you yelling yourself hoarse
for?" So, without uttering a single other word, they repeated
that one beloved word six times in a row, one after another,
and understood one another completely.

F. Dostoevsky

The prosodic structure of an utterance (i.e., intonation, accent, stress, number and location of pauses, . . .) contains information which is important for understanding. Probably early in
an utterance a pattern is begun which rouses certain expectations as to the temporal locations at which some stimuli will happen in the very near future. The weight of this factor is shown in
an experiment of Bosshardt (1980). His subjects hear sentences
like the following:

(8.1)	The student in the cold attic.	writes	his thesis
(8.2)	In the cold attic his thesis.	writes	the student
(8.3)	His thesis in the cold attic.[4]	writes	the student

The task of the subjects is to repeat the sentences immediately
after hearing them; achieving this aim is made a little bit more
difficult by mixing the speech signal with white noise. All three
versions are found to be of about equal difficulty.

In a next step, versions (8.2) and (8.3) were cut into pieces at
the three points indicated by the vertical lines, and then the
pieces were pasted together in the sequence given by (8.1). When
these new versions were presented, the subjects had very great
difficulties in understanding the sentences. Even the perception
of the verb constituent ("writes") suffers, although this constitu-

[4]All three versions in German are perfectly well formed and acceptable, although
(8.2) and (8.3) are not grammatically well formed in English.

ent is at the same position in all three versions and therefore was
not moved or exchanged in the cut-and-pasted versions. Similarly, even though the constituent "the student" is now presented
always in first position, it is much more difficult to comprehend
than it was in the uncut, original version of (8.1).

These findings show that when generating prosodic expectations from the first words of an utterance, the listener not only
takes into consideration what sounds are produced here but also
allows for the fact that these sound the particular way they do
because they are produced at this particular position in the sequence of the utterance. In hearing the cut-and-pasted versions,
the listener is misled in this respect: he hears something in, say,
position 1 which has actually been pronounced in position 3, and
so the listener generates false expectations which then impede
comprehension even of the constituent "writes," which was produced at the very place (in time) that it is heard.

As we see, the listener uses actual prosodical information
and knowledge of possible or probable prosodical information as
cues in understanding an utterance. Cutler (1976) assumes that
the listeners are making use of this suprasegmental information
in such a way that highly informative words are received by a
high-tuned attention; we think, however, that this prosodic code
contains more specific information than merely when to pay attention. Interestingly, the use of this prosodic code seems to take
a rather long time to learn: Hörmann and Bosshardt (1981–82)
found that children's perception of sentences is not impaired by
misleading suprasegmental information in a way comparable to
that of adults.

Independence Thesis and Intention Thesis

These thoughts about the prosodic guidance of listener expectation have of course led us to conceive on a completely different
scale the temporal length of what we view as input for the process
of understanding. If at the beginning we spoke of phonemes, or at
the most of syllables, we can discuss the prosodic findings at all
only by taking into account the environment of a phoneme or of a

word. Naturally this is also true of the listener's syntactic expectations which guide the comprehension of an individual word and/or the structure of a whole phrase of the utterance. In the process of understanding, subprocesses of rather different temporal extension interact. (Or, to put the same fact into other words, the various codes simultaneously decoded by a listener operate with units of different extent.) However, since we can find prosodic and syntactic factors only by looking at larger structures, we have now arrived at the problem of understanding whole phrases, clauses, sentences. This area has been rather thoroughly investigated by psycholinguists. Of the theories of understanding which begin at this point, we can introduce here the most widespread, which says that understanding an utterance means recovering an inner representation of the *linguistic* structure of that particular utterance (Clark 1974; Fodor, Bever, and Garrett 1974). "The linguistic deep structure represents exactly what the people who have understood a sentence know," says Clark (1974: 13). We will call this the *theory of independence* of sentence comprehension because it postulates, as the essence of the understanding process, recovery of the (linguistic deep) structure which permeates the sentence and because both this structure and the process of recovering it are thought to be independent of all other factors. According to this theory, understanding "ends" with the attainment of this linguistically defined condition. On the basis of this condition, a further processing of what has been understood—a processing perhaps in part not linguistically determined—could then possibly begin.

The achievements and the weaknesses of this theory can best be shown if we juxtapose its opposite. We will do this with an example. Let us assume that two people are working or reading in an overheated room. One says to the other, who is sitting near the window,

(8.4) Could you open the window?

When has the listener understood this sentence? According to the theory of independence, it is at the moment when he successfully grasps the linguistic deep structure of the sentence (predicate verb "can" . . . object "window" . . . question form . . .).

What the listener can do with this, after he grasps the linguistic structure, has something to do with the further processing of the sentence, possibly, but nothing to do with the understanding of the sentence. Sentence (8.4) would thus be understood if the listener answered,

(8.5) Probably, if I pulled hard enough

and then resumed working.

The opponents of the thesis of independence would say that this answer is evidence of a misunderstanding. According to their view, the listener would have understood sentence (8.4) if he had stood up and opened the window—or also if he had said,

(8.6) I'd rather not; there would be a draft.

For this alternative theory understanding is achieved if the intention of the speaker is grasped. In contrast to the theory of independence, we call this the *theory of intention*. In this second theory understanding involves, in many cases, going beyond the linguistic structure of the sentence. Understanding, for instance, (8.4) implies that the question form is seen as a request. For followers of this theory, the listener has understood an utterance when he grasps what the speaker means.[5]

If understanding was defined linguistically for the theory of independence, namely, as grasping the linguistic structure of the utterance, then for the representatives of the intention theory it is defined communicatively, namely, as grasping what the speaker means.

Following the basic theme of this book—namely, that language is a tool in the lives of people who deal with one another—we support the intention theory. Understanding language requires that the listener see the utterance of the speaker as an act of meaning and that he allow himself to be carried beyond the lexemes and words by the force that is in it; when understanding

[5]H. Clark, who in earlier publications advocated the independence theory, has adopted (1978) the intention theory. He distinguishes it, however, from a constructivist theory—a distinction we will not adopt in this book.

is successful he is carried to the place where the speaker wants the consciousness of the listener to be.[6]

It should be clear that for the representatives of the theory of independence there is a break between understanding (= establishing a representation of the linguistic structure or the "immediate linguistic awareness" of the propositional structure inherent in the sentence, as Levelt 1978 says) and the further assimilation and processing of what is understood. This break is clearly defined as the grasping of the deep structure, but unfortunately there is no agreement in linguistics about what deep structure itself actually is. For the followers of the intention theory there is no break of this kind; they must concern themselves with the problem as to whether there is *one* end-condition of the process of understanding which can be defined formally at all, or whether we should not conceive of this process as possibly running over a whole series of stages. We will still need to go into this further and to discuss the fact that the concept of understanding necessarily leads beyond mere linguistic understanding.

Before doing so, however, we will present the knowledge which we have about certain partial aspects of understanding utterances which are interesting and important for both theoretical approaches.

Proponents of either theory must be interested in learning *how* the structures which permeate the whole sentence, or clauses, or parts of the sentence, are "extracted" from the stream of sounds reaching the ear of the listener. (For the theory of independence grasping these structures and having a representation of them *is* itself already understanding; for the theory of intention this grasping is in most cases *necessary* for further understanding.[7])

---

[6]This theoretical position is gaining acceptance. "Our attention should focus on the cognitive functioning of hearers in interpreting speech sounds. The central question in communication concerns the relations between words and their users, not between words and other words, or words and other things" (Harris, Begg, and Upfold, 1980:598).

[7]The fact that these (linguistic, syntactic, semantic . . .) structures actually *are* perceived has been already discussed in Chapter 6; remember the click experiments of Fodor and Garrett or the investigations of Johnson and of Engelkamp.

Perceiving a comprehensive structure in a linear stream of speech sounds implies, for most theoretical approaches, a phase of *parsing* by which the words (or lexemes or syllables . . .) are assigned specific functions in that structure. In order to do this, the listener must be able to assess the boundaries between words. (He must decide, for instance, whether the speaker produced "a name" or "an aim.") If this is so, the meaning of these units must be assessed (by looking them up in the "mental lexicon") at a rather early phase of processing the incoming stimulus. On the other hand, in many cases the correct parsing will be a prerequisite for the correct perception of the individual word; we see that the exact "timing" of when what information becomes available and necessary is a ubiquitous problem in this theoretical field.

We will now describe a widely endorsed type of theoretical formulation accounting for structure perception, without going into details which differ from one author to another. This approach (Fodor *et al.* 1974) maintains that the elements of an incoming utterance are first collected in a short-term store. As soon as the material is sufficient for structuring a clause or phrase from it, this is done: it is recoded into a semantic representation and, by this recoding, carried over *en bloc* into another store. Syntactic and lexemic details may get lost in this process. Because this account is firmly anchored in the framework of independence theory, the act of structuring the content of the first store is equivalent to understanding; talking about recoding it into a semantic store is just a different way of formulating what goes on.

This model is based on the common view in the psychology of memory according to which retention is accomplished by a series of storehouses which are used one after another and which differ according to how they code material and according to their retention spans. The incoming material lies in the first (short-term) store in a more or less unstructured form, until it is comprehended *by* recoding it semantically.

What is important is that understanding is discontinuous— we do not understand one word after another, but clause after clause.

Among the main supports for this model are the investigations of Sachs (1967). She read small minitexts, always consisting of only a few sentences, aloud to her subjects, and later read them a further sentence, asking them whether this sentence had been in the original text or not. The new sentence was either identical with a sentence in the text or presented a small syntactic or semantic variation of such a sentence. It was found that if the original and the changed sentences were separated by only a short period of time (in the experiment, if the text that came after the original sentence included fewer than eighty syllables), then the subject noticed every variation. If the separation included more than eighty syllables, then semantic variations were noticed, but not syntactic ones. The recall of the exact wording was thus lost.

Up to now we have stated, in a rather general way, that according to this model the syntactic structure is recognized when the elements of a clause are all stored in some kind of short-term memory; we have not yet said anything about *how* this is done, *how* the syntactic status or function of the elements is recognized. Most answers to this question rely heavily on interpreting certain markers to signal the occurrence of particular syntactic constructions. Kimball (1973) has published a number of rules or strategies for doing this.

One of these rules says: if possible, subsume each incoming unit to what is the last constituent in your tree-structure. We will demonstrate the feasibility by an example in which following this rule leads to failure. When we have

(8.7) The horse raced past the barn fell

our first attempt to structure the incoming utterance according to this single strategy fails when "fell" comes in; we see that we must adopt a more complex structure (by changing "raced" from intransitive to transitive, etc.). In order to avoid the necessity of these late restructurings, very often specific syntactic markers are inserted in an utterance to signal that a more complex structure should be projected into the utterance. In our example,

(8.8) The horse which was raced past. . .

the words "which was" are just such a signal. There is empirical evidence that the inclusion of such signals facilitates recognition of the structure of the utterance:

(8.9) He knew the girl left

is harder to recognize than

(8.10) He knew that the girl left.

Other authors (e.g., Bever 1970) advocate other perceptual strategies for elucidating (slightly differently conceptualized) syntactic structures.

Strategies of Understanding

The concept of strategy perhaps deserves some commentary. In recognizing the linguistic structure inherent in an utterance, it will always be necessary, as we have said before, to use knowledge of various kinds; bottom-up processes must interact with top-down processes. The decision as to *which* top-down processes to apply will very often be made under conditions of insufficient information. We *try* a first strategy, and if it does not work, we *try* a second one.[8] Strategies are, as it were, patent recipes or shortcuts used in the absence of reliable longhand rules. The use of strategies for establishing the structure of an utterance is also required, presumably, by the very fact that the comprehensive structure *and* the individual words must be assessed simultaneously, that is, with no clear-cut order of precedence available.

Strategies of this kind attract our attention particularly in cases in which they lead us astray. If we cling to the rule, "Add every newly arrived word to the latest constituent in your tree-diagram," the headline in the London newspaper

(8.11) Zoo-keeper finds Jaguar queuing for underground ticket

seems, at first, to have a rather astonishing meaning. We bring—erroneously—"queuing" together with the immediately preceding "Jaguar" and we thus get the idea that the Jaguar was standing in line. The sentence is, however, about a zoo-keeper who, while

---

[8]The condition "if it does not work" calls for some mechanisms by which the working of a strategy is evaluated. This is discussed under the term of *sense constancy* in Hörmann (1976/1981).

standing in line, is reading a newspaper and finds a car (a Jaguar) in the advertisements.

The theory of clausal processing just presented is subject to two major objections. The first has to do with the assertion contained in it that the representation of the exact words (sounds) is stored only until the structure of the clause as a whole is understood. Because this understanding is tantamount to a recoding into a further (semantic) storage, it implies a loss of the representation these elements had up to this point. Understanding is, in this view, coupled with recoding by some kind of biological necessity—there should be no exceptions. However, a recent investigation shows that the question as to whether the exact words are retained or not depends—at least in actual communication situations—on pragmatic factors. If the listener assumes, for example, that the utterance reflects the emotional attitude of the speaker in respect to a certain person or thing, then the exact words are retained very well and for very long. This means, however, that the "survival" of only the semantic content, which is so often observed, is *not* a result of any recoding into a different storage which might be necessary at this point (Keenan, McWhinney, and Mayhew 1977).

The second objection is mainly made by Marslen-Wilson and his colleagues (1976, 1978, 1980). This author uses above all "shadowing" experiments in which a text is read aloud to the subject who is to repeat it immediately, with the least possible delay or lag. Several subjects were able to keep this lag at only 250 milliseconds; this corresponds to the length of about one syllable. Thus their listening was in advance of their own pronunciation for at best one syllable (not for a whole clause). If errors occur in this immediate repetition, they should, according to the clausal processing theory, *not* be determined by the syntactic or semantic characteristics of the text, because any syntactic or semantic analysis would require, as we have learned, a processing of the *entire* clause. This kind of syntactic or semantic error should only occur in subjects who are "limping behind" the speaker at quite a distance. The findings of Marslen-Wilson show, however, that the *kind of error* is independent of the extent of the lag in repetition. The kind of error also agrees with the syntactic and semantic features of the text even for minimal lag times. Thus the listener apparently does *not* postpone understanding until the entire clause has come in, but progresses continuously. This author therefore suggests a model which predicts a "direct on-line interaction" instead of a processing in clauses. "The listener can develop at least a preliminary syntactic and semantic analysis of the speech input word-by-word as he hears it" (1980:6).

If we take a closer look, the consequences of these findings may prove to be fatal not only for a clausal processing theory, but for any independence theory. The theory of independence claims, as we recall, that understanding of an utterance is achieved in rigid temporal order: the linguistic deep structure of the utterance must be recovered before any—perhaps context-dependent—additional steps can be taken. The evidence adduced by Marslen-Wilson in shadowing and word-recognition experiments seems incompatible with this kind of model. He postulates, instead,

> A recognition system in which the acoustic-phonetic input can be consistent with a range of possible word-candidates at the moment of recognition, and where, evidently, it is contextual factors that allow a single word-candidate to be selected. . . . Contextual and sensory inputs interact continuously at the same stage of processing. . . . The interactions are not mediated by a discontinuous, two-stage model. (1980: 26)

Marslen-Wilson's is a *distributed processing model* in which recognition is achieved by a large array of individual recognition elements, each of which can integrate sensory and contextual information in order to determine whether the word it represents was actually spoken by the speaker. Throughout the whole sentence, the semantic dimensions structuring the whole discourse dominate processing.

Marslen-Wilson rejects the independence theory of understanding. We agree with him completely but would like to go one step further, to the intention theory.

In our earlier example

(8.4) Could you open the window?

said in an overheated room, we had a first misunderstanding in the form of

(8.5) Probably, if I pulled hard enough.

A supporter of the independence theory would probably say here that the listener really did understand the utterance but that he did not process it further in accordance with the expectations of the speaker. But there is another misunderstanding in addition to the one mentioned in (8.5); here the listener, who was thinking about something else, jumps and asks

(8.12) What should I do?

Apparently the listener did not understand a single word that the speaker said in this case, but he at least gathered vaguely that the speaker was requesting something of him. The listener here knows something about the intention of the speaker. How does he know this? How could he understand that he was supposed to do something, when he understood so little of the individual words and of course the deep structure of the utterance? (He failed also to understand that the speaker produced a question that was "not meant that way.")

These questions urge us to change our conception of understanding.

Levels of Understanding

Does understanding—in the sense of grasping what the speaker means—have only a relatively loose connection with the exact words and with the (deep) structure of the utterance? And further: must understanding be something that is either there or not there? Or could it not be something that is there in different degrees, or on different levels? (We recall here Meumann junior!) In the next step these questions will be carried further, by looking more closely into idioms, semantic anomalies, and metaphor.

Take, for instance, the utterance

(8.13) Fritz kicked the bucket.

How do we understand this sentence? According to the independence theory, we would first pick out its deep structure: noun phrase, verb phrase, second noun phrase, and so on. This would lead to a complete failure of understanding—what the speaker actually means by this utterance is that Fritz died. Somewhere and somehow the process of understanding must here be directed to a completely different track, a fact for which the usual theories of understanding have only to offer the explanation that here the listener *interprets* what he has first understood *verbatim.* But is this *interpretation* a process differing in kind from understanding proper? And we recall our famous misunderstanding (Can you open the window? / What should I do?), where some understanding was achieved *without* any previous word-for-word understanding. We understand what the speaker saying "Fritz kicked the bucket" means because we want to understand him and because understanding him in that way (= Fritz died) is the only way that makes sense.

Much the same argument is true also for the case of semantic anomaly *versus* metaphor.[9] When we hear about a

smiling spring meadow

we understand what the speaker means even though smiling cannot be said of nonanimate objects, according to the selection restrictions in our inner lexicon. We understand it because we want to understand it!

With this a new and decisively important viewpoint is introduced into the discussion. The listener understands the question (8.4) as a request, he understands the idiom in (8.13), he makes a metaphor out of the semantic anomaly "the smiling spring meadow," because he is not happy with not understanding and because he keeps at understanding further until the result of this process, which may run through several steps, has reached a goal which was, in a general form, already vaguely before him: utterances should make sense. In order to reach this criterion, he ignores the fact that (8.4) bears a question mark. He understands (8.4) or

---

[9]A semantic anomaly is said to exist when words are brought together in a syntactically correct sentence in a way that contradicts the meaning of these words. Chomsky's famous sentence "Colorless green ideas sleep furiously" is a semantic anomaly.

(8.14) Couldn't you open the window?

in the very same way as

(8.15) Please open the window.

The listener does this in such a situation (overheated room, working quietly) because only in this way can the utterance of the speaker fit sensibly into his view of the present world.

Two things now become clear. (1) In the process of understanding, the listener also makes use of situative, that is nonlinguistic, factors. If the room were not so warm, he would perhaps understand the utterance differently. (2) Understanding is a goal-oriented process. The speaker, as we have already emphasized, has the intention of directing the consciousness of the listener. Now it becomes recognizable that the listener also has a certain intention in every act of communication: to see the world around him clearly, to make it intelligible.

With this, attempts at developing a theory of the process of understanding move to a different climate, so to speak. According to the usual models, certain steps have an effect in a certain order (phonetic analysis, recognizing deep structure, semantic interpretation, etc.); whatever appears as the end result of these processes, which have a fixed order, *is* "what is understood." Understanding is thus in these models a dependent variable, dependent on an established series of specific factors in the model. But the fact that when it is necessary we understand semantic anomalies as metaphors, understand idioms, understand questions as requests, shows that this kind of model is basically inadequate. The understanding of an utterance is not finished when we have passed through the fixed order of stations of a process model, but rather different factors, probably in changing sequences and combinations, are used as long as it takes for the result to satisfy the listener here and now. He is satisfied when it makes sense.

For this it is necessary that the listener already know what makes sense. This tendency to see the world as sensible whenever possible also confronts us outside of language (and therefore there is also understanding outside of language). We can hardly

perceive an action of a person or even of an animal without assigning a reason for this act. This usually is done by our placing
the action into a larger context, if available, or by our constructing a context that helps us make sense out of the action. If we see
a man running and a woman running in front of him, then he is
chasing her. If the woman is behind him, then he is running
away from her. If he is running alone, then he is jogging. If he is
fat, then he is jogging because he is fat. If he is slim, then he is
slim because he jogs. And so on.

   If we view understanding in this way as a process guided by
its goal, then we are doing something with which we are already
acquainted from the psychology of perception. Human perception
is designed to perceive objects. In the service of this function,
things like variations in brightness or color are often simply ignored, even though they are registered on the retina: we speak of
brightness or color constancy. We perceive a table as having right
angles, even when we walk around it and its shape is grossly
distorted in our eyes: we speak of shape constancy. The visitor
who takes two steps toward us and extends his hand to us does
not double in size, even though we should "actually" see it that
way. The so-called size constancy makes sure that, according to
the particular situation, the organism uses different programs for
the evaluation of the individual information which results from
our perception of distance, of retinal disparity, from the size of
the reflection on the retina, from experience, and so forth. *Different* programs are used so that a *constant* goal can be reached: to
inform the organism about the stable size of an object so that he
can deal with this perceived size.

Sense Constancy

In complete accordance with these acts and mechanisms of perception, we postulate something that we call *sense constancy.*
Just as man is prepared for and directed toward perceiving objects whenever there is a possibility for this, he is also directed
toward perceiving an utterance as sensible.

   When understanding is "making sense (of something) by

placing it in a context," it acquires a constructive aspect: it is more than mere reception. The listener construes a sensible context from what the utterance stimulates and makes possible, from his knowledge of the situation, from his knowledge of the world, and from his motivation. Having established this kind of context, he fits it in with the subjective feeling "now I have understood it" and with the conviction coupled to this that one could act adequately (within the context) if this were necessary.[10]

Understanding as involving a constructive process—what do we know about this process? We can learn something by obstructing it. Bransford and Johnson (1973) presented a group of subjects with a short story:

(8.16) If the balloons popped the sound wouldn't be able to carry since everything would be too far away from the correct floor. A closed window would also prevent the sound from carrying, since most buildings tend to be well insulated. Since the whole operation depends on a steady flow of electricity, a break in the middle of the wire would also cause problems. Of course, the fellow could shout, but the human voice is not loud enough to carry that far. An additional problem is that a string could break on the instrument. Then there could be no accompaniment to the message. It is clear that the best situation would involve less distance. Then there would be fewer potential problems. With face to face contact, the least number of things could go wrong.

Here only a very low-level of understanding is achieved; although the words and the sentences are "clear," the story as a whole does not make sense but rather remains obscure. When the authors, however, presented the same text to another group of subjects who had just seen the picture on the next page (Figure 9), the process of understanding or the construction of understanding could go on to a quite different level, a level satisfactory for the subjects. As we see, a satisfactory level of understanding is achieved by integrating information from different sources (here,

[10]See Deese (1969).

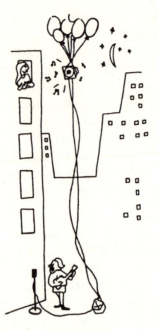

Figure 9. Appropriate context for the balloon *passage.*

story and picture). This has some rather important consequences
which we shall mention briefly:

1. What the listener understands is not so much the text of
   the story (or the verbal utterance of the speaker), but
   rather what the writer of the story (or the speaker) means.
2. What the speaker means may be conveyed to the listener
   via several different "languages" (or: come from several
   different "sources"): the syntactic code, the lexical code,
   prosodical signals, the constraints of the situation, and so
   forth.
3. The integration of these different but simultaneous and
   coordinated "messages" makes understanding a case of
   problem solving.

How is this integration to be conceptualized? Bransford (1973)
points to what goes on by presenting subjects with either of two
sentences:

(8.17) (a) Three turtles rested beside a floating log, and a fish swam beneath them.

(8.18) (b) Three turtles rested on a floating log, and a fish swam beneath them.

In sentence (b) it is suggested (but not said!) that the fish is also under the floating log. It is suggested by the listener's knowledge of the world. The listener draws, as it were, inferences.

That he actually does so was tested by Bransford by presenting his subjects afterwards with a sentence

(8.19) (c) Three turtles rested (beside/on) a floating log and a fish swam beneath it.

Subjects who had previously heard sentence (a) recognized the difference between (a) and (c), whereas subjects who had heard sentence (b) did not recognize any difference in (c).

Bransford's conclusion (see Bransford 1972): what is understood (and stored in memory) is not a representation of the (linguistic) structure of the utterance, but a *semantic description* constructed with the aid of the verbal utterance, but also with the aid of several other factors (in our example, with the aid of our knowledge of physics).

The semantic description is some kind of schema. We have, in our memory, a large number of schemata, which determine to a large extent the structure we impose on what goes on around us, what we perceive, hear, and understand. These schemata are, on the other hand, changed by what is assimilated into them. In recalling and remembering, therefore, listeners are often unable to distinguish between what was actually uttered by the speaker and what the listeners have inferred on the basis of the receiving schema. As Masson (1979) has shown, retrieval of a message heard may be cued by aspects of inferences made while processing the message; this cuing is about as effective as cues that were taken from the actual utterance of the speaker.

Constructing connections or drawing inferences within (or under control of) a schema may be facilitated by several devices which are more or less explicitly used in rhetoric, textbook writing, and the like. Subjects, for instance, are found to read state-

ments exhibiting a consistent point of view faster than statements exhibiting a change of view; consistent statements are
rated as more easily comprehensible (Black et al. 1979). Incoming
information is processed and interpreted in such a way that the
listener or reader develops expectations about what can come
next. In a discourse the integration of two sentences is facilitated
when common information across the pair is first introduced as
new and then repeated as old; here the terms *focus* and *presupposition* which we discussed earlier come in again.

Constructing connections and "missing links" is also evident
in Clark's (1978) example: when we hear

(8.20) Yesterday I went to a wedding. The woman is a doctor

then the use of the definite article in the second sentence is a
signal to see the second sentence as connected to the first one, so
that from our knowledge of the world (that every wedding has a
woman) *and* from the utterance we can draw the conclusion that
the bride is a doctor. The tendency toward making the *whole*
sensible (the utterance heard *and* my knowledge of the world)
often causes the listener to set up bridge constructions which
make sure that the sequencing of the individual utterances becomes a connected text. Whoever hears

(8.21) Yesterday I met two people. The woman was a doctor

must, in order to justify the use of the definite article and to fulfill
the criterion of sensibleness, draw the conclusion that one of the
two people was a woman, but that the other one was not.

With this, we learn something important about the process of
understanding: understanding is not—or at least not only—a recoding or decoding of information "contained" in the message;
understanding is *creating* information. The speaker in (8.21) did
not mention at all that one of the two people he met yesterday was
either a man or a child, but the listener who understands the
speaker knows this afterwards. He knows it because the utterance *suggests* that the empty space of his *semantic description*
be filled out in this way. The utterance suggests it; his organized
knowledge of the world allows it.

Schemata and Frame Semantics

We are brought back once more to the attempts to conceptualize this organized knowledge, these schemata which control the constructive activities of the listener. Perhaps the best way to discuss them is indicated in what Fillmore writes (1976a,b) about *frame semantics:*

> People have in memory an inventory of schemata for structuring, classifying, and interpreting experiences, and they have various ways of accessing these schemata and various procedures for performing operations on them . . . particular words or speech formulas, or particular grammatical choices, are associated in memory with particular frames in such a way that exposure to the linguistic form in an appropriate context activates in the perceiver's mind the particular frame. . . . A frame is a kind of outline figure. . . . If I tell you that I bought a new pair of shoes, you do not know where I bought them or how much they cost, but you know, by virtue of the frame I have introduced into our discourse, that there have got to be answers to these questions.

In another passage, Fillmore compares understanding a text to understanding the scenes of a film, or the frames of a comic strip. Understanding the sentences

(8.22) The boy is sitting up now
(8.23) The boy is sitting down now

is *not* equivalent to having the same visual image in both cases. Understanding these sentences must include an awareness of the earlier scene in the strip or frame. When we hear the story

(8.24) John entered the restaurant, took a seat, and called, "Waiter, may I have the check, please?"

the frame about visiting a restaurant tells us that some important things are missing.

And sense constancy, abhorring this nonsense, offers as an explanation the possibility that John might have been outside the restaurant for two minutes to get some money or something of that sort.

Understanding a speaker very often involves, as we see, going beyond what is said, and this going beyond is controlled by, among other things, the frames in our semantic memory.

On the other hand, the individual words of the utterance add to the construction of the semantic description only what is needed for the context *here*, not everything which could potentially be in it. As an example, take the investigation of Barclay *et al.* (1974). They presented subjects with different sentences like:

(8.25) The man lifted the piano.
(8.26) The man smashed the piano.
(8.27) The man tuned the piano.
(8.28) The man photographed the piano.

Sentence (8.25) talks about the piano as something heavy, sentence (8.26) as something made of wood, (8.27) as something that sounds good, (8.28) as something that looks good. If the subjects are asked after some time, when they have already forgotten almost everything, to remember the object named, then one can help the subjects in group (8.25) by saying, "It was something heavy," those of the (8.26) group with "It was something made of wood," etc. They cannot remember it, however, if we tell the first group "something made of wood" and the second group "something heavy." The word "piano" apparently added to the understanding of the sentence (and with that to its retention) only what in each case was necessary for the construction of a sensible text or semantic description. The sentence as a whole (and especially its verb) thus also adds to the determination of what the individual words are *allowed* to add to understanding. Not all information contained in the word "piano" is used.

Under the influence of information theory and of what was appearing with great acclaim as semiotics (the science of signification), the process of understanding was for a long time viewed as one of decoding. It was viewed as a kind of retranslation of the language signs into the thoughts which contain this same information. Then understanding would indeed be a linguistically determined process, because it would move exclusively in the area of the language code. Now we see that understanding is a creative, constructive act that always goes beyond the information coded in the utterance itself, sometimes not filling out this information completely or ignoring much of it, but always having its goal indicated by the intention of the listener: making the surrounding world, to which the speaker belongs, intelligible *through* the words of the utterance—we say that language is "transparent."[11]

When is this goal reached? How far should the process of construction go? With this we have once again arrived at the question which already appeared at the beginning of the chapter: when have we understood something? It is now clear that understanding can reach different levels. Whoever reads a text for misprints understands it, if probably only at a relatively shallow level. Whoever repeats the same text in the shadowing experiment also understands it. Whoever listens to a text to decide whether it is consistent understands it "more deeply"; and, finally, whoever listens to it so that he can paraphrase it in his own words afterwards understands it still better, on an even deeper level. The concept of the level of processing, which the psychology of language here has taken over from the psychology of memory (Bock 1978; Craik and Lockhart 1972), assigns an important role to the total action in which the understanding of an utterance is embedded.

Our question as to when have we understood can now, after we have become acquainted with the process of understanding as a part of communication binding two people, also be answered from a formal communication-psychological standpoint: the listener has understood whenever the speaker can say, "Yes, that is what I meant" in response to the original listener's utterance or action.

But this is of course unsatisfactory. When a son-in-law asks his visiting mother-in-law irritably,

(8.29) When does your train leave?

then the process of understanding by the listener can reach several different levels, up to and including the one in which she gives the utterance the meaning that the speaker hopes her visit will be

---

[11]For a more extensive discussion of this view see Hörmann (1976/1981). A similar position is taken, e.g., by Harris, Begg, and Upfold (1980).

over soon. What does it mean when the son-in-law then replies that he did not mean it *that* way?

Does the speaker always know exactly *how* he means something? And if he does not know exactly, can understanding then be more precise than meaning? Thus it gradually becomes clear to us that in certain cases there do not exist such precise limits to the process of understanding that we can say with certainty and dependably that we have reached them. In the same way, the investigation of this process by psychologists of language will not have reached its limits for a long time.

Epilogue

> But if you have vitality enough of knowing enough of what you mean, somebody and sometime and sometimes a great many will have to realize that you know what you mean and so they will agree that you mean what you know, what you know you mean, which is as near as anybody can come to understanding anyone.
>
> Gertrude Stein, *Henry James*

References

Austin, J. L. *How to Do Things with Words.* Oxford: Oxford University Press, 1962.

Barclay, J. R., Bransford, J. D., Franks, J. J., McCarrell, N., and Nitsch, K. "Comprehension and Semantic Flexibility." *Journal of Verbal Learning and Verbal Behavior* 13 (1974):471–481.

Bartlett, F. C. *Remembering.* Cambridge: Cambridge University Press, 1932.

Beattie, G. W. "Floor Apportionment and Gaze in Conversational Dyads." *British Journal of Social and Clinical Psychology* 17/1 (1978):7–15.

_____. "Contextual Constraints on the Floor-Apportionment Function of Speaker Gaze in Dyadic Conversations." *British Journal of Social and Clinical Psychology* 18/4 (1979):391–392.

Bever, T. G. "The Cognitive Basis for Linguistic Structures." In *Cognition and the Development of Language,* edited by J. R. Hayes. New York: Books Demand, UMI, 1970.

Bierwisch, M. "Some Semantic Universals in German Adjectivals." *Foundations of Language* 3 (1967):1–36.

Black, J. B., Turner, H., and Bower, G. H. "Episodes as Chunks in Narrative Memory." *Journal of Verbal Learning and Verbal Behavior* 18 (1979):309–318.

271

Bloom, L. M. *Language Development: Form and Function in Emerging Grammars.* Cambridge, Mass.: MIT Press, 1970.

Bloomfield, L. *Language.* New York: Henry Holt, 1933.

Blumenthal, A. L. "Prompted Recall of Sentences." *Journal of Verbal Learning and Verbal Behavior* 6 (1967):203–206.

Blumenthal, A. L., and Boakes, R. "Prompted Recall of Sentences: A Further Study." *Journal of Verbal Learning and Verbal Behavior* 6 (1967):674–676.

Bock, M. "Überschriftspezifische Selektierungsprozesse bei der Textverarbeitung." *Archiv für Psychologie.* 131 (1978):77–93.

Bosshardt, H.-G. "Suprasegmental Structure and Sentence Perception." In *Temporal Variables in Speech,* edited by H. W. Deckert and M. Raupach. The Hague: Mouton, 1980.

Braine, M. D. S. "The Ontogeny of English Phrase Structure: The First Phase." *Language* 39 (1963):1–13.

Bransford, J. D., and Johnson, M. K. "Considerations of some Problems of Comprehension." In *Visual Information Processing,* edited by W. G. Chase. New York: Academic Press, 1973.

Bransford, J. D., Barclay, J. R., and Franks, J. J. "Sentence Memory: A Constructive Versus Interpretive Approach." *Cognitive Psychology* 3 (1972):193–209.

Braunwald, S. R. "Context, Word and Meaning: Toward a Communication Analysis of Lexical Acquisition." In *Action, Gesture, and Symbol. The Emergence of Language,* edited by A. Lock. New York: Academic Press, 1978:485–527.

Brown, R. W. *A First Language.* Cambridge, Mass.: Harvard University Press, 1973.

Brown, R. W., and Gilman, A. "The Pronouns of Power and Solidarity." In *Style in Language,* edited by Thomas A. Sebeok. Cambridge, Mass.: MIT Press, 1960.

Brown, R. W., and Hanlon, C. "Derivational Complexity and Order of Acquisition." In *Cognition and the Development of Language,* edited by J. R. Hayes. New York: John Wiley, 1970.

Bruner, J. "Nature and Uses of Immaturity." *American Psychologist* 7 (1972):1–22.

———. "From Communication to Language—A Psychological Perspective." *Cognition* 3 (1974/75):255–287.

———. "On Prelinguistic Prerequisites of Speech." In *Recent Advances in the Psychology of Language*, III, edited by R. N. Campbell and P. T. Smith. New York and London: Plenum Press, 1978.

———. "Learning How to Do Things with Words." In *Psycholinguistic Research*, edited by D. Aaronson and R. Rieber. Hillsdale, N.J.: Lawrence Erlbaum, 1979.

Bühler, K. *Sprachtheorie.* Jena: Gustav Fischer, 1934.

Buschke, H., and Schaier, A. H. "Memory Units, Ideas, and Propositioning in Semantic Remembering." *Journal of Verbal Learning and Verbal Behavior* 18 (1979):549–563.

Butterworth, B., and Beattie, G. "Gesture and Silence as Indicators of Planning in Speech." In *Recent Advances in the Psychology of Language*, edited by R. N. Campbell and P. T. Smith. New York and London: Plenum Press, 1978:347–360.

Chafe, W. "Language and Memory." *Language* 49 (1973):261–281.

———. "Some Reasons for Hesitating." In *Temporal Variables in Speech. Studies in Honour of F. Goldman-Eisler*, edited by H. W. Dechert and M. Raupach. The Hague: Mouton, 1980:169–180.

Chomsky, N. *Syntactic Structures.* The Hague: Mouton, 1957.

———. *Aspects of the Theory of Syntax.* Cambridge, Mass.: MIT Press, 1965.

Clark, E. V. "Non-linguistic Strategies and the Acquisition of Word Meanings." *Cognition* 2 (1973):161–182.

———. "Knowledge, Context, and Strategy in the Acquisition of Meaning." In *Georgetown University Round Table on Languages and Linguistics*, edited by D. P. Dato. Washington, D.C.: Georgetown University Press, 1975.

Clark, H. H. "Word Associations and Linguistic Theory." In *New Horizons in Linguistics*, edited by J. Lyons. Baltimore: Penguin, 1970.

———. *Semantics and Comprehension.* (Janua Linguarum Minor) The Hague: Mouton, 1974.

———. "Inferring What Is Meant." In *Studies in the Perception of Language*, edited by W. J. Levelt and G. B. Flores d'Arcais. Chicester, N.Y.: John Wiley, 1978.

Clark, H. H., and Clark, E. V. *Psychology and Language: An*

Introduction to Psycholinguistics. New York: Harcourt, Brace, Jovanovich, 1977.

Clark, H. H., and Haviland, S. E. "Comprehension and the Given-New Contract." In *Discourse Production and Comprehension,* edited by R. D. Freedle. Norwood, N. J.: Ablex, 1977.

Clark, R. "What's the Use of Imitation?" *Journal of Child Language* 4 (1977):341–358.

Collins, A. M., and Loftus, E. F. "A Spreading Activation Theory of Semantic Processing." *Psychological Review* 82 (1975):407–428.

Collins, A. M., and Quillian, M. R. "Retrieval Time from Semantic Memory." *Journal of Verbal Learning and Verbal Behavior* 8 (1969):241–248.

————. "Experiments on Semantic Memory and Language Comprehension." In *Cognition in Learning and Memory,* edited by L. W. Gregg. New York: John Wiley, 1972.

Collis, G. M. and Schaffer, H. R. "Synchronization of Visual Attention in Mother-Infant Pairs." *Journal of Child Psychology and Psychiatry* 16/4 (1975):315–320.

Condon, W. S., and Ogston, W. D. "Sound Film Analysis of Normal and Pathological Behavioral Patterns." *Journal of Nervous and Mental Disease* 143 (1966):338–347.

Condon, W. S., and Sander, L. W. "Neonate Movement Is Synchronized with Adult Speech: Interactional Participation and Language Acquisition." *Science* 183 (1974):99–101.

Craik, F. I. M., and Lockhart, R. S. "Levels of Processing: A Framework for Memory Research." *Journal of Verbal Learning and Verbal Behavior* 11 (1972):117–138.

Cutler, A. "Beyond Parsing and Lexical Look-Up: An Enriched Description of Auditory Sentence Comprehension." In *New Approaches to Language Mechanism,* edited by R. J. Wales and E. Walker. Amsterdam: North Holland, 1976.

de Beaugrande, R. *Text, Discourse, and Process: Toward a Multidisciplinary Science of Texts.* Norwood, N. J.: Ablex, 1980.

Deese, J. "Behavior and Fact." *American Psychologist* 24 (1969):515–522.

————. "Thought into Speech." *American Scientist* 66 (1978):314–321.

_____. "Pauses, Prosody, and the Demands of Production in Language." In *Temporal Variables in Speech*, edited by H. W. Dechert and M. Raupach. The Hague: Mouton, 1980:69–84.

Derwing, B. L., and Baker, W. J. "On the Re-integration of Linguistics and Psychology." In *Recent Advances in the Psychology of Language*, edited by R. N. Campbell and P. T. Smith. New York and London: Plenum Press, 1978.

Diver, W. "Phonology as Human Behavior." In *Psycholinguistic Research*, edited by D. Aaronson and R. W. Rieber. Hillsdale, N.J.: Lawrence Erlbaum, 1979:161–186.

Donaldson, M., and Balfour, G. "Less Is More: A Study of Language Comprehension in Children." *British Journal of Psychology* 59 (1968):461–472.

Eimas, P. D. "Speech Perception in Early Infancy." In *Infant Perception: From Sensation to Cognition*, vol. 2, edited by L. B. Cohen and P. Salapatek. New York: Academic Press, 1975.

Engelkamp, J. *Semantische Struktur und die Verarbeitung von Sätzen*. Bern: Huber, 1973.

_____. *Satz und Bedeutung*. Stuttgart: Kohlhammer, 1976.

Ertel, S. "Where Do the Subjects of Sentences Come From?" In *Sentence Production. Developments in Research and Theory*, edited by S. Rosenberg. Hillsdale, N.J.: Lawrence Erlbaum, 1977.

Ertel, S., and Bloemer, W. D. "Affirmation and Negation as Constructive Action." *Psychological Research* 37 (1975):335–342.

Fillenbaum, S., and Rapoport, A. *Structures in the Subjective Lexicon*. New York: Academic Press, 1971.

Fillmore, C. J. "The Case for Case." In *Universals in Linguistic Theory*, edited by E. Bach and R. Harms. New York: Holt, Rinehart, & Winston, 1968.

_____. "Frame Semantics and the Nature of Language." In *Origins and Evolution of Language and Speech*, edited by S. R. Harnad *et al*. Annals of the New York Academy of Sciences, vol. 280. New York, 1976. (a)

_____. "The Need for a Frame Semantics within Linguistics." *Statistical Methods in Linguistics* (1976):5–29. (b)

Flores d'Arcais, G. B. *Cognitive Principles in Language Process-ing.* Rijksuniversiteit Leiden, 1973.

Fodor, J. A., and Bever, T. "The Psychological Reality of Lin-guistic Elements." *Journal of Verbal Learning and Verbal Behavior* 4 (1965):414–420.

Fodor, J. A., Bever, T. G., and Garrett, M. F. *The Psychology of Language: An Introduction to Psycholinguistics and Gener-ative Grammar.* New York: McGraw-Hill, 1974.

Foppa, K. "Mentale Strukturen—Phantasie oder Wirklichkeit." Paper read at the 32nd Congress of the German Psychological Society, Zurich, 1980.

Foss, D. J., and Blank, M. A. "Identifying the Speech Codes." *Cognitive Psychology* 12 (1980):1–31.

Freeman, R. B. "Zerebrale Asymmetrie der Sprachwahrnehmung bei Neugeborenen." Lecture at the 15th Meeting of Experi-mental Psychologists, Erlangen, 1973.

Fromkin, V. "The Non-anomalous nature of anomalous utter-ances." *Language* 47 (1971):27–52.

Fromkin, V. (Ed.). *Speech Errors as Linguistic Evidence.* The Hague: Mouton, 1973.

Gardner, A., and Gardner, B. T. "Teaching Sign Language to a Chimpanzee." *Science* 165 (1969):664–672.

Goldman-Eisler, F. *Psycholinguistics: Experiments in Spon-taneous Speech.* London: Academic Press, 1968.

Greenfield, P. M., and Smith, J. H. *The Structure of Communica-tion in Early Language Development.* New York: Academic Press, 1976.

Greenfield, P. M., Nelson, K.; and Saltzman, E. "The Development of Rulebound Strategies for Manipulating Seriated Cups: A Parallel between Action and Grammar." *Cognitive Psychol-ogy* 3 (1972):291–310.

Grice, H. P. "Logic and Conversation." In *Speech Acts: Syntax and Semantics,* vol. 3, edited by P. Cole and J. L. Morgan. New York: Academic Press, 1975.

Grosjean, F. "Linguistic Structures and Performance Structures: Studies in Pause Distribution." In *Temporal Variables in Speech,* edited by H. W. Dechert and M. Raupach. The Hague: Mouton, 1980:91–106.

Halliday, M. A. K. "Intonation Systems in English." In *Patterns of Language*, edited by A. McIntosh and M. A. K. Halliday. London: Longmans, 1967:111–133.

———. *Learning How to Mean: Explorations in the Development of Language*. London: Edward Arnold, 1975.

Hampton, J. A. 'Polymorphous Concepts in Semantic Memory." *Journal of Verbal Learning and Verbal Behavior* 18 (1979):441–461.

Harris, G., Begg, I.; and Upfold, D. "On the Role of Speaker's Expectations in Interpersonal Communications." *Journal of Verbal Learning and Verbal Behavior* 19 (1980):597–607.

Haviland, S. E., and Clark, H. H. "What's New? Acquiring New Information as a Process in Comprehension." *Journal of Verbal Learning and Verbal Behavior* 13 (1974):512–521.

Hayes-Roth, B., and Thorndyke, P. W. "Integration of Knowledge from Text." *Journal of Verbal Learning and Verbal Behavior* 18 (1979):91–108.

Henley, N. M. "A Psychological Study of the Semantics of Animal Terms." *Journal of Verbal Learning and Verbal Behavior* 8 (1969):176–184.

Herrmann, Th. "Die Situationsabhängigkeit des Sprechens und das Pars-pro-toto-Prinzip. Eine Zwischenbilanz." Report no. 10. Language and Cognition Research Group, University of Mannheim. Mannheim, 1979.

Herrmann, Th., and Deutsch, W. "Psychologie der Objektbenennung." *Studien zur Sprachpsychologie*. Vol. 5. Bern: Huber (1976).

Herrmann, Th., and Laucht, M. "Pars pro toto: Überlegungen zur situationsspezifischen Variation des Sprechens." *Psychologische Rundschau* 28 (1977):247–265.

Höpp, G. *Evolution der Sprache und Vernunft*. Berlin: Springer, 1970.

Hörmann, H. *Psychologie der Sprache*. Heidelberg, 1967. [2nd edition, 1977.]

———. "Semantische Anomalie, Metapher und Witz, oder: schlafen farblose grüne Ideen wirklich wütend?" *Folia Linguistica*. V (1972/73):310–330.

———. *Meinen und Verstehen*. Frankfurt: Suhrkamp, 1976.

_____. *Psycholinguistics*. Translated by H. H. Stern and Peter Leppmann. New York: Springer, 1971. 2nd revised edition, 1979. [Translation of Hörmann, 1967 and 1977.]

_____. *To Mean–To Understand*. Translated by Bogusław A. Jankowski. New York: Springer, 1981.

Hörmann, H., and Bosshardt, H.-G. "Der Einfluss suprasegmentaler Information auf die Sprachwahrnehmung bei 4- bis 6-jährigen Kindern." *Archiv für Psychologie* 134,2 (1981/82):81–104.

Hörmann, H., Pieper, U., and Engelkamp, J. "Zur psychologischen Problematik sogenannter Altersdialekte." *Psychologische Rundschau* 27 (1976):12–27.

Holenstein, E. *Von der Hintergehbarkeit der Sprache*. Frankfurt: Suhrkamp, 1980.

Humboldt, W. von. *Über die Verschiedenheit des menschlichen Sprachbaues* (1827–1829). New printing. Darmstadt: Wissenschaftliche Buchgesellschaft, 1963. [Translated as *Linguistic Variability and Intellectual Development* by George C. Buck and Frithjof A. Raven. Miami: University of Miami Press, 1971. Paperback edition, 1972, University of Pennsylvania Press.]

Innis, R. E. *Karl Bühler: Semiotic Foundations of Language Theory*. New York: Plenum Press, 1982.

Jaffe, J., Stern, D. N., and Perry, J. C. "'Conversational' Coupling of Gaze Behavior in Prelinguistic Human Development." *Journal of Psycholinguistic Research* 2 (1973):321–330.

Jaffe, J., Anderson, S. W., and Stern, D. N. "Conversational Rhythms." In *Psycholinguistic Research: Implications and Applications*, edited by D. Aaronson and R. W. Rieber. Hillsdale, N.J.: Erlbaum, 1979.

Jakobson, R. "Kindersprache, Aphasie und allgemeine Lautgesetze." *Universitets Årsskrift* (Uppsala) 9 (1941):1–83. *Selected Writings* I. The Hague: Mouton, 1962, pp. 328–401. Also published separately as *Child Language, Aphasia, and Phonological Universals*. The Hague: Mouton, 1968.

Jarvella, R. J. "Syntactic Processing of Connected Speech." *Journal of Verbal Learning and Verbal Behavior* 10 (1971): 409–416.

Johnson, N. F. "Language Models and Functional Units of Language Behavior." In *Directions in Psycholinguistics*, edited by S. Rosenberg. New York: Macmillan, 1965.

Johnson-Laird, P. N. *Mental Models: Towards a Cognitive Science of Language, Inference, and Consciousness.* Cambridge, Mass.: Harvard University Press, 1983.

Katz, J. J., and Fodor, J. A. "The Structure of a Semantic Theory." *Language* 39 (1963):170–210.

Kaye, K. "Toward the Origin of Dialogue." In *Studies in Mother–Infant Interaction*, edited by H. R. Schaffer. London: Academic Press, 1977.

Keenan, J. M., MacWhinney, B., and Mayhew, D. "Pragmatics in Memory: A Study of Natural Conversation." *Journal of Verbal Learning and Verbal Behavior* 16 (1977):549–560.

Kempen, G. "Conceptualizing and Formulating in Sentence Production." In *Sentence Production: Developments in Research and Theory*, edited by S. Rosenberg. Hillsdale, N.J.: Lawrence Erlbaum, 1977.

Kimball, J. P. "Seven Principles of Surface Structure Parsing in Natural Language." *Cognition* 2 (1973):15–47.

Kintsch, W. *The Representation of Meaning in Memory.* Hillsdale, N.J.: Lawrence Erlbaum, 1974.

———. "Memory for Prose." In *The Structure of Human Memory*, edited by C. N. Cofer. San Francisco: W. H. Freeman, 1976.

———. "Semantic Memory: A Tutorial." In *Attention and Performance VIII*, edited by R. S. Nickerson. Hillsdale, N.J.: Lawrence Erlbaum, 1980.

Kintsch, W., and Keenan, J. "Reading Rate and Retention as a Function of the Number of Propositions in the Base Structure of Sentences." *Cognitive Psychology* 5 (1973):257–274.

Kintsch, W., and van Dijk, T. A. "Toward a Model of Text Comprehension and Production." *Psychological Review* 85 (1978):363–394.

Kintsch, W., and Vipond, D. "Reading Comprehension and Readability in Educational Practice and Psychological Theory." In *Perspectives on Memory Research*, edited by L. G. Nilsson. Hillsdale, N.J.: Lawrence Erlbaum, 1979.

Kintsch, W., Kozminsky, E., Streby, W. J., McKoon, G., and Keenan, J. M. "Comprehension and Recall of Text as a Function of Content Variables." *Journal of Verbal Learning and Verbal Behavior* 14 (1975):196–214.

Klatt, H.-J. "I stumble . . . in my speech . . . like a hobbled . . . horse . . . hops. The Nature and Length of Pauses in the Readings of Aphasics." *Psychological Research* 41 (1980):199–209.

Labov, W. "The Boundaries of Words and Their Meanings." In *New Ways of Analyzing Variation in English*, edited by C. Bailey and R. Shuy. Washington, D.C.: Georgetown University Press, 1973.

Lakoff, G. *Hedges: A Study in Meaning Criteria and the Logic of Fuzzy Concepts.* Papers from the eighth regional meeting of the Linguistics Society. University of Chicago, Linguistics Department, 1972.

Langendoen, D. T. "Discussion of the Papers by Yakov Malkiel and by E. M. Uhlenbeck." In *The European Background of American Linguistics*, edited by H. M. Hoenigswald. Dordrecht: Foris Publications, 1979:145–151.

Lashley, K. S. "The Problem of Serial Order in Behavior." In *Cerebral Mechanisms in Behavior*, edited by L. A. Jeffress. Hixon Symposium. New York: Wiley, 1951.

Lesgold, A. M. "Pronominalization: A Device for Unifying Sentences in Memory." *Journal of Verbal Learning and Verbal Behavior* 11 (1972):316–323.

Lesgold, A. M., Roth, S. F., and Curtis, M. E. "Foregrounding Effects in Discourse Comprehension." *Journal of Verbal Learning and Verbal Behavior* 18 (1979):291–305.

Levelt, W. J. M. "A Survey of Studies in Sentence Perception 1970–1976." In *Studies in the Perception of Language*, edited by W. J. M. Levelt and G. B. Flores d'Arcais. Chichester: Wiley, 1978.

Linde, C., and Labov, W. "Spatial Networks as a Site for the Study of Language and Thought." *Language* 51 (1975):924–939.

Luria, A. R. "The Directive Function of Speech in Development and Dissolution." *Word* 15 (1959):341–352 and 453–464.

MacNamara, J. "Cognitive Basis of Language Learning in Infants." *Psychological Review* 79 (1972):1–13.

Mandler, J. M., and Johnson, N. S. "Remembrance of Things Parsed. Story Structure and Recall." *Cognitive Psychology* 9 (1979):111–151.

Maratsos, M. "How to Get from Words to Sentences." In *Psycholinguistic Research*, edited by D. Aaronson and R. W. Rieber. Hillsdale, N.J.: Lawrence Erlbaum, 1979.

Marslen-Wilson, W. D. "Linguistic Descriptions and Psychological Assumptions in the Study of Sentence Perception." In *New Approaches to Language Mechanism*, edited by R. J. Wales and E. Walker. Amsterdam: North Holland, 1976.

Marslen-Wilson, W. D., and Tyler, L. K. "The Temporal Structure of Spoken Language Understanding." *Cognition* 8 (1980):1–71.

Marslen-Wilson, W. D., Tyler, L. K., and Seidenberg, M. "Sentence Processing and the Clause Boundary." In *Studies in the Perception of Language*, edited by W. J. M. Levelt and G. B. Flores d'Arcais. Chichester: Wiley, 1978.

Martin, J. G. "Rhythmic (Hierarchical) versus Serial Structure in Speech and Other Behavior." *Psychological Review* 79 (1972):489–509.

Massaro, D. W. "Preperceptual Images, Processing Time, and Perceptual Units in Speech Perception." In *Understanding Language. An Information-processing Analysis of Speech Perception, Reading, and Psycholinguistics*, edited by D. W. Massaro. New York: Academic Press, 1975.

Masson, M. E. J. "Context and Inferential Cuing of Sentence Recall." *Journal of Verbal Learning and Verbal Behavior* 18 (1979):173–186.

McNeill, D. "Natural Processing Units of Speech." In *Psycholinguistic Research*, edited by D. Aaronson and R. W. Rieber. Hillsdale, N.J.: Lawrence Erlbaum, 1979.

Merdian, F. *Kommunikation über Personen. Zur Verarbeitung evaluativer Äusserungen durch den Hörer.* Bochum: Brockmeyer, 1977.

Meuman, E. *Die Entstehung der ersten Wortbedeutungen beim Kinde.* Leipzig: W. Engelmann, 1908.

Miller, G. A. "The Magical Number Seven, Plus or Minus Two." *Psychological Review* 63 (1956):81–97.

_____. "Some Preliminaries to Psycholinguistics." *American Psychologist* 20 (1965):15–20.

_____. "English Verbs of Motion: A Case Study in Semantics and Lexical Memory." In *Coding Processes in Human Memory*, edited by W. A. Melton and E. Martin. New York: Wiley, 1972.

Miller, G. A., and Johnson-Laird, P. N. *Language and Perception.* Cambridge, Mass.: Harvard University Press, 1976.

Miller, G. A., Galanter, E., and Pribram, K. H. *Plans and the Structures of Behavior.* New York: Holt, Rinehart, and Winston, 1960.

Moyer, R. S. "Comparing Objects in Memory: Evidence Suggesting an Internal Psychophysics." *Perception and Psychophysics* 13 (1973):180–184.

Neisser, U. *Cognition and Reality.* San Francisco: Freeman, 1976.

Nelson, K. "Concept, Word, and Sentence: Interrelations in Acquisition and Development." *Psychological Review* 81 (1974):267–285.

Ninio, A., and Bruner, J. "The Achievement and Antecedents of Labelling." *Journal of Child Language* 5 (1978):1–15.

O'Connell, D. C. and Kowal, S. "Prospectus for a Science of Pausology." In *Temporal Variables in Speech*, edited by H. W. Dechert and M. Raupach. The Hague: Mouton, 1980.

Ogden, C. K., and Richards, I. A. *The Meaning of Meaning.* London: Kegan Paul, 1923.

Olson, D. R. "Language and Thought: Aspects of a Cognitive Theory of Semantics." *Psychological Review* 77 (1970):257–273.

Osgood, C. E. "Where Do Sentences Come From?" In *Semantics*, edited by D. D. Steinberg and L. A. Jakobovits. Cambridge: Cambridge University Press, 1971.

Osgood, C. E. "What Is a Language?" In *Psycholinguistic Research*, edited by D. Aaronson and R. W. Rieber. Hillsdale, N.J.: Lawrence Erlbaum, 1979.

Osgood, C. E. *Lectures on Language Performance.* New York: Springer, 1980.

Osgood, C. E., and Bock, K. "Salience and Sentencing: Some Production Principles." In *Sentence Production. Develop-*

ments in Research and Theory, edited by S. Rosenberg. Hillsdale, N.J.: Lawrence Erlbaum, 1977.

Osgood, C. E., Suci, G. J., and Tannenbaum, P. H. *The Measurement of Meaning*. Urbana: University of Illinois Press, 1957.

Paivio, A. *Imagery and Verbal Processes*. New York: Holt, Rinehart, and Winston, 1971.

_____. "Images, Propositions, and Knowledge." In *Images, Perception, and Knowledge*, edited by J. M. Nicholas. Dordrecht: Kluwer, 1977.

Piaget, J. *The Child's Conception of the World*. New York: Harcourt, 1929.

_____. *The Construction of Reality in the Child*. New York: Basic Books, 1954.

Polanyi, M. *The Tacit Dimension*. New York: Doubleday, 1966.

Prentice, J. L. "Effects of Cueing Actor versus Cueing Object on Word Order in Sentence Production." *Psychonomic Science* 8 (1967):163–164.

Pylyshyn, Z. "What Does It Take to Bootstrap a Language?" In *Language and Learning and Thought*, edited by J. MacNamara. New York: Academic Press, 1977.

Repp, B. H., Lieberman, A. M., Eccardt, T., and Pesetzky, D. "Perceptual Integration of Cues for Stop, Fricative and Affricate Manner." *Haskins Laboratory Status Report on Speech Research* SR-53, 2 (1978):61–83.

Rips, L. J., and Turnbull, W. "How Big Is Big? Relative and Absolute Properties in Memory." *Cognition* 8 (1980):145–174.

Rommetveit, R. *On Message Structure*. New York: Wiley, 1974.

Rosch, E. "On the Internal Structure of Perceptual and Semantic Categories." In *Cognitive Development and the Acquisition of Language*, edited by T. E. Moore. New York: Academic Press, 1973:111–144.

_____. "Cognitive Representations of Semantic Categories." *Journal of Experimental Psychology* 104, 3 (1975):192–233.

Rosch, E. C. B., Mervis, W. D., Gray, W. D., Johnson, D. M., and Boyes-Braem, P. "Basic Objects in Natural Categories." *Cognitive Psychology* 8 (1976):382–439.

Rumelhart, D. E. "Notes on a Schema for Stories." In *Representa-*

tion and Understanding, edited by S. A. Bobrow and A. M. Collins. New York: Academic Press, 1975.

Sachs, J. S. "Recognition Memory for Syntactic and Semantic Aspects of Connected Discourse." *Perception and Psychophysics* 2 (1967):437–442.

Sacks, H.; Schegloff, E. A.; and Jefferson, G. "A Simplest Systematics for the Organization of Turn-Taking for Conversation." *Language* 50 (1974):686–735.

Saussure, F. de. *Course in General Linguistics,* translated by Wade Baskin. New York: Philosophical Library, 1959. [First published 1916.]

Scaife, M., and Bruner, J. S. "The Capacity for Joint Visual Attention in the Infant." *Nature* 253 (1975):265–266.

Schane, S. A. "A Survey of Generative Phonology." In *Psycholinguistic Research,* edited by D. Aaronson and R. W. Rieber. Hillsdale, N.J.: Lawrence Erlbaum, 1979.

Schank, R. C., and Wilks, Y. "The Goals of Linguistic Theory Revisited." *Lingua* 34 (1974):301–326.

Schatz, M. "On the Development of Communicative Understandings: An Early Strategy for Interpreting and Responding to Messages." *Cognitive Psychology* 10 (1978):271–301.

Schegloff, E. A., and Sacks, H. "Opening up Closings." *Semiotica* 8 (1973):289–327.

Schlesinger, I. M. "Production of Utterance and Language Acquisition." In *The Ontogenesis of Grammar,* edited by D. Slobin. New York: Academic Press, 1971.

———. "The Role of Cognitive Development and Linguistic Input in Language Acquisition." *Journal of Child Language* 4 (1977a):153–169.

———. *Production and Comprehension of Utterances.* Hillsdale, N.J.: Lawrence Erlbaum Associates, 1977b.

———. "Semantic Assimilation." Paper presented at the Conference on Language Development, Nijmegen, 1979.

Schmidt, S. J. *Texttheorie.* Munich: Fink, 1973.

Schönbach, P. *Soziolinguistik.* In *Perspektiven der Linguistik* II, edited by W. A. Koch. Stuttgart: Kröner, 1974:156–177.

Searle, J. R. *Speech Acts.* Cambridge: Cambridge University Press, 1969.

Shugar, G. W. "Text Analysis as an Approach to the Study of Early Linguistic Operations." In *The Development of Communication*, edited by N. Waterson and C. Snow. Chichester: Wiley, 1978.

Slobin, D. (Ed.). *The Ontogenesis of Grammar*. New York: Academic Press, 1971.

―――. "Cognitive Prerequisites for the Acquisition of Grammar." In *Studies of Child Language Development*, edited by C. A. Ferguson and D. I. Slobin. New York: Holt, Rinehart and Winston, 1973.

Smith, E. E., Shoben, E. J., and Rips, L. J. "Structure and Process in Semantic Memory: A Featural Model for Semantic Decision." *Psychological Review* 81 (1974):214–241.

Snow, C. "Mother's Speech to Children Learning Language." *Child Development* 43 (1972):549–565.

―――. "The Conversational Context of Language." In *Recent Advances in the Psychology of Language*, III, edited by R. N. Campbell and P. T. Smith. New York: Plenum Press, 1978.

Straight, H. S. "Psycholinguistics: A Review Essay." *The Canadian Journal of Linguistics* (1977):169–195.

Studdert-Kennedy, M. "Speech Perception." *Language and Speech* 23 (1980):45–66.

Sudnow, D. *Ways of the Hand: The Organization of Improvised Conduct*. Cambridge, Mass.: Harvard University Press, 1978.

Tannenbaum, P. H., and Williams, F. "Generation of Active and Passive Sentences as a Function of Subject and Object Focus." *Journal of Verbal Learning and Verbal Behavior* 7 (1968):246–250.

Terbuyken, G. *Sprechform, Situationsstruktur und Verstehensprozess. Zur kommunikativen Funktion formaler Merkmale gesprochener Sprache*. Bochum: Brockmeyer, 1975.

Terrace, H. S., and Bever, T. G. "What Might Be Learned from Studying Language in the Chimpanzees?" In *Origins and Evolution of Language and Speech*, edited by S. R. Harnad et al. *Annals of the New York Academy of Sciences*, vol. 280. New York, 1976.

Thorndyke, P. W. "Cognitive Structures in Comprehension and

Memory of Narrative Discourse." *Cognitive Psychology* 9 (1977):77–110.

Tolman, E. C. "Cognitive Maps in Rats and Men." *Psychological Review* 55 (1948):189–208.

van der Geest, T. "The Development of Communication: Some Non-verbal Aspects." In *Developmental Kinesics*, edited by R. St. Clair and B. Hoffer. Baltimore: University Park Press, 1980.

Vipond, D. "Micro- and Macroprocesses in Text Comprehension." *Journal of Verbal Learning and Verbal Behavior* 19 (1980):276–296.

Wakefield, J. A., Doughtie, E. B., and Yomb, B. H. L. "The Identification of Structural Components of an Unknown Language." *Journal of Psycholinguistic Research* 3 (1974):261–270.

Walker, C. H., and Meyer, B. J. F. "Integrating Different Types of Information in Text." *Journal of Verbal Learning and Verbal Behavior* 19 (1980):263–275.

Whorf, B. L. *Language, Thought, and Reality*, edited by J. B. Carroll. Cambridge, Mass.: MIT Press, 1956.

Wittgenstein, L. *Philosophical Investigations*, translated by Elisabeth Anscombe. Oxford: Basil Blackwell, 1958.

Wundt, W. *Völkerpsychologie*. Leipzig: Engelmann, 1900.

Yekovich, F. R., Walker, C. H., and Blackman, H. S. "The Role of Presupposed and Focal Information in Integrating Sentences." *Journal of Verbal Learning and Verbal Behavior* 18 (1979):535–548.

Name Index

287

Subject Index